FOUNDATIONS OF PUBLIC INTERNATIONAL LAW

General editors: MALCOLM EVANS AND
PHOEBE OKOWA

INTERNATIONAL LAW AND THE USE OF FORCE

International Law
and the
Use of Force

CHRISTINE GRAY

OXFORD
UNIVERSITY PRESS

OXFORD

UNIVERSITY PRESS

Great Clarendon Street, Oxford OX2 6DP

Oxford University Press is a department of the University of Oxford.
It furthers the University's objective of excellence in research, scholarship,
and education by publishing worldwide in

Oxford New York

Athens Auckland Bangkok Bogotá Buenos Aires
Cape Town Chennai Dar es Salaam Delhi Florence Hong Kong Istanbul
Karachi Kolkata Kuala Lumpur Madrid Melbourne Mexico City Mumbai
Nairobi Paris São Paulo Shanghai Singapore Taipei Tokyo Toronto Warsaw

and associated companies in Berlin Ibadan

Oxford is a registered trade mark of Oxford University Press
in the UK and certain other countries

Published in the United States
by Oxford University Press Inc., New York

British Library Cataloguing in Publication Data
Data available

Library of Congress Cataloging in Publication Data
Data available

ISBN 0–19–876528–2
ISBN 0–19–876527–4 (pb)

3 5 7 9 10 8 6 4 2

Typeset by J&L Composition Ltd, Filey, North Yorkshire
Printed in Great Britain
on acid-free paper by
T.J. International Ltd, Padstow, Cornwall

General Editors' Preface

Few topics in international law arouse as much interest as the use of force. Indeed, the very origins of the discipline lie in attempts to wrestle with the question of when force might legitimately be used within the international arena. It shapes and defines the subject. It is, then, most fitting that the first volume to appear in the Foundations of Public International Law Series should address international law and the use of force.

Since 1945 there has been a sustained attempt to place limitations upon unilateral use of force by states and it was envisaged that this would be balanced by the capacity of the UN Security Council to exercise a monopoly over the use of force for the common good of the international community. This, of course, proved to be unattainable for most practical purposes during the cold war years. The cold war is over, but other problems have emerged which ensure that the perennial problems surrounding the legality of the use of force will remain the subject of fierce debate and fundamental doctrinal difference.

In keeping with the aims of the Series, Christine Gray surveys and explores the current pattern of legal regulation in a manner which combines clarity in presentation with rigour in academic scrutiny. If the issues raised are themselves timeless, the point of departure is clearly contemporary and firmly grounded in recent state practice as well as the pronouncements of the International Court of Justice. Indeed, one of the hallmarks of this work is the way in which state practice is drawn into the jurisprudential debate, producing a synthesis which is both stimulating and satisfying. Difficult questions are posed and challenging conclusions are drawn and this is as it should be. Even if the law in this area were easy to state—and it is not—it would still be difficult to apply. It is a sign of the increasing maturity of international law that it is able to face up to this truth whilst continuing to search for a way forward that preserves and enhances the rule of law within the international community. If that means replacing the platitudinous orthodoxies of a previous era with the ever-more complex and perplexing outcomes of evolution and innovation in law and practice, then this a price well worth paying. One does, however, need a reliable guide through the resulting thickets and this volume is offered in the expectation that it will not only fulfil that function with distinction, but will itself mould the manner in which the legal regulation of the use of force is perceived and examined for years to come.

Malcolm D. Evans
Phoebe N. Okowa

Contents

Abbreviations

ADF	Arab Defence Force
ANC	African National Congress
CIA	Central Intelligence Agency
CIS	Commonwealth of Independent States
ECOMOG	Economic Community of West African States Monitoring Group
ECOWAS	Economic Community of West African States
FMLN	Frente Farabundo Martí para la Liberación Nacional
FNLA	Frente Nacional de Libertação de Angola
FRY	Federal Republic of Yugoslavia
IAEA	International Atomic Energy Authority
IGAD	Intergovernmental Authority on Drought and Development
ILC	International Law Commission
IPTF	United Nations International Police Task Force
MINURCA	United Nations Mission in the Central African Republic
MISAB	Inter-African Force in the Central African Republic
MONUA	United Nations Observer Mission in Angola
MONUC	United Nations Observer Mission in the Democratic Republic of Congo
MPLA	Movimento Popular de Libertação de Angola
NAM	Non-Aligned Movement
NPFL	National Patriotic Front of Liberia
OAS	Organization of American States
OAU	Organization of African Unity
OECS	Organization of East Caribbean States
ONUC	United Nations Operation in the Congo
ONUCA	United Nations Observer Group in Central America
ONUMOZ	United Nations Operation in Mozambique
ONUSAL	United Nations Observer Mission in El Salvador
OSCE	Organization for Security and Cooperation in Europe
PLO	Palestine Liberation Organization
RUF	Revolutionary United Front
RENAMO	Resistencia Nacional Moçambicana
SADC	Southern African Development Community
SWAPO	South West Africa People's Organization
UAR	United Arab Republic
UNAMET	United Nations Mission in East Timor
UNAMIC	United Nations Advance Mission in Cambodia
UNAMIR	United Nations Assistance Mission for Rwanda

UNAMSIL	United Nations Mission in Sierra Leone
UNAVEM	United Nations Angola Verification Mission
UNCRO	United Nations Confidence Restoration Operation in Croatia
UNEF	United Nations Emergency Force
UNFICYP	United Nations Peace-keeping Force in Cyprus
UNGOMAP	United Nations Good Offices Mission in Afghanistan and Pakistan
UNIFIL	United Nations Interim Force in Lebanon
UNITA	União Nacional para a Independência Total de Angola
UNITAF	Unified Task Force
UNMIBH	United Nations Mission in Bosnia and Herzegovina
UNMIH	United Nations Mission in Haiti
UNMIK	United Nations Mission in Kosovo
UNMOGIP	United Nations Military Observer Group in India and Pakistan
UNMOP	United Nations Mission of Observers in Prevlaka
UNMOT	United Nations Mission of Observers in Tajikistan
UNOMIG	United Nations Observer Mission in Georgia
UNOMIL	United Nations Observer Mission in Liberia
UNOMSIL	United Nations Observer Mission in Sierra Leone
UNOMUR	United Nations Observer Mission Uganda/Rwanda
UNOSOM	United Nations Operation in Somalia
UNPREDEP	United Nations Preventive Deployment Force
UNPROFOR	United Nations Protection Force
UNTAC	United Nations Transitional Authority in Cambodia
UNTAES	United Nations Transitional Administration for Eastern Slavonia
UNTAET	United Nations Transitional Administration in East Timor
UNTAG	United Nations Transition Assistance Group
WEU	Western European Union

1
Law and force

The end of the Cold War has not brought peace; early hopes for a New World Order have not been realized. As the UN Secretary-General said in his Report to the General Assembly in 1995, 'At the time [the end of the Cold War], there was a widespread belief that when no longer fuelled by rival major powers the many regional conflicts flaring in different parts of the world would be quickly extinguished.'[1] In fact many Cold War conflicts were terminated, even if only temporarily, with the assistance of the UN; settlements were reached with regard to Namibia, Mozambique, Angola, Central America, Afghanistan, and Cambodia. But many of the old conflicts continued. Some of these date back to the establishment of the UN; among the first conflicts ever considered by the Security Council were those between India and Pakistan and between Israel and Arab states. These disputes have continued off and on for the last fifty years and are to a large extent still unresolved. Moreover, new wars have continued to erupt, almost all within states; in 1998 there was a resurgence of conflict after a decline since 1992.[2]

An overview of conflict in 1999 gives a bleak picture, especially in Africa. Civil conflict or violent unrest—the line between the two is not always clear—occurred in Sierra Leone, Burundi, Guinea-Bissau, Democratic Republic of Congo (DRC), Congo (Brazzaville) Sudan, Somalia, and Uganda; many of these conflicts spilled over into neighbouring states and threatened the stability of their regions. Fighting also took place within Sri Lanka, Colombia, Comoros, Chad, Peru and Burma. Separatist struggles continued in Georgia (Abkhazia), Russia (Chechenya), Federal Republic of Yugoslavia (Kosovo), East Timor, and Moldova (Dnestr). The end of Cold-War involvement has not brought a final end to conflict in Angola or Afghanistan. China threatened Taiwan with force to recover the territory. Border clashes occurred in Kashmir, between Bangladesh and India, Ethiopia and Somalia, North and South Korea; Turkey pursued Kurds into Iraq; Israel mounted operations into Lebanon. Full-scale fighting broke out again in a major inter-state conflict between Ethiopia and Eritrea that had begun in 1998.

In many of these 1999 conflicts the UN played a role in seeking a solution or in running a peacekeeping operation. It established major operations in East Timor and in Kosovo; it maintained peacekeeping forces in Africa, Europe, the Middle East, and Asia. But, as Jamaica said, 'As many nations

---

[1] 1995 UNYB 3 at 4.   [2] Report of the UN Secretary-General (A/54/1 para 7).

grew weary of the burdens of peacemaking and peacekeeping, the challenge to find new paths and stability through avoiding conflict became more critical.'[3] Attention in the UN Security Council has recently begun to focus on conflict prevention and the study of the causes of conflict; after 'the maintenance of international peace and security' the second purpose of the United Nations set out in Article 1 of the UN Charter is to 'take effective collective measures for the prevention and removal of threats to the peace and for the suppression of acts of aggression or other breaches of the peace'. But even here differences between states have emerged: whereas developed states argue that the rule of law, respect for human rights and democracy are crucial to the avoidance of conflict, China and Russia insist that conflict prevention must be consistent with the rules of the UN Charter and that only clearly expressed consent on the part of states could serve as the legal basis for the use of the tools of preventive action. Developing states tend to stress the interrelationship of underdevelopment and conflict, and the importance of disarmament, demobilization, and rehabilitation after conflicts.[4]

This chapter has two main interrelated themes: first, the problems with the identification of international law on the use of force in the light of the fundamental disagreements between states and between commentators, and, second, the role of international law in this area and the complexities of any inquiry into its effectiveness.

IDENTIFICATION OF THE LAW

The starting point for any examination of the law is the prohibition of the use of force in Article 2(4) of the UN Charter.[5] Irrespective of whether the UN Charter is seen as a revolutionary departure from existing customary international law on the use of force or as a codification of rules that had already undergone a major shift in the twentieth century,[6] the Charter system was a marked departure from that of the League of Nations and the language of Articles 2(4) and 51[7] provides a new terminology and the first

---

[3] SC 4174th meeting, UN Press Release SC/6892.   [4] Ibid.

[5] Article 2(4): 'All Members shall refrain in their international relations from the threat or use of force against the territorial integrity or political independence of any state, or in any other manner inconsistent with the Purposes of the United Nations.'

[6] See, for example, the debate between Bowett, *Self-Defence in International Law* (1958) and Brownlie, *International Law and the Use of Force by States* (1963).

[7] Article 51: 'Nothing in the present Charter shall impair the inherent right of individual or collective self-defence if an armed attack occurs against a Member of the United Nations, until the Security Council has taken measures necessary to maintain international peace and security. Measures taken by Members in the exercise of this right of self-defence shall be immediately reported to the Security Council and shall not in any way affect the authority and responsibility of the Security Council under the present Charter to take at any time such action as it deems necessary in order to maintain or restore international peace and security.'

expression of the basic rules in their modern form. This book will examine the use of force since the Charter; the focus will be on state and UN practice under the Charter.

But the rules of the Charter on the use of force are brief and cannot constitute a comprehensive code. The provisions in Articles 2(4) and 51 are very much a response to the Second World War and are accordingly directed to inter-state conflict. It is now a commonplace that such conflicts, or at any rate large-scale inter-state conflicts, have proved to be the exception in the years since 1945; and that civil wars, with or without outside intervention, have outnumbered traditional inter-state wars. Cross-border guerrilla incursions and limited inter-state fighting in border areas have been the norm rather than all-out wars between states. The struggles of national liberation movements for independence during the decolonization process also did not fit easily into the framework of Articles 2(4) and 51. The evolution of rules to cover these conflicts has been a complex process. Even in inter-state conflicts the apparently simple words of the Charter have given rise to fundamental differences between states.

This is one of the most controversial areas of international law; even from the early days of the UN many disagreements between states (between developed and developing, between East and West) as to the law were apparent. The prohibition of the use of force led to fundamental divisions as to whether the prohibition of the 'use of force' included economic coercion, the scope of the right of self-defence, the right to use force to further self-determination and to intervene in civil wars. These differences emerged in the context of the Cold War and the decolonization process. The end of the Cold War, the dominance of the USA as the one remaining superpower, and the virtual end of decolonization now call for a reappraisal of international law on the use of force by states and by UN forces. How far should the Charter be interpreted to allow the use of force to restore or further democracy, to restore order in a state without an effective government, to further the right to self-determination outside the decolonization context, to respond to terrorist attacks on nationals abroad? How far should the UN Security Council exercise centralized control over these and other uses of force?

How, if at all, can these controversies, old and new, be resolved? A central question is whether it is possible to use state practice to arrive at an authoritative interpretation of the Charter or to supplement its brief provisions. Is it possible to find standards by which to assess the legality of states' actions and which advisers can use to give guidance to states? Given that state practice includes the actual use of force, the justification offered by states for it, the response of other states inside and outside the UN and other organizations, and their public positions in debates on general resolutions of the General Assembly on the use of force, as well as an extensive treaty practice including friendship treaties, non-aggression pacts, border treaties, mutual defence agreements and regional arrangements, how are universal rules to be extracted? Or is this a misguided undertaking? Should the Charter be seen as open to dynamic and changing interpretation on the basis of subsequent state practice or should the prohibition of the use of force in Article 2(4) rather be seen as having a fixed meaning, established in 1945 on the basis of the meaning of the words at that date in the light of the preparatory works and the aims of the founders?[8]

The International Court of Justice in the *Nicaragua* case apparently regarded the Charter provisions as dynamic rather than fixed, and thus as capable of change over time through state practice. It said that 'The UN Charter . . . by no means covers the whole area of the regulation of the use of force in international relations' and went on to explain how the Charter provisions on self-defence needed to be interpreted in the light of customary international law.[9] On the fundamental principles as to the use of force contained in Article 2(4) the parties agreed that the Charter provisions represented customary law and the Court accepted this without going into the question of how far the meaning of Article 2(4) was fixed or how far it had evolved over time. The Court did, however, go into the question of what amounted to a use of force under Article 2(4) not amounting to an armed attack under Article 51.[10] It also accepted the possibility of the development of new law on forcible intervention allowing a new exception to the prohibition of the use of force in Article 2(4). That is, it seems to have accepted the possibility of a dynamic interpretation of Articles 51 and 2(4) based on the development of state practice.[11]

Almost from the time of the creation of the UN the states parties have worked to elaborate on the provisions of the UN Charter on the use of force in General Assembly resolutions. Western states have often evinced some unease about this process; thus the USA has asserted that there is no lack of understanding of Article 2(4). During the Cold War the UK and the USA tended to argue that Article 2(4) should be treated as the last word,

---

[8] Ford, 'Legal Processes of Change: Article 2(4) and the Vienna Convention on the Law of Treaties', 4 Journal of Armed Conflict Law (1999) 75.

[9] *Case Concerning Military and Paramilitary Activities in and against Nicaragua* (hereafter *Nicaragua* case) ICJ Reports (1986) 14 at para 176.   [10] *Nicaragua* case para 191–5.

[11] The Court's approach to customary international law in the *Nicaragua* case, at para 183, was traditional; it stressed the need for practice and *opinio juris* and made clear that universal compliance was not necessary. The Court was much criticized, not so much for this traditional doctrine, but for its application of it in the pursuit of the rules of international law. It was criticized for inferring *opinio juris* from General Assembly resolutions and for not undertaking a wide survey of practice. But, as the Court said, the parties were in agreement that Article 2(4) was customary law. It is not surprising that the Court's inquiry into customary international law was relatively brief. See Gray, 'The Principle of Non-Use of Force', in Lowe and Warbrick (eds), *The United Nations and the Principles of International Law* (1994), 33.

for fear that any modification would be to the advantage of the Soviet Union.[12] But the Western states have come to accept the legal significance and customary international law status of certain of these resolutions. This process of elaboration on the UN Charter began with the 1949 *Resolution on the Essentials of Peace*. The ICJ in the *Nicaragua* case in 1986 singled out the 1975 *Definition of Aggression*[13] and the 1970 *Declaration on Friendly Relations*[14] to help it to identify customary international law on the non-use of force. These resolutions have since been supplemented by the 1987 *Declaration on the Non-Use of Force*.[15] But even though these resolutions adopted unanimously or by consensus may be seen as authoritative interpretations of the UN Charter or as contributing to the formation of customary international law,[16] they often leave controversial issues unresolved.

Typically the price of consensus has been ambiguity on the crucial issues that divide states. The drafting history of the resolutions reveals more about the views of states than the resolutions themselves do.[17] Thus the central question of the scope of the right of self-defence is not dealt with in the General Assembly resolutions. This issue divides states which take a wide view, such as the USA, Israel, and in the past South Africa and, to a lesser extent, the UK and France, from the vast majority of other states. These states claim a right to use force to protect nationals abroad, to take anticipatory self-defence, and to respond to terrorism as part of self-defence. The vast majority of states reject such claims. But it seems that states preferred to avoid any substantial provision on this question of self-defence and this enabled them to maintain their opposing positions. During the debates on the 1987 *Declaration on the Non-Use of Force* only the USA and Australia spoke out expressly in favour of anticipatory self-defence; the other states were able to maintain their positions simply

---

[12] Gray, 'The Principle of Non-Use of Force', in Lowe and Warbrick (eds), *The United Nations and the Principles of International Law* (1994), 33.   [13] GA Res 3314.

[14] GA Res 2625.

[15] GA Res 42/22 (1988); see Treves, 'La Déclaration des Nations Unies sur le renforcement de l'efficacité du principe du non-recours à la force', 33 AFDI (1987) 379.

[16] *Nicaragua* case para 188; *Legality of the Threat or Use of Nuclear Weapons*, ICJ Reports (1996) 226 at para 70.

[17] Though there are problems in assessing the question how far what states say in these debates is significant. They may change their views; clearly their views at any particular time are influenced by the disputes in which they are directly involved or in which they are interested. Typically states may attack each other and set out their own justifications for force during the general debates; during the drafting of the *Declaration on the Non-Use of Force* Iran and Iraq, Cyprus and Turkey and the Arab states and Israel all criticized each other. It is important to see the statements in the context of the time in which they were made. Views expressed in debates on the adoption of declarations may be modified later in response to particular conflicts. Thus the former Soviet bloc at first opposed the inclusion of indirect aggression in aggression and armed attack, but later apparently abandoned this view with regard to Czechoslovakia and Afghanistan.

through the omission of any provision on self-defence apart from the general formula that 'States have the inherent right of individual or collective self-defence if an armed attack occurs, as set forth in the Charter of the UN'.[18]

Also the General Assembly resolutions could not settle the controversies that divided developed and developing states as to the meaning of 'force', as to the right to use force in the furtherance of self-determination for colonial peoples or to recover territory illegally seized by another state. Nor did the resolutions resolve the dispute as to the legality of use of nuclear weapons.[19] These differences manifested themselves during the debates on the *Declaration on Friendly Relations* from 1962; the same differences continued to divide states during the ten years' drafting of the *Declaration on the Non-Use of Force* and the end product did not constitute any real advance on the *Declaration on Friendly Relations*.[20]

And if we turn to other actions and statements of states to interpret or supplement the Charter and the General Assembly resolutions, how is the legal significance of such practice to be assessed? Can state practice be used to resolve the differences between states or is it impossible to find universal standards in this context? It is important not to exaggerate these differences and to keep them in perspective. For the vast mass of actual use of force reveals that states almost always agree on the content of the applicable law; it is on the application of the law to the particular facts or on the facts themselves that the states disagree. Of course it may be difficult to keep these three categories entirely separate, as is clear from the rather repetitive judgment of the International Court of Justice in the *Nicaragua* case. The Court made the distinction between the facts, the law and the application of the law to the facts, but it found itself unable to maintain a strict distinction, especially between the last two categories.

It is clear that in the overwhelming majority of cases of inter-state use of force both states involved invoke self-defence against an armed attack by the other state. In numerical terms, the commonest use of force since the Second World War has been the limited cross-frontier action. The only disagreement in the mass of these cases is over the questions of fact whether there was a cross-border incursion or who began the conflict. This may occur in up to a hundred minor incidents a year. The UN may receive reports from both sides but is not often in a position to assign

[18] A/72326; see Treves, 'La Déclaration des Nations Unies sur le renforcement de l'efficacité du principe du non-recours à la force', 33 AFDI (1987) 379; Gray, 'The Principle of Non-Use of Force', in Lowe and Warbrick (eds), *The United Nations and the Principles of International Law* (1994), 33.

[19] *Legality of Threat or Use of Nuclear Weapons*, ICJ Reports (1996) 226.

[20] The issues of economic blockade of landlocked states and environmental modification also emerged. The remaining differences between developed and developing states are summarized at A/40/41.

responsibility. Thus the vast mass of state practice, even if one of the parties is breaking the law, does not lead to any need to reappraise the content of the law. Similarly, in civil wars states seem from their practice to agree that forcible intervention to help the opposition overthrow the government is unlawful whereas assistance to a government may be legal. This is the position consistently expressed by states since the Second World War.[21] The questions that divide the intervening states are questions of fact, and application of the law to those facts: who invited help; was there a genuine invitation; was it a civil war or mere internal unrest; was there already foreign intervention? State responses to forcible intervention show a lack of doubt about the law; they generally condemn if they think the intervening state was trying to interfere.

But the mass of practice on minor episodes has naturally received relatively little academic examination. The focus of writers, especially American writers, has been on US practice and, to a lesser extent, the practice of Israel; they have been less concerned with the use of force in Africa and Asia or even with the use of force in the former Soviet Union or involving China. There is also comparatively little discussion of the law on the use of force in continental European journals; these journals also show a rather more surprising concentration on US practice and relatively little discussion of the use of force by their own states or by their own former colonies.

This focus on US practice is in part to be explained by the fact that the USA often offers rather fuller articulations of its legal position than do other states using force. Also many of these episodes are unlike the vast mass of state practice in that they do reflect differences between states as to the applicable law; the state using force takes a controversial position as to the content of the law in order to justify its use of force. The protection of nationals, as in Iran, Grenada, and Panama, the extension of this doctrine of self-defence to cover actions in response to terrorism against Libya in 1986, against Iraq in reaction to the alleged assassination attempt on ex-President Bush in 1993, and against Afghanistan and Sudan in 1998, all produced clear divisions between states, apparent in the debates on these particular incidents and in those on the law-making resolutions. In contrast, the USSR has generally put forward in attempted justification of its use of force legal doctrines that were unexceptionable in themselves; it was their application that was controversial. The USSR claimed invitation by the government and collective self-defence to justify its intervention in Hungary, Czechoslovakia and Afghanistan. In these episodes the disagreement was on the facts (had there been an invitation, who had given

---

[21] Doswald-Beck, 'The Legal Validity of Military Intervention by Invitation of the Government', 56 BYIL (1985) 189; see Chapter 3 below.

the invitation, was there outside intervention?) rather than as to the law. The natural focus of writers on controversial episodes where the law relied on by the states using force was not generally agreed, rather than on the mass of state practice where the law was not controversial, may have the side-effect of giving a misleading overall picture. The impression that emerges may be one of greater uncertainty than the total picture would justify. How far does looking at the broader picture of all states' uses of force produce a different view of the law from that produced simply on the basis of more limited practice? In any one year newspaper reports give the largest list of conflicts; many of the minor episodes reported are never referred to the UN. Some conflicts may be referred to the UN in state communications but may not be officially debated; some conflicts may be debated but not lead to the adoption of a resolution or a statement; if a resolution is adopted, it may be legally indeterminate.

In early years it was more common for minor incidents to be referred to the UN and debated. Higgins wrote in 1963 that even minor episodes were the subject of condemnation by the Security Council; this is no longer the case.[22] Should the episodes in which the UN has been involved be considered more important in the establishment or confirmation of legal rules? In practice it is not surprising that they tend to attract more academic discussion. But states have various motives for choosing to refer or not to refer matters to the UN and whether or not to seek a debate. In the early years the UN Yearbook specifically listed 'Matters raised but which the Security Council did not consider'; these tended to be matters dealt with by the OAS and this heading was later dropped.[23] The Secretary-General in his annual report has from time to time mentioned the failure of states to refer their conflicts to the UN; he has acknowledged that they may have had good reasons for this, but also has said that failure to turn to the UN may bring the organization into disrepute.[24]

It may be that willingness to refer a conflict to the UN indicates that the state taking the initiative to make the reference is acting lawfully or that it has confidence in the legality of its position, but this does not necessarily mean that the primary concern in making the reference is to secure peaceful settlement. Sometimes states try to argue that the reference to the Security Council is in itself provocative, designed to internationalize the conflict and not appropriate. Thus, for example, Yemen in 1966 said that

[22] Higgins, *The Development of International Law through the Political Organs of the United Nations* (1963) at 181.
[23] This covered events in 1948–9 on the Costa Rica border, and between Haiti/Dominican Republic; in 1950, Dominican Republic allegations against groups in Cuba and Guatemala; in 1954, Guatemala; in 1955, Costa Rica. At this time there was a serious debate as to priority of jurisdiction between the UN and regional organizations, but this has not been a controversial issue in recent years: Simma, *The United Nations Charter: A Commentary* (1994) at 708.   [24] For example, 1978 UNYB 5.

the complaint by the UK of an air attack on its colonial territory of South Arabia by Yemen should not go to the Security Council; the issue raised by the UK was a minor matter, the alleged incursion of an aircraft, and what was really at stake was the need for the UK to allow the reunification of Yemen.[25] Again in 1946 the question of USSR involvement in Iran was referred to the Security Council by the USA, even though the question was near to peaceful resolution.[26] In 1972 Portugal and the UK argued that a use of force by Portugal against Senegal should not go to the Security Council because Portugal had admitted the violation, ordered criminal proceedings against those responsible and offered compensation. But the states voting for the resolution condemning Portugal replied that the Security Council intervention was justified because the episode was not an isolated one; it was part of Portugal's continuing illegal colonialism.[27]

The Security Council clearly has an important role, but there is controversy as to whether its findings are conclusive as to legality, illegality, and as to the content of the applicable norms. How far is the law developed by institutions? That is, do states acting collectively through the UN have a more important role than they do outside the UN in the interpretation and application of the UN Charter? Does the Security Council have the final say as to not only what is an act of aggression, threat to the peace or breach of the peace under Chapter VII of the Charter, but also as to what is a threat or use of force under Article 2(4) or an armed attack and as to whether a state is acting in self-defence under Article 51? This question as to the scope of Security Council powers is topical because the end of the Cold War has brought vastly increased activity of the Security Council. Whereas commentators used to discuss the problem of the inactivity of the Security Council, now they concern themselves with difficulties over the legitimacy of its actions.[28]

The debate as to whether judicial review of the Security Council's resolutions on the use of force is possible and desirable has revived with the end of the Cold War; this issue whether it should be the International Court of Justice rather than the Security Council that has the final word in making determinations under Article 39 and deciding on action under Chapter VII has come up before the International Court of Justice in recent cases. Thus in the *Lockerbie* case Libya argued that a Security Council resolution was invalid because the Security Council was not entitled to find a threat to the peace under Article 39 such as to justify it in passing a

---

[25] 1966 UNYB 190 at 192.   [26] 1946 UNYB 327; Crockett, *The Fifty Years War* (1995), 59.
[27] 1972 UNYB 136.
[28] Brownlie, 'The Decisions of the Political Organs of the UN and the Rule of Law', in Macdonald (ed.), *Essays in Honour of Wang Tieya* (1994), 91; Caron, 'The Legitimacy of the Collective Authority of the Security Council', 87 AJIL (1993) 552; Bedjaoui, *The New World Order and the Security Council: Testing the Legality of its Acts* (1994).

binding resolution under Chapter VII.[29] And in the *Application of the Convention on the Prevention and Punishment of the Crime of Genocide* case the Court was asked to pronounce on the validity of the Security Council arms embargo on the whole of the former Yugoslavia imposed in Security Council Resolution 713, and to determine whether the embargo was invalid because it conflicted with the right of self-defence of Bosnia-Herzegovina under the UN Charter.[30] To date, the International Court of Justice has avoided a categorical answer to the sensitive question as to whether it may allow judicial review of Security Council decisions. Commentators are divided as to whether in principle judicial review should be available or whether it would be incompatible with the primary responsibility of the Security Council for the maintenance of international peace and security 'in order to ensure prompt and effective action by the United Nations' under Article 24 of the UN Charter.[31]

But the Court did make clear in its discussion of admissibility in the *Nicaragua* case that it does not regard itself as excluded from deciding on cases involving ongoing armed conflict, including decisions as to collective self-defence. The USA argued that

the Application was inadmissible because each of Nicaragua's allegations constitutes no more than a reformulation of a single fundamental claim that the United States is engaged in an unlawful use of armed force, or breach of the peace, or acts of aggression against Nicaragua, a matter which is committed by the Charter and by practice to the competence of other organs, in particular the United Nations Security Council. All allegations of this kind are confided to the political organs of the Organization for consideration and determination; the United States quotes Article 24 of the Charter, which confers upon the Security Council 'primary responsibility for the maintenance of international peace and security'.[32] The provisions of the Charter dealing with the ongoing use of armed force contain no

---

[29] *Cases concerning Questions of Interpretation and Application of the 1971 Montreal Convention arising from the Aerial Incident at Lockerbie, Jurisdiction and Admissibility*, ICJ Reports (1998); 37 ILM (1998) 187.   [30] Provisional Measures, ICJ Reports (1993) 3, 325.

[31] Gowlland-Debbas, 'The Relationship between the International Court of Justice and the Security Council in the Light of the Lockerbie case', 88 AJIL (1994) 643; Graefrath, 'Leaving to the Court what belongs to the Court', 4 EJIL (1993) 184; Franck, 'The Powers of Appreciation: Who is the Ultimate Guardian of UN Legality', 86 AJIL (1992) 519; Alvarez, 'Judging the Security Council', 90 AJIL (1996) 1.

[32] Article 24 of the UN Charter provides:

1. In order to ensure prompt and effective action by the United Nations, its Members confer on the Security Council primary responsibility for the maintenance of international peace and security, and agree that in carrying out its duties under this responsibility the Security Council acts on their behalf.
2. In discharging these duties the Security Council shall act in accordance with the Purposes and Principles of the United Nations. The specific powers granted to the Security Council for the discharge of these duties are laid down in Chapters VI, VII, VIII, and XII.
3. The Security Council shall submit annual and, when necessary, special reports to the General Assembly for its consideration.

recognition of the possibility of settlement by judicial, as opposed to political means.[33]

Nicaragua replied that this US argument failed to take account of the fundamental distinction between Article 2(4), which defines a legal obligation to refrain from the threat or use of force, and Article 39, which establishes a political process. The International Court of Justice chose to deal with this question together with the argument advanced by the USA that the subject matter of the application, the ongoing exercise of the inherent right of individual or collective self-defence under Article 51 of the Charter, was outside the subject matter jurisdiction of the Court. Article 51 provides a role in such matters only for the Security Council. Nicaragua replied that Article 51 does not support the claim that the question of the legitimacy of actions assertedly taken in self-defence is committed exclusively to the Security Council. The International Court of Justice asserted the right of the Court to resolve any legal questions. But it seemed to have some sympathy with the argument that determinations of aggression under Article 39 of the UN Charter could be dealt with only by the Security Council. In a rather obscure passage the Court said that the USA had misrepresented the Nicaraguan case as relating to Chapter VII when in fact it concerned Article 2(4), and for this reason could properly be brought before the principal judicial organ of the UN for peaceful settlement.[34] The implication seems to be that matters under Chapter VII could not properly be entertained by the Court.

The Court said that the Security Council had only primary, not exclusive, authority under Article 24 of the UN Charter; moreover, the Court had not in the past shied away from cases merely because they had political implications or involved serious elements of the use of force. The USA itself had brought cases involving armed attacks: 'As to the inherent right of self-defence, the fact that it is referred to in the Charter as a "right" is indicative of a legal dimension; if in the present proceedings it becomes necessary for the Court to judge in this respect between the parties it cannot be debarred from doing so by the existence of a procedure for the States concerned to report to the Security Council in this connection.'

Encouraged by this reasoning, states have recently brought several cases to the Court on this sensitive subject matter of the use of force. Cameroon brought a boundary case against Nigeria, in which it also made allegations that Nigeria had illegally undertaken cross-border incursions;[35] Iran sued the USA in two cases arising out of US involvement in the 1980–88

---

[33] *Nicaragua case (Jurisdiction and Admissibility)* ICJ Reports (1984) 551, para 89.
[34] Ibid. at para 94.
[35] In 1998 the Court found jurisdiction (ICJ Reports 1998); Nigeria has since brought counter-claims against Cameroon also alleging illegal use of force.

Iran/Iraq conflict, first, the *Oil Platforms* case,[36] and, second, a case arising out of the shooting down of the Iran Airbus by a US warship;[37] Yugoslavia brought cases against ten NATO states for their bombing campaign over Kosovo;[38] Pakistan sued India for shooting down a Pakistani aircraft over Pakistani air-space;[39] DRC sued Burundi, Uganda, and Rwanda for acts of armed aggression perpetrated in flagrant violation of the UN Charter; it claimed that the invasion by respondent state troops on 2 August 1998 in an attempt to overthrow the government and establish a Tutsi regime was a violation of the DRC's sovereignty and territorial integrity[40] This recent trend makes it possible that the Court will for the first time since the *Nicaragua* case begin to play a central role in the development of the law on the use of force.[41]

The question has also arisen of the role of the General Assembly and its relationship to the Security Council in the development and application of the law in this area. Chapter IV of the UN Charter gives some guidance on the role of the General Assembly and the division of functions between the two organs of the UN. Under Article 10 the General Assembly may make recommendations to member states or to the Security Council; Article 11(1) says that the General Assembly may consider the general principles of cooperation in the maintenance of international peace and security and may make recommendations with regard to such principles; Article 11(2) sets out a division as far as *action* is concerned: 'any such question on which action is necessary should be referred to the Security Council'; Article 11(3) authorizes the General Assembly to call the attention of the Security Council to situations likely to endanger international peace and security.[42] Article 12 is designed to avoid conflict between the two organs; it provides that whilst the Security Council is exercising in respect of any dispute or situation the functions assigned to it in the Charter, the General Assembly shall not make any recommendation with regard to that dis-

---

[36] The Court found jurisdiction in ICJ Reports (1996) 803.

[37] The *Case concerning the Aerial Incident of 3rd July, 1988* was settled: 35 ILM (1996) 550.

[38] *Legality of the Use of Force*, ICJ Reports (1999), 38 ILM (1999) 950. The Court refused provisional measures on the basis that it lacked *prima facie* jurisdiction on the merits of the case: see Chapter 2.

[39] *Aerial Incident of 10 August 1999 (Pakistan v India)*.The Court decided that it had no jurisdiction to decide this case: ICJ Reports (2000).

[40] *Armed Activities on the Territory of the Congo*. The Court ordered provisional measures: ICJ Reports (2000). There were two further cases where there was no basis for jurisdiction but the claimant state invited the defendant to accept the case.

[41] The issue of whether the Security Council has the exclusive and final right to make determinations as to the occurrence of acts of aggression also caused problems in the work of the International Law Commission on the Draft Code of Offences against the Peace and Security of Mankind and later on the Statute of the International Criminal Court.

[42] Simma, *The UN Charter: A Commentary* (1994) at 254; Bailey and Daws, *The Procedure of the UN Security Council* (3rd edn, 1998) at 281, and see Chapter 6 below.

pute or situation unless the Security Council so requests. That is, both the General Assembly and the Security Council may discuss questions to do with the use of force and make recommendations, but the Charter scheme empowered only the Security Council to make binding decisions on action in this area under Article 25 and it was the Security Council that was to have the primary role.[43]

The question therefore arises how far condemnation or approval or discussion by the Security Council and by the General Assembly are of equal importance in interpreting the Charter and developing the law on the use of force by states. Both are fora in which states can set out their legal justifications for the use of force and appeal to other states for support; accordingly it does not seem appropriate to try to distinguish between the two fora with regard to the statements in debates and in explanation of votes.[44] As regards the significance of resolutions, the General Assembly may be more representative, but it was the Security Council that was expressly assigned primary responsibility for the maintenance of international peace and security. Nevertheless, the General Assembly has passed resolutions not only confirming condemnation already made by the Security Council but also condemning behaviour when a veto or threat of a veto prevented a Security Council resolution from being adopted.

At times Western powers have challenged the right of the General Assembly to use terms such as 'aggression' contained in Chapter VII of the UN Charter on the ground that the General Assembly should not override the discretion of the Security Council. For example, in 1981 the UK objected to the General Assembly using the phrase in relation to South Africa's actions against the front-line states.[45] Again Canada, speaking on the General Assembly resolution on the Israeli bombing of the Iraqi nuclear reactor, argued that the General Assembly should not use the term 'acts of aggression'; it was a matter for the Security Council to make such determinations.[46] The USA denounced the repeated condemnation of Israel for this attack as a ritualistic exercise which failed to make a positive contribution to resolving the Middle East conflict; the Security

---

[43] See Chapter 6 below. On the complex question of which Security Council resolutions are binding, see Bailey and Daws, *The Procedure of the UN Security Council* (3rd edn, 1998) at 263.

[44] In more recent years since the end of the Cold War and the virtual end of decolonization General Assembly debates and resolutions have generally become different in tone, often adopted by consensus. Also, the use of the Security Council as a mini-General Assembly, with many non-member states claiming the right to address the Council, was criticized by Western states during the Cold War (for example, by Australia, S/PV 2620, which said that the Security Council should not be used as a forum for confrontation in this way); this practice is now much less common: see Bailey and Daws, *The Procedure of the UN Security Council* (3rd edn, 1998) at 154.   [45] 1981 UNYB 228.

[46] 1982 UNYB 425.

Council had itself condemned Israel for this action. Sweden opposed certain passages of General Assembly Resolution 38/180A calling for states to refrain from supplying weapons to Israel, to suspend economic and financial dealings, and to sever diplomatic, trade, and cultural links. Sweden said that these were matters for the Security Council and that the resolution could not be reconciled with the division of responsibilities between the General Assembly and the Security Council.[47] That is, Western states have made it clear that they do not regard General Assembly resolutions as authoritative determinations under Chapter VII.

The assessment of Security Council and General Assembly practice may not be simple. After a debate member states may choose neither to pass a resolution nor to make a statement. And in their debates states are often cautious in their language; they may not always use legal language in their assessment of the justification for a use of force. They may choose rather to express sympathy or understanding of the action taken. For example, the UK, in its reaction to controversial uses of force by the USA, has from time to time adopted forms of words that allow it to offer support or sympathy but to stop short of an unequivocal endorsement of the legal argument of the USA; to a casual observer this statement may appear to offer support for the US legal argument, but in fact it does not go so far.

The resolutions and statements of the Security Council and the resolutions of the General Assembly tend not to use the language of the Charter in Articles 2(4) and 51, nor to refer to them expressly; when they do refer to these Articles it is normally to recall them in general terms in the preamble of the resolution.[48] The Security Council in particular may not be concerned to determine legality; its role in the maintenance of international peace and security may lead it to choose to avoid any attribution of responsibility for breach of the law. Its resolutions may be indeterminate; a condemnation may be interpreted as limited to the particular facts, simply a condemnation of the particular use of force in the particular circumstances or as a pronouncement on the general law invoked by the states using force. Even when the Security Council does condemn it generally does so on the particular facts, in order to secure consensus and perhaps to secure the strongest condemnation possible. That is, the resolution makes no general pronouncement on the legality of, for example, anticipatory self-defence or the protection of nationals; it condemns the

---

[47] 1983 UNYB 330.

[48] The *Repertoire of Practice of the Security Council* and the *Repertoire of Practice of UN Organs* list such express references. It is noteworthy that the Security Council has not expressly concerned itself to identify threats of force: see Sadurska, 'Threats of Force', 82 AJIL (1988) 239. On threats of force under Article 2(4), see *Nicaragua* case, ICJ Reports (1986) 14 at para 227; *Legality of Threat or Use of Nuclear Weapons*, ICJ Reports (1996) 226 at para 47.

particular use of force. These episodes do not provide express confirmation that the general right invoked to justify the use of force is not part of international law, but if there is no example of a particular type of force escaping condemnation, that is persuasive evidence against that doctrine.

In contrast, the views expressed in the debates on the particular uses of force or in the general debates on law-making resolutions will be more revealing of states' views of the legal position and will reflect the doctrinal divergence behind the resolutions. A resolution condemning a particular use of force may reflect very different views of the legal position; the different states voting for the resolution may have done so for very different reasons and on the basis of different views of the law. Thus, for example, some states would reject the legality of a use of force simply because it was taken in protection of nationals abroad or was anticipatory; others would not reject all such actions in principle but would condemn the action on the particular facts because it was disproportionate or unnecessary. In the case of South Africa, Portugal, and Israel some states regarded any claim by these states to use force in self-defence against neighbouring states as defective because they were acting to further illegal policies or illegal occupation; other states accepted the possibility of self-defence by South Africa, Portugal, and Israel, but looked at each incident on its facts.

It may be argued that condemnation of a particular use of force by the Security Council or General Assembly is conclusive or at least persuasive as to illegality. Condemnation of another state by a state with whom it normally has close relations, as when the UK condemns a use of force by the USA or the USA condemns a use of force by Israel, is exceptionally strong evidence of illegality. Franck makes a convincing case with regard to the General Assembly that states tended even during the Cold War to vote in a principled way in responding to a use of force by a superpower or by a third world state; there was not a double standard on the part of most states except for the superpowers themselves and their close supporters.[49] But a slight doubt arises because occasionally both the General Assembly and the Security Council seemed willing to condemn a state for a particular episode because of its past record. Examples of this can be found in the regular condemnations of Portugal and later of South Africa for particular uses of force. It seems that because these states were acting in furtherance of apartheid and colonialism there was a readiness to condemn for individual uses of force even without clear evidence with regard to the particular incident. Such doubts about the evidence led Western states sometimes to abstain on certain resolutions. An example

---

[49] Franck, 'Of Gnats and Camels: Is there a Double Standard at the United Nations?', 78 AJIL (1984) 811.

is the episode in 1969 when the UK and Spain did not join in the votes condemning Portugal for actions against Senegal, Zambia, and Guinea. The UK said that the Security Council was not dealing with Portuguese policy in Africa, but with a specific incident for which it was not justified to condemn Portugal.[50] Other states argued that self-defence could not be invoked to perpetuate colonialism with regard to Guinea and Portugal.[51] Similarly in 1976 the USA refused to condemn South Africa for its use of force against Zambia on the ground that the episode needed further investigation.[52] If this apparent scrupulousness on the part of the UK and the USA is taken at face value, then condemnations may not be conclusive evidence of illegality in these cases. However, these were special cases and there are no apparent equivalents today.

The more difficult question and one that has given rise to greater controversy among writers is whether, if condemnation is evidence of illegality, the converse is true. Is failure to condemn evidence of legality? Not necessarily so, for there are many reasons for a failure to condemn.[53] Indeed, the practice of the Security Council shows a distinct reluctance to condemn; even a finding of responsibility is unusual. Even if there is an investigation of a use of force where there are conflicting claims by the two sides there may be no conclusion as to responsibility and no blame.[54] Similarly the UN Secretary-General, in his many reports on conflicts to the Security Council, generally avoids the attribution of responsibility unless expressly asked to pronounce on this, as, for example, when the Security Council asked him to report on the responsibility for the start of the Iran/Iraq war in 1980. He is also generally very careful in his public statements not to attribute blame for breach of the law on the use of force. It is also common for the Security Council and the General Assembly's initial response to a conflict to be to avoid any finding of responsibility and simply to call for an end to all intervention.

Thus the Security Council unanimously passed Resolution 479 at the outbreak of the Iran/Iraq conflict; this called upon Iran and Iraq to refrain immediately from any further use of force and to settle their dispute by peaceful means. More recently the resurgence of conflict in Kashmir and the outbreak of conflict between Ethiopia and Eritrea led the Security Council again simply to call for peaceful settlement. With regard to the latter conflict, the Security Council subsequently imposed an arms

---

[50] 1969 UNYB 137.   [51] 1969 UNYB 140.   [52] 1976 UNYB 166.

[53] See Barsotti, 'Armed Reprisals', in Cassese (ed.), *Current Legal Regulation of the Use of Force* (1986), 79. For example, states on the Security Council or the General Assembly may think that, although the legality of a particular use of force is open to question, the acts should not be condemned because they were morally or politically justified. (As, for example, with the failure to condemn Israel in 1967 over the Entebbe raid, the Tanzanian invasion of Uganda to overthrow Idi Amin or the split vote on the condemnation of the US use of force against Panama.)   [54] As with Iran/Iraq in 1974, 1974 UNYB 252.

embargo on *both* states in Resolution 1298. Express findings of aggression (or of aggressive acts) are extremely unusual. It has been only states which were in some sense seen as outlaws which have been condemned for aggression by both the Security Council and the General Assembly; Portugal when it refused to relinquish its colonial possessions, Southern Rhodesia after its unilateral declaration of independence, Israel after its occupation of the West Bank, Gaza and other territory, South Africa during apartheid and its occupation of Namibia, and Indonesia after its invasion of East Timor. Express condemnation by name is also unusual, although it may nevertheless be clear which state is being criticized. For example, in 1983 the General Assembly passed Resolution 38/10 on Central America by consensus; it asserted in general terms the duty of all states to refrain from the threat of use of force, and the inalienable right of all peoples to decide on their own form of government free from all foreign intervention, coercion or limitation; it then condemned the acts of aggression against the sovereignty, independence, and territorial integrity of the states of the region, but did not name any specific state as responsible.[55] Similarly when Turkey invaded Cyprus, Iran attacked commercial shipping during the Iran/Iraq war, the USA intervened in Grenada and Nicaragua, resolutions passed by the Security Council and the General Assembly condemned the behaviour, but did not name the state responsible.

If there is no condemnation of a particular use of force by the Security Council because a permanent member actually uses its veto, or threatens to use its veto, it would seem to be even harder to argue that the use of force is therefore legal.[56] A few writers have, however, made this argument and have asserted that failure of the Security Council to condemn (whether because of the veto or not) constitutes acquiescence by other states and helps to undermine the prohibition on the use of force or intervention and to support controversial doctrines of international law, such as a right of pro-democratic intervention or the right to use force in retaliation for terrorist attacks or the right to use force to protect nationals abroad.[57] This unusual approach to the assessment of state practice discounts the statements of states and ignores widespread condemnation; it also discounts not only general resolutions of the General Assembly on the use of force but also the massive network of treaties which reinforce

[55] 1983 UNYB 197.

[56] The US government took this position with regard to regional action under Chapter VIII; failure to condemn was argued to constitute authorization by the Security Council: see Chapter 7 below.

[57] D'Amato, *International Law: Process and Prospect* (2nd edn, 1995), Chapter 6; Weisburd, *Use of Force* (1997); Arend and Beck, *International Law and the Use of Force* (1993), Chapter 10. On pro-democratic invasions, see Chapter 2 below; on force against terrorist attacks and the protection of nationals, see Chapter 4 below.

the prohibitions of the use of force and of intervention; it gives decisive weight to the action of the state using force. This clearly privileges powerful states and especially the permanent members of the Security Council who, through the veto or threat of veto, can create new customary international law in reinterpretation of the Charter. In a more extreme version of this argument, some have argued that even Security Council or General Assembly condemnation of a particular use of force, if it is not followed by any action against the state condemned, also constitutes acquiescence.[58] Some, like D'Amato, have used these arguments mainly to argue that controversial US actions are lawful; others have applied it to challenge the customary status of the prohibition on force.[59] Both these approaches discount what states say in reaction to the use of force by other states; they claim that the absence of a Security Council or General Assembly resolution or of any sanctions against the state using force means that its behaviour should be seen not as a breach of international law but as the emergence of a new right to use force.

The effect of this argument is compounded by the fact that some of these writers also discount what the states using force actually say in justification of their use of force and try to extract new rights to use force on the basis of the actions of the states using force. That is, they ignore the fact that states generally do not claim revolutionary new rights to use force, but try to defend their use of force by claiming self-defence or other legal justifications. They say that the state practice should be reinterpreted in the light of what the state could or should have said to explain its actions. Thus, if the action could be favourably described as humanitarian intervention or pro-democratic intervention, then this supports the emergence of such a doctrine, even though states do not invoke these new rights but base their use of force on traditional doctrines. The Court in the *Nicaragua* case refused to take this approach in its consideration of the question whether a new customary law right of forcible intervention to assist opposition forces to overthrow governments had become established. For the Court, the fact that states did not claim a new right of intervention was a decisive factor in the rejection of the emergence of any new customary law right. States in fact justified their interventions by invoking the doctrine of collective self-defence; they did not claim a new right to use force in response to invitations from opposition forces.[60]

Clearly there can be no common ground in the assessment of the significance of states, practice between those writers who discount what

[58] Weisburd, ibid.; Arend and Beck, ibid.
[59] Arangio-Ruiz, *The UN Declaration on Friendly Relations and the system of sources of international law* (1979). Franck, 'Who killed Article 2(4)?', 64 AJIL (1970) 809, and reply by Schacter, 'The Reports of the Death of Article 2(4) are greatly exaggerated', 65 AJIL (1971) 544.   [60] *Nicaragua* case para 207.

states say and those who take the more traditional view adopted by the International Court of Justice in the *Nicaragua* case.[61] It is only a few writers who take this extreme position of treating General Assembly or Security Council condemnation as support and ignoring the actual language of states. This approach has been subjected to serious criticism,[62] but it cannot be ignored because recently with regard to Kosovo there were signs that some states were putting forward such arguments in their attempt to justify the NATO action. That is, they were arguing that past practice should be reinterpreted to support a doctrine of humanitarian intervention.[63]

EFFECTIVENESS OF THE PROHIBITION OF THE USE OF FORCE

The question as to how far divergences from the prohibition on the use of force should be seen not as breaches but rather as exceptions to or modifications of the prohibition is crucial also to any assessment of the role of international law in this area. There is widespread scepticism as to the 'effectiveness' of international law on the use of force. Is this justified? The gap between the prohibition of the use of force and the practice seems striking to some commentators, but this divergence should not necessarily be taken as proving the ineffectiveness or pointlessness of the law in this area. Conversely, international law should not be assumed to be effective in the sense of controlling or influencing state behaviour just because state behaviour is in fact in compliance with it.

As the ICJ put it in the *Nicaragua* case, in a now very well-known passage in its discussion of whether the prohibition of the use of force does represent customary international law:

It is not to be expected that in the practice of States the application of the rules in question should have been perfect, in the sense that States should have refrained, with complete consistency, from the use of force or from intervention in each other's internal affairs. The Court does not consider that, for a rule to be established as customary, the corresponding practice must be in absolutely rigorous conformity with the rule. In order to deduce the existence of customary rules, the Court deems it sufficient that the conduct of States should, in general, be consistent with such rules, and that instances of State conduct inconsistent with a given rule should generally be treated as breaches of that rule, not as indications of the recognition of a new rule. If a State acts in a way prima facie incompatible

---

[61] Farer, 'Human Rights in Law's Empire: The Jurisprudence War', 85 AJIL (1991) 117.

[62] Mullerson, 'Sources of International Law: New Tendencies in Soviet Thinking', 83 AJIL (1989) 494 at 505; Brownlie, 'The UN Charter and the Use of Force 1945–1985', in Cassese (ed.), *The Current Legal Regulation of the Use of Force* (1986) at 491. Akehurst, 'Letter', 80 AJIL (1986) 147.   [63] See Chapter 2 below.

with a recognized rule, but defends its conduct by appealing to exceptions or justifications contained within the rule itself, then whether or not the State's conduct is in fact justifiable on that basis, the significance of that attitude is to confirm rather than to weaken the rule.[64]

But the insistence that breaches may be seen as strengthening rather than negating rules cannot be taken too far without losing plausibility.

In this as in other areas, it is fundamentally misguided to attribute to international law an exclusive role in controlling state behaviour; it tends to be non-lawyers rather than lawyers whose expectations are unreasonably elevated and who attack international law as having no significant role when there is anything less than perfect compliance. As in the national sphere, legal rules are only one among a variety of factors that may influence behaviour.

Questions as to whether international law does influence state behaviour involve a study of the role of international law in national decision-making; this requires empirical work on the internal decision-making processes. The focus must shift from the artificial legal entity, the state, to the politicians and officials actually making the decisions on the use of force and the response to the use of force by others. But there are all sorts of practical problems with this type of empirical work. Studies such as that of Chayes on the 1962 Cuban Missile Crisis remain unusual.[65] Access to the material on national decision-making may be possible only many years after the events in question. Thus the role of the law in the UK decision-making process in the 1956 Suez Crisis came to light only thirty years later when the official papers could finally be published.[66] And generalization may not be justified; just because the officials and politicians used international law in one way in one episode it does not follow that the same approach would be adopted in different circumstances. That is, the question of the impact of international law on national decision-making is not easily resolved, if at all. In the absence of such empirical research the matter remains one for inference from public statements and actions of states. Simple conclusions as to effectiveness may not be possible. Writers differ fundamentally in their interpretation of state practice; thus some claim that 'non-intervention is preached but not practised' and that states assert a principle with which they do not comply.[67] Some have said that the prohibition on the use of force is not customary law because states had used force both before and after the Charter and the reactions of other states were often ambiguous and

---

[64] *Nicaragua* case para 186.   [65] Chayes, *The Cuban Missile Crisis* (1987).

[66] Marston, 'Armed Intervention in the 1956 Suez Canal Crisis: The Legal Advice Tendered to the British Government', 37 ICLQ (1988) 773.

[67] Lowe, 'The Principle of Non-intervention: Use of Force', in Lowe and Warbrick (eds), *The United Nations and the Principles of International Law* (1994), 72.

inadequate.[68] Others say that, broadly, states comply with the law outlawing the use of force.

One of the issues that has given rise to the most significant scepticism as to effectiveness of the prohibition of the use of force is the question as to whether breach of the law on the use of force is cost free, whether states may break the law and get away with it. This question also is not susceptible of a simple answer. The UN collective security system was generally incapacitated during the Cold War, although regional organizations did impose sanctions in some cases.[69] It is notorious that the only use of Chapter VII enforcement action involving armed force was in Korea, and the legal status of even that action was controversial. The only uses of UN economic sanctions were against Southern Rhodesia and South Africa. The Security Council and the General Assembly from time to time issued condemnations of the use of force by states in their resolutions. The question of how far a simple condemnation by the Security Council or the General Assembly or a regional organization operated as a disincentive, even in the absence of any formal collective sanction, is not a simple one. Again there can be no conclusive answer without looking behind the state façade, but it is clear from public information that states argue and negotiate to try to avoid condemnation; the price may be intangible, but it is one that states using force do not want to have to pay. The set-piece Security Council and General Assembly debates in which they repeated year after year their condemnation of earlier uses of force by certain states fulfilled a symbolic role.[70] Thus year after year the General Assembly voted to condemn the Israeli attack on the Iraqi nuclear reactor, Vietnam's intervention in Cambodia, and the USSR invasion of Afghanistan.[71] Of course a hazard of this practice is that the General Assembly is then trapped into continuing, because to stop would give the message that the behaviour is somehow now accepted.

The rules of international law in this area clearly also serve a declaratory function; they set out the goal to be aimed at, the ideal that states adhere to. This symbolic function is apparent in the *African Charter* and the 1984 General Assembly *Declaration on the Right of Peoples to Peace*, for example, when they assert the right of peoples to national and international peace and security.[72] Many resolutions of the UN General Assembly have been passed to reassert and develop the rules in the Charter. As was explained above, typically the Western states have been suspicious of

---

[68] Arangio-Ruiz, *The UN Declaration on Friendly Relations and the system of sources of international law* (1979).   [69] See Chapter 7 below.

[70] Bleicher, 'The Legal Significance of Recitation of General Assembly Resolutions', 63 AJIL (1969) 444; Sloan, 'General Assembly Resolutions Revisited', 58 BYIL (1987) 41.

[71] It is interesting that after Iraq invaded Kuwait the ritual inclusion of the nuclear reactor question was dropped.   [72] 21 ILM (1981) 58.

such resolutions and their ritual reaffirmation of existing rules. They have seen them as pointless and/or dangerous, pointless in that they add nothing to the UN Charter and dangerous in so far as they may depart from it. It is easy to be cynical about such resolutions, especially when they are advocated by states such as the USSR, contemporaneously involved in aggression against others. China and Albania both regarded the proposal for the 1987 *Declaration on the Non-Use of Force* as a fraudulent abuse. Much of the debate over the 1987 Declaration was taken up by political point-scoring about breaches of the general rules that states were solemnly debating. But small and new states typically have supported the drafting of general resolutions on the use of force. They have been willing to seek consensus and not simply to use their majority in the General Assembly. Some of the suspicion of general statements of principle misses the point that many states were still colonies at the time of the adoption of the Charter by the fifty-one original member states and that they had come to want to take part in the public reaffirmation of its most important rules. Moreover, the drafting of substantive rules has from the start been accompanied by concern over the functioning of the UN system. To accompany the general resolutions on the use of force the General Assembly has worked endlessly, and often on the initiative of the Western states, on resolutions with a more practical focus, such as the *Declaration on the Strengthening of International Security*, and on Questions concerning the UN Charter and the Strengthening of the Role of the UN, Good Neighbourliness and so on.

Given the problems of any empirical investigation into 'effectiveness', it is all the more important to look at international law on the use of force in terms of the language used by states. Given that in fact they choose to use this language to explain their behaviour and to respond to that of others, anyone involved in any way in advising states or in assessing their actions will have to be able to engage in this discourse. Simple assertions that this use of language is mere cynical manipulation of the rules, and no more than *ex post facto* rationalization for actions reached on other grounds, are not justified in the absence of empirical evidence that this is in fact the case and are no more plausible than the opposite version that states are in fact influenced by law. Of course, it is common for states to offer other justifications as well; it is rare for a state to use the language of international law exclusively. They also offer political explanations, criticisms, and justifications, but with only a tiny number of exceptions they take care to offer a legal argument for their use of force. It is very rare for them not even to try to provide a legal justification.

The rare instances when states seem to have made a deliberate decision not to give a legal explanation stand out. The absence of any real attempt at a legal justification by the USA, the UK, and France for the protection of the Kurds in 1991 and by Turkey for its incursions into Iraq in pursuit of Kurds is unusual and seems to indicate considerable doubt as to the legality of these actions.[73] Even when politicians do occasionally say that they will no longer observe international law restrictions on the use of force, as was sometimes the case during the Reagan era when the administration suggested that it was not necessary to comply with international law in response to an enemy, an evil empire that did not itself observe the law, the USA continued to offer legal argument in the Security Council.[74] Rather than not even attempt a legal justification, commonly states offer what may seem weak or unconvincing arguments. But it is always important to allow for different viewpoints; even when two opposing states both invoke self-defence they may both believe they have right on their side. Often it is a series of arguments that are offered, maybe differing over time, in order or emphasis. This combination of a series of different justifications is typical legal reasoning, often apparent in arguments in court; a whole series of arguments of differing strengths is included on the chance that one of them may appeal to one particular audience. During the Cold War a constraint on this rhetoric was the consideration that the language of states in their interpretation and application of the UN Charter could operate as a precedent and later be invoked against them.[75] The end of the Cold War has apparently weakened this constraint, at any rate as far as NATO member states are concerned.

[73] On the protection of the Kurds in Iraq, see Chapter 2 below; on Turkey's incursions into Iraq, see Chapter 4 below.
[74] Kirkpatrick, the US representative to the UN, said that 'unilateral compliance with the Charter's principles of non-intervention and non-use of force may make sense in some instances but is hardly in itself a sound basis for either US policy or for international peace and security': 'Law and Reciprocity', 1986 ASIL 59.
[75] As Franck graphically illustrates in Franck and Weisband, *Word Politics* (1972).

2
The prohibition of the use of force

The central rule on the use of force, the prohibition of the threat or use of force contained in Article 2(4) of the UN Charter, is currently the subject of fundamental disagreement. Although states and commentators generally agree that the prohibition is not only treaty and customary law but is also *ius cogens*,[1] there is no comparable agreement on the exact scope of the prohibition. This controversy has come to the fore dramatically in the recent use of force by NATO in Kosovo in 1999. States and commentators expressed their fundamental disagreements about the legality of this intervention in terms of Article 2(4). Some claimed that a new right to humanitarian intervention was emerging; others that the NATO action was a flagrant breach of the UN Charter.

The current debate is a reincarnation of earlier disagreements on the interpretation of Article 2(4). Here these will be set out in outline only. Writers disagreed as to whether Article 2(4) reflected existing customary international law or whether it was in 1945 a radical departure from previous customary law, to be narrowly interpreted. The controversy centred on the second part of Article 2(4): should the words 'against the territorial integrity or political independence of any state, or in any other manner inconsistent with the Purposes of the United Nations' be construed as a strict prohibition on all use of force against another state or did they allow the use of force provided that the aim was not to overthrow the government or seize the territory of the state and provided that the action was consistent with the purposes of the UN?[2] Many US commentators argued during the Cold War that the interpretation of Article 2(4) depended on the functioning of the UN collective security system, and therefore that the inability of the Security Council to act because of the veto meant that Article 2(4) should be read to allow the

---

[1] *Case Concerning Military and Paramilitary Activities in and against Nicaragua (Merits)*, ICJ Reports (1986) 14, para 190. See Christenson, 'The World Court and Jus Cogens', 81 AJIL (1987) 93; Ronzitti, 'Use of Force, Jus Cogens and State Consent', in Cassese (ed.), *The Current Legal Regulation of the Use of Force* (1986), 147; Weisburd, 'The Emptiness of the Concept of ius cogens, as Illustrated by the Law in Bosnia-Herzegovina', 17 Michigan Journal of International Law (1995–6) 591.

[2] Bowett, *Self-Defence in International Law* (1958) at 152; Brownlie, *International Law and the Use of Force by States* (1963); Cot and Pellet, *La Charte des Nations Unies* (1991) at 115; Simma (ed.), *The Charter of the United Nations: A Commentary* (1994), 106; Schindler and Hailbronner, *Die Grenzen des völkerrechtlichen Gewaltverbots* (1986); Waldock, 'The Regulation of the Use of Force by Individual States in International Law', 81 RCADI (1952) 415.

use of force to further 'world public order' or the principles and purposes of the UN.[3]

For many years this doctrinal disagreement was of limited practical significance in that states themselves rarely made any attempt to interpret Article 2(4) in this narrow fashion; they did not in fact claim that their use of force was justified because it did not aim to seize the territory or overthrow the government of another state or because the UN system was not working. They did not, on the basis of a narrow interpretation of Article 2(4), claim a legal right to use force for humanitarian intervention or to overthrow governments in the name of democracy or some other political system. The argument of the UK in the *Corfu Channel* case remained a relatively isolated example; it claimed that its use of forcible intervention in Albanian waters to recover evidence that might indicate who was responsible for the destruction of two British warships by mines did not violate Article 2(4) because its action did not threaten the territorial integrity or the political independence of Albania. The famous rejection of this argument by the ICJ has been interpreted in fundamentally divergent ways, either as a complete rejection of the narrow interpretation of Article 2(4) or as a more limited rejection of the UK claim on the particular facts. The Court said it 'can only regard the alleged right of intervention as the manifestation of a policy of force such as has in the past given rise to most serious abuses and such as cannot find a place in international law. It is still less admissible in the particular form it would take here—it would be reserved for the most powerful states.'[4]

Similarly there were indications that Israel also took a narrow interpretation of Article 2(4) over the Entebbe incident in 1976; when hijackers diverted an aircraft bound for Tel Aviv to Uganda, Israeli forces mounted a successful rescue operation in Uganda. The main argument of Israel in the Security Council was expressly based on self-defence of its nationals, but it also put forward an interpretation of Article 2(4) by the writer O'Connell as allowing the limited use of force when UN machinery was ineffective.[5] This line was not taken up by other states in the Security Council debate, except perhaps by the USA in its passing reference to the breach of Uganda's sovereignty as only temporary.[6] The Israeli argument

---

[3] This debate is conveniently summarized in the articles by Reisman, 'Coercion and Self-determination: construing Charter Article 2(4)' and the reply by Schacter, 'The Legality of Pro-democratic Invasion', 78 AJIL (1984) 642, 646. See also Farer, 'Human Rights in Law's Empire: the Jurisprudence War', 85 AJIL (1991) 117; Franck, 'Who Killed Article 2(4)', 64 AJIL (1970) 809; Henkin, 'The Reports of the Death of Article 2(4) are Greatly Exaggerated', 65 AJIL (1971) 544.

[4] ICJ Reports (1949) 4 at 34. The ICJ, in the *Nicaragua* case para 202, construed this as a blanket condemnation of intervention.

[5] SC 1942nd meeting, para 102; 1976 UNYB 315.

[6] SC 1941st meeting, para 92, 27 October 1983.

on Article 2(4) was expressly rejected by Sweden; it said: 'The Charter does not authorize any exception to this rule except for the right of self-defence and enforcement measures undertaken by the Council under Chapter VII of the Charter. This is no coincidence or oversight. Any formal exceptions permitting the use of force or of military intervention in order to achieve certain aims, however laudable, would be bound to be abused, especially by the big and strong, and to pose a threat, especially to the small and weak.'[7] The overwhelming majority of states speaking in the debate regarded Israel's action as a breach of Article 2(4). Those who did not condemn Israel did not expressly defend the legality of its action in terms of a narrow interpretation of Article 2(4).

More significantly, when the USA justified its invasion of Grenada in 1983 it suggested in the Security Council that Article 2(4) should not be seen in isolation: 'the prohibitions against the use of force in the Charter are contextual, not absolute. They provide justification for the use of force in pursuit of other values also inscribed in the Charter, such values as freedom, democracy, peace.'[8] But earlier in the debate the USA had relied on the right to protect its nationals in danger and on an invitation by the Governor-General of Grenada to justify its action. Thus in the Entebbe and Grenada incidents the narrow interpretation of Article 2(4) as a less than absolute prohibition of the use of force was not crucial to the state using force: the USA and Israel also put forward other arguments to justify their actions, and the interpretation of Article 2(4) played only a subsidiary and not a decisive role in determining the legality of the intervention. The question of the interpretation of Article 2(4) plays a more decisive role in the debate over humanitarian intervention.

HUMANITARIAN INTERVENTION

Until recently unilateral humanitarian intervention was not put forward as a legal doctrine by states. The Indian action in Bangladesh (1971) which helped the people to secure independence from Pakistan and to end repression,[9] the Tanzanian action in Uganda (1979) which led to the overthrow of Idi Amin[10] and the Vietnamese invasion of Cambodia (1978) which led to the overthrow of Pol Pot[11] were not in fact justified by India, Tanzania, and Vietnam on the basis of humanitarian action; rather, the states using force focused mainly on self-defence. The first two episodes avoided condemnation by the Security Council or the General Assembly,

---

[7] SC 1940th meeting, para 121.   [8] SC 2491st meeting, para 53; 1983 UNYB 211.
[9] 1971 UNYB 144; Franck and Rodley, 'After Bangladesh: The Law of Humanitarian Intervention by Military Force', 67 AJIL (1973) 275.   [10] 1979 UNYB 262.
[11] 1979 UNYB 271.

but the last, although it was at least as persuasive a case for humanitarian intervention, divided states partly on Cold War lines (and partly because of the regional rivalry between Vietnam and China) and was repeatedly condemned by the General Assembly.[12] Many states, including France and the UK, said that violations of human rights could not justify the use of force.[13]

During the Cold War it was writers rather than states that argued in favour of the doctrine of humanitarian intervention as a justification for the use of force by states.[14] In 1982 the UK Foreign and Commonwealth Office had expressed considerable doubt as to the existence of such a doctrine, saying that it was very controversial: the state practice to which advocates of the right of humanitarian intervention had appealed provided an uncertain base on which to rest such a right. Not least this was because history had shown that humanitarian ends were almost always mixed with other, less laudable motives for intervening, and because often the humanitarian benefits of an intervention were either not claimed by the intervening state or were only put forward as an *ex post facto* justification of the intervention. In fact 'the best case that can be made in support of humanitarian intervention is that it cannot be said to be unambiguously illegal'.[15] The absence of the express invocation of the right by states did not, however, deter some writers from arguing that all or some of the above episodes were actually part of state practice supporting a legal right to humanitarian intervention because the states using force *should have* or *could have* used this justification.[16]

These writers ignored the General Assembly resolutions on the use of force which outlawed forcible intervention in absolute terms. The *Friendly Relations Declaration* excludes the right to intervene and makes no provision for humanitarian intervention.[17] The *Definition of Aggression*

---

[12] As, for example, in GA Res 34/22.

[13] 1979 UNYB 271 at 274. This intervention in Cambodia was retrospectively said by the Netherlands in the debate over NATO action in Kosovo to have been a genuine humanitarian intervention. It said that it was a shameful episode in the 1980s when the UN had been more indignant at a Vietnamese military intervention in Cambodia, which almost all Cambodians had experienced as a liberation, than at three years of Khmer Rouge genocide (UN Press Release SC/6686; SC 4011th meeting, 10 June 1999).

[14] See, for example, Lillich (ed.), *Humanitarian Intervention and the United Nations* (1973); Teson, *Humanitarian Intervention: An Inquiry into Law and Morality* (2nd edn, 1997).

[15] 'UK Materials on International Law', 57 BYIL (1986) 614.

[16] See Chapter 1 above; Lillich (ed.), *Humanitarian Intervention and the United Nations* (1973); D'Amato, *International Law: Process and Prospect* (2nd edn, 1995), D'Amato, 'The Invasion of Panama was a Lawful Response to Tyranny', 84 AJIL (1990) 516; Teson, *Humanitarian Intervention: An Inquiry into Law and Morality* (2nd edn, 1997) at 192.

[17] GA Res 2625 (1970). For a discussion of the status of this resolution and of its provisions of the use of force, see Arangio-Ruiz, *The UN Declaration on Friendly Relations and the System of the Sources in International Law* (1972); Gray, 'The Principle of Mon-use of Force', in Lowe and Warbrick (eds), *The United Nations and the Principles of International Law* (1994), 33.

provision that 'no consideration of whatever nature, whether political, economic, military or otherwise, may serve as a justification for aggression' also supports this.[18] These writers also explained away the rejection of forcible humanitarian intervention by the ICJ in the *Nicaragua* case as either simply mistaken or limited to the particular facts.[19] The USA did not actually invoke the doctrine of humanitarian intervention to justify its support for the *contras* in their attempt to overthrow the government of Nicaragua or to justify its direct use of force in mining Nicaraguan ports and bombing oil installations. The Court nevertheless considered whether the protection of human rights might provide a legal justification for the US use of force. The Court said, 'While the USA might form its own appraisal of the situation as to respect for human rights in Nicaragua, the use of force could not be the appropriate method to monitor or ensure such respect. With regard to the steps actually taken, the protection of human rights, a strictly humanitarian objective, cannot be compatible with the mining of ports, the destruction of oil installations, or again with the training, arming and equipping of the contras.'[20] This can be seen as either a complete rejection of any right to use force to protect human rights or as merely a finding that the particular US action did not further any humanitarian objective.[21]

Recent years have seen a shift in state practice and a polarization between NATO states on the one hand and Russia and China on the other. Certain states have now been prepared to rely more openly on a legal doctrine of humanitarian intervention. The first signs of this emerged in the UK justification of the operations which it undertook with the USA and France to protect the Kurds and Shiites in Iraq after the 1991 Iraq/Kuwait conflict.[22] During the UN-authorized operation to drive Iraqi forces out of Kuwait the Kurds and Shiites had been encouraged by the coalition states to rebel against the government, but the cease-fire resolution passed by the Security Council made no provision for the protection of the Kurds in northern Iraq and the Shiites in the south. When the operation to drive Iraqi forces out of Kuwait was over, the government of Iraq turned on the Kurds and Shiites. At first the members of the Security Council treated

---

[18] GA Res 3314 (1974).

[19] For example, Kritisiotis, 'Reappraising Policy Objections to Humanitarian Intervention', 19 Michigan Journal of International Law (1998) 1005; Teson, *Humanitarian Intervention: An Inquiry into Law and Morality* (2nd edn, 1997) at 270.   [20] *Nicaragua* case para 268.

[21] The Court drew a distinction between forcible intervention and genuine humanitarian assistance at para 242. It said 'There can be no doubt that the provision of strictly humanitarian aid to persons or forces in another country, whatever their political affiliations or objectives, cannot be regarded as unlawful intervention, or as in any other way contrary to international law.'

[22] See Gray, 'After the Ceasefire: Iraq, the Security Council and the Use of Force', 65 BYIL (1994) 135.

this as an internal question for Iraq, a clear sign that there was no well-established doctrine of humanitarian intervention at that time. But under pressure from France the Security Council returned to the matter and passed Resolution 688. This called on Iraq to end the repression of its civilian population and to allow access to international humanitarian organizations, but it does not authorize the use of force to help the Kurds and Shiites. The resolution was not passed under Chapter VII and it expressly recalled Article 2(7) of the UN Charter prohibiting the UN from intervention in matters within domestic jurisdiction. Even so, those states which abstained or voted against the resolution did so because they saw it as an illegitimate intervention in Iraqi internal affairs and not a matter for the Security Council.

Despite the absence of express authority from the Security Council, the USA, the UK, and France nevertheless forcibly intervened to protect the Kurds and Shiites in Iraq. They proclaimed safe havens and forced Iraqi troops to leave these areas. They did not offer any explicit legal justification for their action; they did not put forward in the Security Council the doctrine of humanitarian intervention as the justification for their action. Indeed, they did not at this time seem to feel the need to put forward any legal justification. The operation was not condemned by the Security Council or the General Assembly. The USA, the UK, and France subsequently proclaimed no-fly zones over north and south Iraq and continued to patrol Iraqi air-space in order to protect the Kurds and Shiites. This was also done without Security Council authority. When Iraq lodged protests with the Security Council the USA, the UK, and France replied by saying that their measures were designed to prevent Iraqi repression. They also said that they were acting in support of Resolution 688. This apparent attempt to bring their action within an implied authorization by Security Resolution in the absence of any express authorization provided a pattern that was to be followed in the future.[23]

Later the UK did openly espouse the doctrine of humanitarian intervention. It modified its earlier position that the most that could be said about humanitarian intervention was that it was 'not unambiguously illegal'. From August 1992 it moved gradually towards an expression of the doctrine of humanitarian intervention as the justification for the actions in Iraq. It did so not in the Security Council, but in statements and publications in the UK. The Foreign and Commonwealth Office said that international law develops to meet new situations: 'We believe that international intervention without the invitation of the country concerned can be justified in cases of extreme humanitarian need. This is why we were

---

[23] See Lobel and Ratner, 'Bypassing the Security Council: ambiguous authorization to use force, cease-fires and the Iraqi inspection regime', 93 AJIL (1999) 124.

prepared to commit British forces to *Operation Haven*, mounted by the coalition in response to the refugee crisis involving the Iraqi Kurds. The deployment of these forces was entirely consistent with the objectives of SCR 688.'[24] But it did not explain *how* this alleged change in the law had come about. If Article 2(4) of the UN Charter is a dynamic provision open to changing interpretation over time, what developments in fact justified a new interpretation? The UK later elaborated on the doctrine of human-itarian intervention, putting forward conditions which could govern its use. First, there should be a compelling and urgent situation of extreme humanitarian distress which demanded immediate relief; the other state should not be able or willing to meet the distress and deal with it; there should be no practical alternative to intervening in order to relieve the stress, and also the action should be limited in time and scope.[25] This UK espousal of the doctrine of humanitarian intervention seems to have been the first open support by a state since the establishment of the UN.

Confrontations between Iraq and the coalition planes patrolling the no-fly zones occurred in 1991 and 1992; they escalated in 1993 when the coali-tion forces mounted a major operation against Iraqi missile sites and again in 1999 when a long series of confrontations occurred. The legal jus-tifications put forward by the USA, the UK, and France assumed the legal-ity of the no-fly zones; they said that their pilots had the right of self-defence to cover action against Iraqi planes and missile sites.[26] The protests of Iraq did not lead to condemnation by the Security Council or the General Assembly. But the escalation of activity in 1999 was discussed by the Security Council; Russia and China condemned the use of force in the no-fly zones by the US and UK aircraft.[27] The UK replied that its oper-ations were purely reactive and not aggressive. The no-fly zones were necessary both to limit Iraq's capacity to oppress its own people and to monitor its compliance with obligations. The USA agreed with this ration-ale.[28] The implication was that the no-fly zones were justified partly on humanitarian grounds and partly on the basis of implied authority under

[24] 'UK Materials on International Law', 63 BYIL (1992) 824.
[25] Ibid. at 826, 827. Many of the writers who support a legal right to humanitarian inter-vention similarly have tried to produce guidelines to govern its exercise; see, for example, Lillich (ed.), *Humanitarian Intervention and the United Nations* (1973); Verwey, 'Humanitarian Intervention Under International Law', 32 Netherlands International Law Review (1985) 357; Teson, *Humanitarian Intervention: An Inquiry into Law and Morality* (2nd edn, 1997); Charney, 'Anticipatory Humanitarian Intervention in Kosovo', 93 AJIL (1999) 834.
[26] France ended its participation in the operation in 1996. The actions in 1999 went further than previous use of force in that the coalition rules of engagement were expanded to cover not only response to an armed attack, but also pre-emptive action against Iraqi missile sites and command and control centres. See Keesings (1999), 42754, 42811, 42866.
[27] SC 4008th meeting, 21 May 1999.
[28] 'Contemporary Practice of the United States Relating to International Law', 93 AJIL (1999) 470 at 478.

Security Council resolutions. It is interesting that the doctrine of humanitarian intervention was not expressly put forward as a legal argument; this clearly indicates caution about relying on the doctrine as a legal justification for the use of force.

KOSOVO: A NEW ROLE FOR NATO

The NATO action in Kosovo in 1999 marked a further development and revealed a fundamental split as to the legality of humanitarian intervention.[29] The legal arguments of states for and against this action will be discussed in detail in order to illuminate the doctrinal debate about Article 2(4), its relation to Chapter VII, and the practical importance of this debate. It was clear that this bombing campaign against Yugoslavia in protection of the Kosovo Albanians marked a new departure for NATO, which was moving away from its original role as an organization for collective self-defence. With the end of the Cold War it had sought a new role for itself; from 1990 it had begun to redefine itself.[30] It had agreed on the need to transform the Atlantic Alliance 'to reflect the new, more promising era in Europe'. It adopted a new strategic concept in 1991. This said that risks to allied security were less likely to result from calculated aggression against the territory of the allies, but rather from the adverse consequences of instabilities that may arise from the serious economic, social, and political difficulties, including ethnic rivalries and territorial disputes which are faced by many countries in Central and Eastern Europe. These tensions could lead to crises inimical to European stability and even to armed conflicts which could involve outside powers or spill over into NATO countries, having a direct effect on the security of the Alliance. Moreover, Alliance security must also take account of the global context; security interests could be affected by other risks, including proliferation of weapons of mass destruction, disruption of the flows of vital resources, and actions of terrorism and sabotage. Accordingly NATO would have to be prepared to undertake management of crises. In pursuance of this new role NATO became involved in the 1991–95 conflict in the former Yugoslavia and used force other than in collective self-defence. But in this conflict its member states were specifically authorized to use force by the Security Council.

---

[29] 'Editorial Comments: NATO's Kosovo Intervention', 93 AJIL (1999) 824–60; Kritsiotis, 'The Kosovo Crisis and NATO's application of armed force against the Federal Republic of Yugoslavia', 49 ICLQ (2000) 330.

[30] On NATO's redefinition of its role up to February 1999 and on the NATO action with regard to Kosovo up to this date, see Simma, 'NATO, the UN and the use of force: Legal Aspects', 10 EJIL (1999) 1.

After this action further changes were made to NATO's strategic concept. The 1991 new strategic concept had still emphasized that 'The Alliance is purely defensive in purpose.' This phrase has disappeared from the newest strategic concept adopted in 1999. NATO was now not only to ensure the defence of its members but also to contribute to peace and security in the 'Euro-Atlantic region'. NATO would undertake new missions, including conflict prevention and crisis management. This redefinition of NATO was made specifically in response to the events in Kosovo. The member states, in announcing the 1999 strategic concept explained that:

The continuing crisis in and around Kosovo threatens to further destabilise areas beyond the Federal Republic of Yugoslavia. The potential for wider instability underscores the need for a comprehensive approach to the stabilisation of the crisis region in South-Eastern Europe. We recognise and endorse the crucial importance of making South-Eastern Europe a region free from violence and instability. A new level of international engagement is thus needed to build security, prosperity and democratic civil society, leading in time to full integration into the wider European family.[31]

Nevertheless, when NATO resorted to force to protect ethnic Albanians in Kosovo there was still some ambivalence in the official NATO statements as to the precise legal justification for its action against Yugoslavia. NATO did not on the whole clearly and expressly invoke humanitarian intervention as a legal doctrine; the initial authorization by the North Atlantic Council of air strikes in January 1999 said only that the crisis in Kosovo was a threat to the peace and security of the region; the NATO strategy was to halt the violence in Kosovo and thus avert a humanitarian catastrophe.[32] When *Operation Allied Force* actually began in March 1999 the NATO justification focused primarily on moral and political rather than expressly legal justifications for the action. The Secretary-General of NATO said that all efforts to achieve a negotiated, political solution to the Kosovo crisis had failed and they were taking action to support the political aims of the international community. The military aim was to disrupt the violent acts being committed by the Serb army and to weaken their ability to cause further humanitarian catastrophe. They wished thereby to support international efforts to secure Yugoslav agreement to an interim political settlement: 'We must halt the violence and bring an end to the humanitarian catastrophe now unfolding in Kosovo.'[33] Implicitly this seems to be a claim to humanitarian intervention; it also claims to be an action to further the aims of the international community. That is, NATO seemed to be relying in part on a doctrine of implied authorization by the

---

[31] NATO Press Release NAC-S(99)64.
[32] NATO Press Release 99/12, 30 January 1999.   [33] NATO Press Release 1999 (040).

Security Council to justify the legality of its use of force.[34] The official NATO statements left some uncertainty as to whether they were relying on an autonomous doctrine of humanitarian intervention or whether the Security Council resolutions and the doctrine of implied authorization had been a necessary part of the legal justification for the action initiated in March 1999.

In Security Council meetings a variety of arguments were put forward for and against the NATO air strikes. Those attacking the NATO action accused it of a clear violation of the UN Charter; they focused on the absolute prohibition of the use of force in Article 2(4), the primary role of the Security Council in the maintenance of international peace and security under Article 24 of the UN Charter, and the need for Security Council authorization under Chapter VII of the Charter rather than uni- lateral action. Some of the member states assumed NATO was a regional organization under Chapter VIII of the Charter and therefore limited also by the specific requirement in Article 53 that any enforcement action be authorized by the Security Council.[35]

The UN Secretary-General, speaking in response to the start of the NATO air strikes reminded states of the primary responsibility of the Security Council for the maintenance of international peace and security; this was explicitly acknowledged in the NATO Treaty. Therefore the Council should be involved in any decision to resort to force.[36]

At the first emergency Security Council meeting called immediately after the start of the NATO air attacks, states supporting the action said it was taken as a last resort to prevent a humanitarian catastrophe after the failure of all diplomatic efforts to find a peaceful solution.[37] Security Council resolutions had recognized that the situation in Kosovo was a threat to regional peace and security and invoked Chapter VII of the UN Charter. The USA took the line that NATO had acted to avert a humani- tarian catastrophe and deter future aggression and repression in Kosovo. The UK offered a relatively extensive legal argument; it said, 'The action being taken is legal. It is justified as an exceptional measure to prevent an overwhelming humanitarian catastrophe . . . Every means short of force has been tried. In these circumstances, and as an exceptional measure on grounds of overwhelming humanitarian necessity, military intervention is legally justifiable. The force now being used is directed exclusively to

[34] This reflects the justification offered by NATO for its earlier threat of force against Yugoslavia in October 1998; at that time the North Atlantic Council based itself more ex- plicitly on Security Council resolutions. See Simma, 'NATO, the UN and the use of force: Legal Aspects', 10 EJIL (1999) 1.   [35] See Chapter 7 below.
[36] www.un.org/News/dh/latest.htm, 24 March 1999.
[37] SC 3988th meeting, 24 March 1999.

averting a humanitarian catastrophe, and is the minimum necessary for that purpose.'

At the subsequent Security Council meeting called two days later to vote on a resolution condemning the use of force by NATO the Security Council rejected the resolution by three votes in favour (China, Namibia, and Russia) to twelve against.[38] The draft resolution affirmed that the uni-lateral use of force by NATO constituted a violation of Article 2(4), Article 24 (on the primacy of the Security Council), and Article 53 (on the need for Security Council authorization of enforcement action by regional organizations). Those speaking against the NATO action (Cuba, India, Russia, China, Ukraine, and Belarus) were clear that this was a gross vio-lation of the Charter, whereas those defending the action concentrated on the continuing violence by the government of Yugoslavia against the peo-ple of Kosovo.

Those defending the NATO action offered a variety of legal arguments. They stressed the earlier Security Council resolutions passed under Chapter VII calling on Yugoslavia to stop its actions. Although these res-olutions did not expressly authorize the use of force by NATO, several states seemed to argue that they nevertheless justified the NATO action. Thus France spoke of the fact that the Security Council had adopted three resolutions under Chapter VII. In Resolution 1199 the Council had reaf-firmed that the deterioration of the situation posed a threat to regional peace and security and made a number of demands on Yugoslavia. In Resolution 1203 the Council had demanded that the agreements between Yugoslavia, the OSCE, and NATO should be implemented. As Yugoslavia had not done so, NATO's action had responded to this failure. The Netherlands took a similar approach; it said that 'The NATO action fol-lowed directly from resolution 1203, in conjunction with the flagrant non-compliance on the part of Yugoslavia. Given its complex background, the action could not be allowed to be described as unilateral use of force.' Slovenia also took a similar line; it stressed that the Security Council had declared the situation a threat to regional peace and security, had spelled out the requirements for the removal of the threat and the fact that these requirements had been flagrantly violated by Yugoslavia. The Security Council's responsibility in this area was primary but not exclusive, so NATO had been entitled to act. The USA was apparently less concerned to offer a specifically legal justification. It mentioned the violation of res-olutions by Yugoslavia, and then said simply that 'NATO's actions were completely justified. They were necessary to stop the violence and to pre-vent a further deterioration of peace and stability in the region.'

---

[38] SC 3989th meeting, 26 March 1999.

The adoption by the Security Council of Resolution 1244, passed after the agreement on principles of a political solution to end the Kosovo crisis, did not mark a retrospective acceptance of the legality of the NATO action or of humanitarian intervention.[39] Many states, including some of those like Slovenia and Canada who had supported the NATO action, stressed their relief that the Security Council was again taking a central role. Those who had opposed the action took this line even more strongly. Thus Russia said that it was glad that NATO had recognized that the Security Council was the body primarily responsible for the maintenance of peace and security. China maintained its view that NATO had 'seriously violated the Charter of the United Nations and norms of international law, had undermined the authority of the Security Council, and had, hence, set an extremely dangerous precedent in the history of international relations'. Because the resolution failed fully to reflect China's principled stand China had difficulties with it, but in view of the fact that Yugoslavia had accepted the peace plan; that NATO had suspended its bombing; and that the draft resolution reaffirmed the purposes and principles of the UN Charter and the primary responsibility of the Security Council and also reaffirmed the commitment of all member states to the sovereignty and territorial integrity of Yugoslavia, China abstained rather than veto the resolution. It is noteworthy that Latin American states (Costa Rica, Brazil, and Mexico) continued to express concern about the use of force by NATO without Security Council authorization.

LEGALITY OF USE OF FORCE: THE CASE BEFORE THE INTERNATIONAL COURT OF JUSTICE

As well as attacking the legality of the NATO action in the Security Council Yugoslavia brought an action against ten of the nineteen NATO member states before the International Court of Justice; it alleged that by taking part in the bombing each respondent was in breach of the obligation not to use force and also that by taking part in training terrorists (the Kosovo Liberation Army) each respondent was in breach of its obligation not to intervene in the affairs of another state. During the request for provisional measures Yugoslavia set out its position on the intervention at some length. Its argument was in two parts: first, there is no right to humanitarian intervention in international law and, second, even if there were such a right, the modalities chosen by NATO, the air strikes, could not constitute humanitarian intervention. In the oral argument Yugoslavia

---

[39] See the debate leading up to the adoption of the resolution, SC 4011th meeting, 10 June 1999.

said that the prohibition in Article 2(4) was unqualified. The preparatory work of the Charter indicated that intervention for special motives was ruled out by the inclusion of the phrase 'against the territorial integrity or political independence of any State'. The subsequent practice of states had not produced a departure in international law; such a departure would be a major aberration and would require consistent and substantial evidence. Such a change in customary law had not been proved by any NATO member state. This position was confirmed in the *Friendly Relations Declaration*, which excludes the right to intervene in absolute terms; the *Definition of Aggression* provision that 'no consideration of whatever nature, whether political, economic, military or otherwise, may serve as a justification for aggression' also confirmed this. The Yugoslav argument went on to quote writers opposed to humanitarian intervention and the 1984 UK Foreign and Commonwealth Office position that humanitarian intervention was of doubtful legality.

The second stage of Yugoslavia's argument was that on the facts of the case the NATO action could not qualify as humanitarian intervention.[40] Yugoslavia claimed that there was no genuine humanitarian purpose. Moreover, the modalities selected disqualified the action as a humanitarian one. Bombing populated areas of Yugoslavia from a height of 15,000 feet could not qualify. The selection of a bombing campaign was disproportionate to the declared aims of the action. In order to protect one minority in one region all the other communities in the whole of Yugoslavia were placed at risk of intensive bombing. The pattern of targets and the geographical extent of the bombing indicated broad political purposes unrelated to humanitarian issues. Finally, major considerations of international public order disqualified the bombing as a humanitarian action. NATO states had intervened in civil war in Kosovo. The threats of massive force went back seven months before the NATO action and were intended to produce a dictated result. The massive air campaign was planned in order to force Yugoslavia to accept NATO demands. There was no attempt to obtain Security Council authorization.

At the provisional measures stage most of the respondent states said that they did not want to go into the merits of the case and they limited themselves to descriptions of atrocities in Kosovo as background to their argument that Yugoslavia's claim for provisional measures should be rejected. But Belgium did go into the law on the use of force in order to

---

[40] Simma, 'NATO, the UN and the use of force: Legal Aspects', 10 EJIL (1999) 1, argued that the NATO action could not be seen as humanitarian intervention, but was rather reprisals or countermeasures. Many commentators expressed concern that the bombing campaign was not appropriate humanitarian action; the only true humanitarian action would have been a ground operation. The ICJ, in the *Nicaragua* case para 268, rejected the use of force to secure respect for human rights.

offer a legal justification of the NATO action. It argued that the armed intervention was in fact 'based on' Security Council resolutions. This is another instance of the argument of implied Security Council authorization. However, Belgium said that it was necessary to go further and set out the doctrine of humanitarian intervention. There was an obligation to intervene to prevent the humanitarian catastrophe which was occurring and which had been established by the Security Council resolutions, in order to protect those essential human rights which had also achieved the status of *ius cogens*. NATO had never questioned the political independence of the territorial integrity of Yugoslavia; this was not an intervention directed against the territorial integrity or political independence of Yugoslavia. It was intended to save a population in danger and so it was compatible with Article 2(4) of the Charter, which only prohibited those interventions directed against territorial integrity or political independence. This is an express adoption of the narrow interpretation of Article 2(4).

Belgium invoked as precedents the intervention by India in Bangladesh, Tanzania in Uganda, and even the intervention of Vietnam in Cambodia, despite its repeated condemnation by the General Assembly. It also invoked the ECOWAS actions in Liberia and Sierra Leone on the ground that these interventions had not been expressly condemned by the competent organs of the UN.[41] Also Belgium said that the rejection by the Security Council of the Russian draft resolution condemning the NATO action confirmed that the action was legal. The Security Council had decided that there was a humanitarian catastrophe and that the situation was a threat to the peace. It was clear from the resolutions that Yugoslavia was responsible for this state of affairs. The UN Secretary-General had said that, 'Emerging slowly, but I believe surely, is an international norm against the violent repression of minorities that will and must take precedence over concerns of State sovereignty.' The intervention was also intended to safeguard the security of the whole region. These Belgian arguments, relying on what states did rather than what they said and on failure to condemn by the UN, follow the approach of those writers who had argued for a right of humanitarian intervention before this was expressly adopted by any state.

Other respondent states did not go into the legal justification for the NATO action. The USA listed a variety of justifications: that the action was to avert humanitarian catastrophe, that there was a threat to the security of the neighbouring states, that there had been serious violations of human rights by Yugoslavia, and that the Security Council had determined the

---

[41] On Liberia and Sierra Leone, see Chapter 7 below.

existence of a threat to international peace and security and had under Chapter VII demanded a halt to such violations.

The UK, in response to the Yugoslav accusation that the doctrine of humanitarian intervention had only been relied on at a late stage by NATO, and was therefore of doubtful plausibility as a justification, denied this accusation and briefly repeated the position it had put forward in the Security Council that the NATO action was designed to avert humanitarian catastrophe. In October 1998 NATO had focused primarily on implied authorization by the Security Council, but it had also included reference to the need to avert humanitarian catastrophe. The argument by Yugoslavia highlighted the (apparently deliberate) lack of clarity in the NATO position and its unwillingness expressly to rely only on the doctrine of humanitarian intervention. Yugoslavia's argument was designed to indicate that there was considerable uncertainty about the doctrine, preventing its unequivocal support by NATO.

The Court refused provisional measures in all ten cases brought by Yugoslavia against NATO member states.[42] It did not pronounce on the legality of NATO's use of force, but it did indicate concern. In all the cases it said:

Whereas the Court is deeply concerned with the human tragedy, the loss of life, and the enormous suffering in Kosovo which form the background of the present dispute, and with the continuing loss of life and human suffering in all parts of Yugoslavia; Whereas the Court is profoundly concerned with the use of force in Yugoslavia; Whereas under the present circumstances such use raises very serious issues of international law; Whereas the Court is mindful of the purposes and principles of the United Nations Charter and of its own responsibilities in the maintenance of peace and security under the Charter and the Statute of the Court; Whereas the Court deems it necessary to emphasize that all parties appearing before it must act in conformity with their obligations under the United Nations Charter and other rules of international law, including humanitarian law.[43]

Thus the controversy over the legality of humanitarian intervention continues. Many states in many different fora within the UN in 1999 have subsequently made a point of stressing that they regarded the NATO action as illegal.[44] The arguments put forward by states in the Security

[42] The Court refused provisional measures on the ground that it did not have *prima facie* jurisdiction on the merits of the case; see Gray, 49 ICLQ (2000) 730.

[43] ICJ Reports (1999), 38 ILM (1999) 950. The reasoning of the Court in its denial of provisional measures made it unlikely that the Court would find that it has jurisdiction to give a decision on the merits of these cases.

[44] For example, the Non-Aligned Movement rejected humanitarian intervention as having no legal basis in the UN Charter or in the general principles of international law, UN Press Release GA/SPD/164, 18 October 1999; see also the Fourth Committee debate on peacekeeping, GA/SPD/164-6; Special Committee on UN Charter, UN Press Release L/2919 and the Opening Debate of the 1999 General Assembly, GA/9606.

Council and before the International Court of Justice show vividly the fundamental differences on the law on humanitarian intervention. States are divided on treaty interpretation and on the significance of state practice. Does Article 2(4) of the UN Charter allow humanitarian intervention? The states who argued in favour of this saw humanitarian intervention as an emerging right; this indicates that they saw Article 2(4) as open to changing interpretation over time and not with a fixed meaning. They did not argue that the right of humanitarian intervention existed in 1945. But the basis for the claim that this change in meaning has taken place is not clear. Apparently it rests in part on an argument that the law of human rights has developed since 1945 to such an extent that certain human rights are now *ius cogens* just as the prohibition on the use of force is *ius cogens*. But it does not follow from the mere fact that human rights may now be *ius cogens* that this overrides the prohibition on the use of force. For this further, crucial step in the argument it would be necessary to show not only that human rights are accepted and recognized by the international community of states as a whole as a norm from which no derogation is permitted, but also that states have accepted the right to use force to protect them.

Those who opposed the interpretation of Article 2(4) to allow humanitarian intervention saw it as a prohibition that cannot be altered without universal agreement. To confirm this view they also invoked the General Assembly resolutions on the use of force which outlawed forcible intervention in absolute terms. They stressed the primary responsibility of the Security Council under Chapter VII in order to exclude unilateral action. This also seems to have been the final conclusion of the Secretary-General. In spite of his acceptance that human rights were not an internal matter, he wrote in his 1999 *Report on the Work of the Organization*: 'What is clear is that enforcement action without Security Council authorization threatens the very core of the international security system founded on the Charter of the UN. Only the Charter provides a universally accepted legal basis for the use of force.'[45]

Therefore it seems necessary for those states supporting humanitarian intervention on the basis that it is an emerging or a new right to show how the change in the law that they rely on has come about. They have tried to show that state practice supports their argument as to the meaning of Article 2(4). A certain amount of revisionism in the interpretation of past practice has proved attractive to some states. The Belgian arguments on the significance of state practice in Uganda, Bangladesh, and Cambodia relied on what states did rather than on what they said to justify their interventions. But the UN Secretary-General was not willing to go so far.

[45] A/54/1 at para 66.

He argued that, in all three of the cases mentioned, what justified the action in the eyes of the world was the internal character of the regimes the intervening states acted against. Yet at the time in all three cases the international community was divided and disturbed because these interventions were unilateral. The states in question had no mandate from anyone else to act as they did. He concluded that most would prefer to see such decisions taken collectively by an international institution, and surely the only institution competent to assume that role was the Security Council.[46]

During the Kosovo crisis some of the states in favour of humanitarian intervention also argued that humanitarian action by the UN or authorized by the UN, as in Yugoslavia and Somalia, or taken by a regional organization and acquiesced in by the UN, as in Liberia and Sierra Leone, showed the existence of a general doctrine of humanitarian intervention and the right of states to act unilaterally.[47] This was the position of Slovenia in the Security Council and of Belgium before the International Court of Justice.[48] It is difficult to see how this argument can be sustained. The UN actions in Somalia and the former Yugoslavia were within the Charter scheme, even if such actions were not initially envisaged by the drafters of the UN Charter. Member states were specifically authorized to use force in those states for humanitarian ends by the Security Council under Chapter VII. The regional actions in Liberia and Sierra Leone were justified by ECOWAS as regional peacekeeping with the consent of the host state; the response by the Security Council was cautious. It did not authorize force except to secure compliance with an arms embargo under Article 41 of the UN Charter or on the basis of a peace agreement between the parties.[49] It is very doubtful whether this UN-authorized state action or regional peacekeeping could amount to a basis for a new right of humanitarian intervention not expressly authorized by the Security Council, such as the action over Kosovo.[50]

---

[46] 1998 (3) UN Chronicle 3.

[47] Some states even went so far as to suggest an obligation to intervene, but the limited and selective state practice cannot support such a doctrine. As Cuba argued, there have been many other terrible violations of human rights where no humanitarian intervention was undertaken: SC 4011th meeting, see also UN Press Release SC/6686.

[48] For Slovenia's argument, see SC 3989th meeting, 26 March 1999.

[49] For a detailed discussion of the ECOWAS action in Liberia and the Security Council response, see Nolte, 'Restoring Peace by Regional Action', 53 Zeitschrift für ausländisches öffentliches Recht und Völkerrecht (1993) 603; and Gray, 'Regional Arrangements and the UN Collective Security System', in Fox (ed.), *The Changing Constitution of the United Nations* (1997), 91.

[50] Similarly the legality of the earlier action against Iraq in protection of the Kurds and Shiites in Iraq after the 1991 Iraq/Kuwait conflict is doubtful. It is striking that the states using state practice to support a right to humanitarian intervention in Kosovo did not refer to this action.

For those states who do support the legality of humanitarian intervention the operation in Kosovo has left some basic issues as to the scope of the right unclear. The official position of NATO seemed to reflect a fundamental division as to the legal basis for the operation. It remains doubtful whether the NATO operation could be a precedent for unilateral action by one state rather than a regional organization or other group of states. The constant stress on the Security Council resolutions by certain states indicates that they were putting forward a doctrine of implied authorization by the Security Council; they were not arguing for a unilateral right of humanitarian intervention. Alternatively, a less restrictive view of the scope of the doctrine would be that, although Security Council authorization is not necessary, a determination by it under Chapter VII of the existence of a threat to international peace and security and of the imminence of humanitarian disaster is crucial. The question as to the appropriate modalities for humanitarian intervention also remains.

The UK has continued to take a lead role in the development of the doctrine. The Foreign Secretary recently set out a framework to guide intervention in response to massive violations of humanitarian law and crimes against humanity.[51] The framework was built on six principles. First, an intervention is an admission of failure of prevention. We need a strengthened culture of conflict prevention. Second, we should maintain the principle that armed force should only be used as a last resort. Third, the immediate responsibility for halting violence rests with the state in which it occurs. Fourth, when faced with an overwhelming humanitarian catastrophe, which a government has shown it is unwilling or unable to prevent or is actively promoting, the international community should intervene. Intervention in internal affairs is a sensitive issue, so there must be convincing evidence of extreme humanitarian distress on a large scale, requiring urgent relief. It must be objectively clear that there is no practicable alternative to the use of force to save lives. Fifth, any use of force should be proportionate to achieving the humanitarian purpose and carried out in accordance with international law. The military action must be likely to achieve its objectives. Sixth, any use of force should be collective. No individual country can reserve to itself the right to act on behalf of the international community. The Foreign Secretary said that the intervention in Kosovo was a collective decision, backed by the nineteen members of NATO; his preference would be that, wherever possible, the authority of the Security Council should be secured. It remains to be seen whether this framework will be adopted by other states, but the continuing opposition of China, Russia, and the Non-Aligned Movement (NAM) to intervention

---

[51] http://www.fco.gov.uk/news/speechtext.asp?3989, 20 July 2000.

without Security Council authority means that the doctrine is far from firmly established in international law.

Thus the debate as to the proper interpretation of Article 2(4) has proved to be of practical significance in relation to humanitarian intervention. In contrast, the current claims by some writers that states may use force in 'pro-democratic' invasions to ensure democratic government in a foreign state have not proved attractive to states.[52] The political goals underlying the use of force may include the re-establishment of 'democratic' government, but this has not led states to espouse a legal doctrine of 'pro-democratic' invasion.

A RIGHT OF PRO-DEMOCRATIC INTERVENTION

As with humanitarian intervention before the Kosovo action, the right of pro-democratic invasion has not generally been put forward as a legal argument by states. Originally certain US commentators argued that Article 2(4) was not an absolute prohibition of the use of force, but should be interpreted in the light of the Chapter VII provisions for a collective security system. Because of the failure of the UN collective security system during the Cold War, Article 2(4) could be interpreted to allow the use of force to further 'world public order' and to justify 'pro-democratic' invasions by the USA, though not 'pro-socialist' invasions by the USSR.[53] There were indications of this approach in the US justification for its intervention in Grenada.[54] Clearly this argument has now been overtaken by events in so far as it was based on the inaction of the Security Council during the Cold War. However, the argument has not been abandoned and its proponents have chosen to shift their emphasis; the doctrine is no longer predicated on the breakdown of the UN system. They now focus on the legality of force if this is designed to further purposes of the UN such as the protection of human rights. The end of the Cold War and the collapse of communist governments in Eastern Europe brought assertions that there was now a right of peoples to democratic governance and perhaps even a right of third states to use force to help a people to assert that right.[55] Perhaps the most striking illustration of this was the claim by

---

[52] For a detailed discussion of this debate, see Roth, *Governmental Illegitimacy in International Law* (1999).

[53] Reisman, 'Coercion and self-determination: construing Charter Article 2(4)', 78 AJIL (1984) 642; Reisman, 'Sovereignty and Human Rights in Contemporary International Law', 84 AJIL (1990) 866; D'Amato, 'The Invasion of Panama was a Lawful Response to Tyranny', 84 AJIL (1990) 516; Teson, *Humanitarian Intervention: An Inquiry into Law and Morality* (2nd edn, 1997).	[54] See page 26.

[55] Franck, 'The Emerging Right to Democratic Governance', 86 AJIL (1992); Franck, *Fairness in International Law and Institutions* (1995); Crawford, 'Democracy and International

some in the USA that Russia could forcibly intervene in Romania to help overthrow the government which was brutally punishing demonstrators who were trying to secure a change of government and to install democratic government in 1989.[56]

But it is clear that state practice cannot support such a new right. In its intervention in Panama at the end of 1989 the USA deliberately did not offer the restoration of democracy as a legal justification. In Panama former President Noriega had refused to accept the results of elections held in the middle of 1989 in which Endara was elected President. In December 1989 the USA forcibly intervened. Its legal argument, expressed in a letter to the Security Council, was that it was acting in self-defence in protection of US nationals in Panama.[57] The USA distinguished between its legal justification and its goals; the latter ostensibly included the defence of democracy in Panama. In the Security Council debate on the US intervention no state put forward a legal right to use force to restore democratic government. The USA itself expressly distinguished between its legal justification for the intervention, which was self-defence of its nationals, and its political interest in the protection of democracy. Its representative said, 'I am not here today to claim a right on behalf of the United States to enforce the will of history by intervening in favour of democracy where we are not welcomed. We are supporters of democracy but not the gendarmes of democracy, not in this hemisphere or anywhere else . . . We acted in Panama for legitimate reasons of self-defence and to protect the integrity of the Canal Treaties.'[58] Other states in the Security Council debate did not offer any support for a doctrine of pro-democratic intervention. Thus commentators wishing to assert a legal right of pro-democratic intervention have to discount not only the condemnation by the General Assembly and the OAS but also the express words of the US government and its

Law', 44 BYIL (1993) 113; Fox, 'The Right to Political Participation in International Law', 17 Yale Journal of International Law (1992); Roth, *Governmental Illegitimacy in International Law* (1999); Murphy, 'Democratic Legitimacy and the Recognition of States and Governments', 48 ICLQ (1999) 545.

[56] Reisman, 'Allocating Competences to Use Coercion in the Post-Cold War World', in Damrosch and Fischer (eds), *Law and Force in the New International Order* (1991) 26 at 36.

[57] S/21035; 1989 UNYB 172.

[58] S/PV 2902. In its intervention in the Dominican Republic in 1965 the USA had similarly offered a mixture of legal and political justifications. It said that the aim of its action was to make the Dominican Republic safe for democracy and to prevent the formation of another communist government in the western hemisphere. But it also put forward legal justifications for this, its first overt military intervention since the Second World War. The invocation of regional action by the OAS did not serve to legitimate the intervention. As later in the Nigerian intervention in the name of ECOWAS in Sierra Leone, so here military dictatorships intervened in the name of democracy. For a fuller discussion of the US intervention in the Dominican Republic, see Franck and Weisband, *Word Politics* (1972), 96.

deliberate choice not to put this argument forward as a legal justification for its intervention.[59]

In contrast, the forcible intervention to restore democratic government in Haiti was authorized by the UN. After the overthrow of Haiti's first democratically elected government in a coup in 1991 the Security Council declared that the situation constituted a threat to international peace and security under the UN Charter.[60] However, it showed distinct caution; it referred expressly to the unique and exceptional circumstances in making this determination. The subsequent resolutions authorizing sanctions and authorizing member states to create a multinational force to facilitate the departure of the junta and the prompt return of the legitimately elected President also recognized 'the unique character of the present situation in Haiti and its deteriorating, complex and extraordinary nature requiring an exceptional response'.[61] It may be inferred that the Security Council was anxious that its action should not be seen as setting a precedent, even for future UN action, let alone for unilateral intervention. The overthrow of democratic rule or the annulment of democratic elections in, for example, Burma (1990), Algeria (1991), Nigeria (1993), Niger (1996), and Pakistan (1999) did not produce any UN authorization of the use of force or even of sanctions.

Another episode which has been argued to support a right to humanitarian action or forcible action to restore a democratically elected government is that of Sierra Leone. The government elected under UN supervision after a prolonged civil war was overthrown by a coup in 1997. Nigeria, acting in the name of ECOWAS, used force to restore the legitimate government. The basis for the legality of the ECOWAS action was the express consent of the democratically elected President both before and after the coup in May 1997. ECOWAS itself based its use of force on specific authorization by the Security Council of force to implement an arms embargo and on the limited right of self-defence of the peacekeeping force. The Security Council did not condemn the use of force, but it did not give any express approval until after the presence of ECOMOG was legitimized by a peace agreement.[62] It seems to go too far to argue that these instances of UN and regional action show a right for states unilaterally to use force to restore democratic government.[63]

---

[59] D'Amato, 'The Invasion of Panama was a Lawful Response to Tyranny', 84 AJIL (1990) 516. Against this, Henkin, 'The Invasion of Panama under International Law: A Gross Violation', 29 Columbia Journal of Transnational Law (1991) 293; Nanda, 'The validity of UN Intervention in Panama under International Law', 84 AJIL (1990) 494.

[60] SC Res 841; 1991 UNYB 151; Agora, 'The 1994 US Action in Haiti', 89 AJIL (1995) 58.

[61] SC Res 940; UN Publications, Blue Book Series Volume 11, *Les Nations Unies et Haiti* (1996).   [62] See Chapter 7 below.

[63] Even if it were possible to extrapolate from this limited practice of Haiti and Sierra Leone a unilateral right of pro-democratic intervention, these two instances could be argued to support only a limited right, only in cases where there have been UN-supervised elections and the results of the election have not been accepted.

FORCE AND SELF-DETERMINATION

The argument over whether Article 2(4) allows pro-democratic invasion mirrors the earlier debate as to whether it allows the use of force to further the right of a people to self-determination. This issue produced bitter divisions between states during the decolonization period, but is now of considerably reduced practical importance[64] and will be discussed only briefly. The debate was over the right of national liberation movements in pursuit of self-determination to use force and, more controversially, over the right of other states to assist them in their forcible pursuit of independence.

After the Second World War those states which resisted decolonization were met by force. France encountered violent independence movements in Tunisia, Morocco, and Algeria and recognized their independence; similarly the UK was hastened out of Malaya, Kenya, and Cyprus and the Netherlands out of Indonesia. When India forcibly drove Portugal out of its colony, Goa, in 1961 and itself annexed the territory, the outlines of the legal argument over the right to use force against colonial powers emerged in the Security Council debates. States divided as to whether Portugal's continued occupation of Goa amounted to aggression and a breach of Article 2(4) because the territory formed an integral part of India or whether India's use of force to seize the territory was itself a violation of Article 2(4).[65] Some states argued that the issue should be seen as one of colonialism; this was the position of India, the USSR, Ceylon (now Sri Lanka), Liberia, and the UAR. Other states – the colonial powers Portugal, the UK, and France, and the USA—said that the issue was one of the illegal use of force to settle territorial disputes. The divisions within the Security Council prevented the adoption of any decisive resolution.

Later in the 1960s, in response to Portugal's refusal to give independence to Guinea-Bissau, Angola, and Mozambique, South Africa's occupation of Namibia and perpetuation of apartheid, and the declaration of independence by a white minority government in Rhodesia, certain newly independent and socialist states began more clearly to claim a legal right not only to self-determination but also for national liberation movements to use force under international law, and for third states to use force to help them. The colonial powers and Western states resisted such claims.

The first major General Assembly resolution on the right to decolonization, Resolution 1514 (1960), the *Declaration on the Granting of Independence to Colonial Peoples*, made no mention of force. The first General Assembly

---

[64] It is still a divisive issue in UN debates on the definition of terrorism.

[65] 1961 UNYB 129; see Higgins, *The Development of International Law Through the Political Organs of the United Nations* (1963), 187.

resolution claimed to assert a right to use force was passed, 74–6–27, in 1964 in response to the denial of self-determination by Portugal, South Africa, and Rhodesia; Resolution 2105 'Recognizes the legitimacy of the struggle by the peoples under colonial rule to exercise their right to self-determination and independence and invites all states to provide material and moral assistance to the national liberation movements in colonial territories'. But there was a deliberate ambiguity here, repeated in many subsequent resolutions: the word 'struggle' was taken by some states to mean armed struggle and by other states to mean peaceful struggle. The colonial powers and the USA opposed any express assertion of the right of a people in international law to use force to pursue self-determination, let alone the right of third states to intervene in support of national liberation movements.

The drafting history of the general 'law-making' resolutions on the use of force reveals the continuing disagreement between states; consensus was attained only at the price of ambiguity. Resolutions deliberately masked the differences between states. The arguments as to the legality of the use of force in pursuit of self-determination took different forms; there was no clear focus to the legal debate leading to this or to other resolutions.[66] Sometimes the issue was framed in terms of Article 2(4): the use of force by a people with the right of self-determination was not covered by the prohibition in Article 2(4) and states had the right to assist them in their struggles. An alternative focus was that colonialism was in itself an unlawful use of force, amounting to aggression and a breach of Article 2(4); if so, the people were said to have the right to use force in self-defence, not just in response to violent repression but in order to drive out the colonial power.[67] Related debates concerned the international nature of self-determination conflicts and the applicability of Chapter VII of the UN Charter and of the humanitarian law on international rather than internal armed conflict.[68]

The *Friendly Relations Resolution* (1970) avoided a direct statement of the right of a people to use force and of states to assist them; it did this in order to achieve consensus. Rather, it focused on the duty of states not to use force against a people with the right of self-determination, a simple

[66] See Wilson, *International Law and the Use of Force by National Liberation Movements* (1988), 130; Abi-Saab, 'Wars of National Liberation and the Geneva Conventions and Protocols', 165 RCADI (1979–IV) 363; Grahl-Madsen, 'Decolonization: The Modern Version of a Just War', 22 German Yearbook of International Law (1979) 255; Falk, 'Intervention and National Liberation', in Bull (ed.), *Intervention in World Politics* (1984), 119.

[67] Dugard, 'The OAU and Colonialism: An Inquiry into the plea of self-defence as a justification for the use of force in the eradication of colonialism', 16 ICLQ (1967) 157; Rosenstock, 'The Declaration of Principles of International Law Concerning Friendly Relations: A Survey', 65 AJIL (1971) 713.

[68] See Wilson, *International Law and the Use of Force by National Liberation Movements* (1988).

corollary of the right of the people. It said, 'Every State has the duty to refrain from any forcible action which deprives peoples . . . of their right to self-determination and freedom and independence. In their actions against, and resistance to, such forcible action in pursuit of the exercise of the right to self-determination, such people are entitled to seek and to receive support in accordance with the purposes and principles of the Charter.' Again this deliberately does not unequivocally set out any right of national liberation movements or of sympathetic states to use force.

This focus on the prohibition of the use of force against a people with the right of self-determination, rather than on the more controversial right of a national liberation movement to use force, enabled states to join in condemnation of the use of force by colonial powers to deprive people of their right of self-determination. Those supporting the use of force by colonial peoples condemned any use of force by Portugal, South Africa and Israel against those seeking self-determination; the former colonial powers and western states tended to condemn the particular use of force by a colonial power as unnecessary and disproportionate rather than deny it any right to use force in self-defence.[69]

Other law-making resolutions were also drafted in ambiguous terms in order to secure consensus. The best known is the provision in the 1974 *Definition of Aggression*, Article 7, that

Nothing in this Definition . . . could in any way prejudice the right to self-determination, freedom and independence, as derived from the Charter, of peoples forcibly deprived of that right and referred to in the Declaration on Principles of International Law concerning Friendly Relations and Cooperation among States in accordance with the Charter of the United Nations, particularly peoples under colonial and racist regimes or other forms of alien domination; nor the right of these peoples to *struggle* to that end and to seek and receive support, in accordance with the principles of the Charter and in conformity with the above-mentioned Declaration.[70]

The Security Council passed many resolutions on situations in colonies using this ambiguous term.[71]

Early General Assembly resolutions on Portuguese colonies and on the situation in Namibia affirmed the legitimacy of the struggle of the peoples in these territories 'by all means at their disposal'.[72] It is interesting that here and elsewhere the word legitimacy is used rather than legality. This resolution was still sufficiently ambiguous to allow abstention rather than

[69] See Chapter 4 below.
[70] See 1974 UNYB 845 for an account of the debate on this point.
[71] For example, SC Res 386, 392, 428, 445.
[72] GA Res 2708, 2652, 3295; in the debates many states spoke in favour of the armed struggle (1974 UNYB 156).

opposition by Western states. In contrast, those resolutions, whether general or passed in response to specific conflicts, which did expressly spell out the right to use armed force in pursuit of self-determination met with opposition from colonial powers and other Western states.[73] Thus from 1973 the annual resolution on 'The importance of the universal realization of the right of peoples to self-determination and of the speedy granting of independence to colonial countries and peoples for the effective guarantee and observance of human rights' contained in paragraph 2 an affirmation of support for 'armed struggle'. This formula was finally abandoned in 1991 when the resolution reverted to the formula 'all available means'.[74] Similarly the 1981 *Declaration on the Inadmissibility of Intervention*, Resolution 36/103, said that the right and duty of states to support self-determination included the right of these people to wage both political and armed struggle. Such resolutions did not secure consensus.[75]

There has been less discussion of the theoretically even more controversial right of states to provide forcible help to peoples with the right of self-determination. States were divided on this issue on the same lines as on the question whether a people with the right of self-determination had a right in international law to use force.[76] The resolutions adopted by consensus assert a right to help peoples and urge such help for front-line states and others involved in the struggle against colonial, alien, and racist domination without specifying the right to use force. For example, the Security Council resolutions commending Angola and Mozambique for their support to the people of Zimbabwe in their 'struggle' deliberately used this ambiguous term.[77]

But in practice the southern African front-line states, those neighbouring Portuguese colonies, and the neighbours of Israel were not willing openly to assert such a right to use force to assist the national liberation movements operating from their territories. Such states typically denied that they were helping liberation movements; this was clearly because Portugal, South Africa, and Israel used force against neighbouring states from which national liberation movements were operating. In doing so they claimed to be acting in self-defence against attacks for which neighbouring states were responsible on the ground that states were providing

---

[73]   GA Res 3070, 97–5–28; South Africa GA Res 39/72, 1984 UNYB 128 at 130.
[74]   GA Res 46/87 (1991); 47/82 (1992); GA Res 48/94 (1993). The last such resolution 49/151, was passed in 1994.   [75] 1981 UNYB 145; GA Res 36/103 (120–22–6).
[76]   Zambia, Senegal, and Guinea asserted the right to use force in support of national liberation movements under Article 2(4) of the UN Charter, *Repertoire of the Practice of UN Organs*, No. 4, 45; China called on all states to help national liberation movements, *Repertoire of the Practice of the Security Council 1972–74*, 172.
[77]   SC Res 445. Also SC Res 428 affirmed the right of Angola to help the people of Namibia in similar terms.

assistance to national liberation movements or were tolerating their presence. Such claims were rejected in principle by developing and communist states on the basis that Portugal, South Africa, and Israel could not lawfully invoke self-defence because they were using force to maintain their illegal possessions against people with the right of self-determination. Colonial powers and Western states did not go so far.[78] The Court in the *Nicaragua* case deliberately and expressly left this question out of its consideration of the law on the prohibition of intervention to assist opposition forces. It said that 'The Court is not here concerned with the process of decolonization; this question is not in issue in the present case.'[79] Judge Schwebel was critical of this express disclaimer; he said that the implication was that the Court had endorsed a special exception for wars of national liberation.[80]

In contrast to this division between states over the right of national liberation movements and states to use force to further self-determination, there has been general agreement that irredentist claims did not justify the use of force. That is, the use of force to recover pre-colonial title (on the basis that the colonial title is invalid and that therefore the use of force does not violate Article 2(4) because the state using force has title to the territory) is not generally accepted. India's annexation of Goa is the only instance where the UN has eventually acquiesced in the 'recovery' of territory by force, despite its initial condemnation by a majority of states in the Security Council—apparently on the basis that the Indian action in fact furthered the self-determination of the inhabitants.[81] Subsequent use of this argument based on pre-colonial title has been rejected by the UN. Morocco's claim to Western Sahara on the basis of a title preceding that of the colonial power, Spain, and Indonesia's claim to East Timor on the basis of pre-colonial title preceding that of Portugal were not regarded as justification for the forcible seizures of these territories in 1976.[82] Slow progress has subsequently been made in both cases to secure the right to self-determination of the people.[83] Argentina's use of force in 1982 to terminate the colonial occupation of the Falklands (Malvinas) by the UK did not meet with support. Even those who backed Argentina's claim to the Falklands said that it should have used peaceful means to resolve the dispute; Iraq's invasion of Kuwait in 1990 on the pretext that it had pre-colonial title was even more strongly condemned.[84] That is, such claims are not treated as a special case; they have not been treated differently from other claims by states using force that they are not in breach of

---

[78] See Chapter 4 below.   [79] *Nicaragua* case para 206.
[80] Dissenting Opinion para 179–80.   [81] See Korman, *The Right of Conquest* (1996), 267.
[82] Ibid. at 281 on East Timor; on Western Sahara, see Franck, 'The Stealing of the Sahara', 70 AJIL (1976) 694.   [83] On East Timor, see Chapter 6 below.
[84] See Korman, *The Right of Conquest* (1996) at 275, 292.

Article 2(4) as they are not using force against the territorial integrity of another state because it is in fact their own territory. Such claims are currently being made by China with regard to its right to use force to recover Taiwan.[85] These claims are clearly inconsistent with the duty established in Article 2(3) of the UN Charter, and elaborated on in the *Friendly Relations Resolution* and the *Definition of Aggression*, to settle disputes, including territorial and boundary disputes, peacefully.

Now that the decolonization process is almost complete, and now that South Africa has given up apartheid and its occupation of Namibia, and the Palestinians are apparently on the way to eventual statehood, the debate over the right of a people to seek self-determination through the use of force, with the help of third states, has lost much of its bitterness.[86] The extension of the right of self-determination outside the colonial context in the break-up of the USSR, Yugoslavia, and Czechoslovakia has not brought with it any state support for the use of force for this end.[87] There is no support for the right to use force to attain self-determination outside the context of decolonization or illegal occupation. Still less is there any support by states for the right of ethnic groups to use force to secede from existing states. But when claims to secession, or even to more limited autonomy, are met with forcible repression, as in the cases of Kosovo, the Chechens, and the Kurds, the use of force against a people may strengthen its case for self-determination.[88]

---

[85] China's policy is not to rule out or renounce the use of force to recover Taiwan; its language became more threatening in the run-up to Taiwan's 2000 Presidential elections: Keesings (2000) 43412.

[86] On remaining colonial territories, see 1995 UNYB 236.

[87] The Yugoslavia Arbitration Commission in Opinion 2 (31 ILM (1992) 1497) affirmed the right of self-determination of the Bosnian Serbs, but denied that this gave them the right to use force to alter existing boundaries.

[88] See Supreme Court of Canada, *Reference re Secession of Quebec*, 37 ILM (1998) 1340 at 1372.

3

Invitation and intervention: civil wars and the use of force

It is notorious that Article 2(4), drafted in response to the Second World War, was addressed to inter-state conflicts. It says, 'all Member States shall refrain in their *international relations* from the threat or use of force'. Internal conflicts were seen as a domestic matter except in so far as they might constitute a threat to international peace and security under Chapter VII of the UN Charter.[1] But in fact large-scale inter-state conflicts have been exceptional since 1945; most inter-state conflicts have been limited to border actions. More common have been civil wars, whether purely civil or fuelled by outside involvement or which have spilled over into neighbouring states. As well as direct intervention in civil wars through their regular armies states have used indirect intervention through support to irregular forces and also more limited forms of intervention. This chapter will focus on the law applicable to the use of force and intervention in such conflicts.

The rules prohibiting forcible intervention in civil conflict have been developed through General Assembly resolutions designed to elaborate on the UN Charter rules on the use of force and to supplement the express prohibitions of intervention in the constituent instruments of the major regional organizations.[2] An early general provision was included in General Assembly Resolution 375 (1949) on the *Rights and Duties of States*; this said that every state has the duty to refrain from intervention in the internal or external affairs of any other state and that every state has the duty to refrain from fomenting civil strife in the territory of another state and to prevent the organization within its territory of activities calculated to foment such civil strife. Similar provision was included in Resolution 2131 (1965) on the *Inadmissibility of Intervention*; this said, 'No state has the right to intervene, directly or indirectly, *for any reason whatever*, in the internal or external affairs of any other state. Consequently, armed intervention and all other forms of interference or attempted threats against the personality of the state or against its political, economic, and cultural elements, are condemned.' The 1970 *Friendly Relations Resolution* followed the same approach; it spelled out the content of the prohibition of the use of force as regards civil conflict. It said, 'Every State has the duty to refrain

---

[1] See Chapter 6 below.
[2] Arab League Pact (70 UNTS 237) Article 8; OAS Charter (119 UNTS 48) Article 15; OAU Charter (479 UNTS 70) Article 3.

from organizing, instigating, assisting or participating in acts of civil strife or terrorist acts in another State or acquiescing in organized activities within its territory directed towards the commission of such acts, when the acts referred to in the present paragraph involve a threat or use of force.' The duty of non-intervention added to this the duty not to foment, finance, incite or tolerate subversive, terrorist or armed activities directed towards the violent overthrow of the regime of another state and the duty not to interfere in civil strife in another state.

The status of these rules on forcible intervention in civil wars is no longer controversial; it was their application that led to fundamental divisions during the Cold War when the superpowers and others waged proxy wars in Africa, Latin America, and Asia. The previous chapter centred on the debate as to the proper interpretation of Article 2(4); this chapter will show that in the vast majority of cases of forcible intervention in a civil war it is not the identification but the application of the law that leads to difficulty. That is, there is a general consensus between states as to the principles to be applied to forcible intervention in civil conflicts, but in practice the disagreements as to the facts and as to the application of the law to those facts can fundamentally divide states.

RECENT APPLICATION OF THE LAW ON INTERVENTION IN CIVIL WARS:
AFRICA AFTER THE COLD WAR

The conflict which started in the diamond-rich Democratic Republic of Congo (DRC), formerly Zaire, in 1998 serves as an example, though perhaps an unusually complex one, illustrating the type of conflict that has been common since the Second World War.[3] After thirty-two years in power President Mobutu, supported by France throughout the Cold War, was overthrown by Kabila in May 1997 with the help of forces from some of the nine neighbouring states. Uganda and Rwanda helped Kabila partly because they were concerned to stop insurgents operating from the territory of the DRC challenging their governments. But when President Kabila came to power he himself used these insurgent forces and was seen as betraying his former allies; Uganda and Rwanda turned against him.[4] President Kabila sought help from Zimbabwe and Angola and they sent forces to support him in August 1998. They were apparently motivated in part by hostility to ex-President Mobutu; he had for many years

---

[3] For an account of events in the DRC, see Keesings (1998, 1999).

[4] On 23 June 1999 the DRC brought an action before the International Court of Justice against Burundi, Uganda and Rwanda for acts of armed aggression in August 1998. On 1 July 2000 the ICJ ordered Provisional Measures ordering the parties to refrain from any armed action.

supported UNITA opposition forces in Mozambique which had operated against their governments. Mobutu had continued to back UNITA even after the USA and South Africa had abandoned it. Congo (Brazzaville), Central African Republic, Sudan, Chad, and Gabon also promised help to Kabila. Thus a civil conflict in the DRC was fuelled by outside involvement from many states because conflicts in their states had spilled over into the DRC and because the DRC had played a role in the conflicts in other states.[5]

The Security Council, in Resolution 1234 (1999), expressed its concern at the continuation of hostilities and stressed its firm commitment to preserving the national sovereignty, territorial integrity, and political independence of the DRC. It said it was concerned at reports of measures by forces opposing the government of President Kabila in violation of the national sovereignty and territorial integrity of the country and recalled the inherent right of individual or collective self-defence in accordance with Article 51 of the UN Charter. It then deplored the continuing fighting and the presence of foreign troops in a manner inconsistent with the principles of the Charter of the UN and called upon those states to bring to an end the presence of these uninvited forces. This resolution reflects the duty not to use force against another state and also the duty not to intervene in its internal affairs. It is based on the legal right of the government of the DRC to seek help and the illegality of the behaviour of the foreign states using force to overthrow that government. It shows that the Security Council regarded the conflict as a mixture of civil war and interstate conflict and that it took a clear position: aid to the government was permissible; intervention or force to overthrow the government was not.

This resolution is stronger than the earlier reaction of the Security Council when President Mobutu was overthrown by Kabila with the help of Rwanda and Uganda in 1997. The Security Council then simply expressed concern at the deteriorating situation in the region and called on the revolutionary forces led by Kabila to accept an immediate cessation of hostilities and the implementation of a peace plan.[6] The Security Council subsequently expressed its support for the people of the DRC as they began a new period in their history. However, it also rejected outside intervention. It said that the Council respected the legitimate national aspirations of the people of the DRC to achieve peace, national reconciliation and progress in the political, economic, and social fields to the benefit of all, and opposed any interference in its internal affairs. It called for the withdrawal of all external forces.[7]

---

[5] As a reflection of their involvement six states signed the Lusaka Cease-fire Agreement for the DRC on 15 July 1999: Keesings (1999) 43051; UN Press Release SC/6711.

[6] S/PRST/1997/11.   [7] S/PRST/1997/31.

Again, when civil war broke out in Congo (Brazzaville) in 1997, Angola
intervened and sent troops to support the opposition forces, which then
secured victory. The Security Council, in a Presidential Statement, condemned outside intervention; it expressed concern about the grave situation and called for an end to hostilities. It condemned all external
interference, including the intervention of foreign forces, in violation of
the Charter of the UN and called for the immediate withdrawal of all foreign forces.[8]

The Security Council reaction to these interventions in civil conflict was
a clear reaffirmation of the prohibition of forcible intervention. Resolution
1234 on the DRC used the language both of Article 2(4) and of the rules
on intervention. This statement of the applicable rules by the Security
Council reflects the reasoning of the Court in the *Nicaragua* case, of para-
mount importance in this area.

THE *NICARAGUA* CASE[9]

This case was brought by Nicaragua against the USA both for the unlawful use of force against the government of Nicaragua and for its intervention through its support for military and paramilitary activities of the
opposition *contra* forces. The part of the judgment which deals with the
use of force and non-intervention provides an authoritative statement of
the law on this area; it has proved relatively uncontroversial among commentators, in contrast to the critical response from many US writers to the
Court's reasoning on collective self-defence.[10] Indeed, there was consensus between the USA and Nicaragua as to the applicable law.[11]

Issues of classification played a central role in this case. Did the actions
of the USA constitute an illegal use of force against Nicaragua under the
customary international law rule codified in Article 2(4)? Were its actions
an unlawful intervention against the government of Nicaragua? If so,
could they be justified as collective self-defence or collective countermeasures in protection of Costa Rica, Honduras, and El Salvador against an
armed attack or unlawful intervention by Nicaragua?[12] The Court undertook an examination of the prohibition of intervention and of the scope of
the prohibition of the use of force; it elaborated on the content of these
two sets of rules and on the relationship between them. As regards the
identification of the customary law on the prohibition of the use of force
codified in Article 2(4), the Court used the *Friendly Relations Resolution*
principles on the use of force quoted at the start of this chapter on the

---

[8] S/PRST/1997/47.   [9] ICJ Reports (1986) 14.   [10] See Chapter 5 below.
[11] *Nicaragua* case para 184.   [12] On collective self-defence, see Chapter 5 below.

duty not to organize civil strife in another state in support of an opposition party.[13] It also set out the basic law on intervention at some length: 'The principle of non-intervention involves the right of every sovereign state to conduct its affairs without outside interference; though examples of trespass against this principle are not infrequent, the Court considers that it is part and parcel of customary international law.'[14] It invoked the *Corfu Channel* case, General Assembly resolutions and inter-American practice as authority for the principle of non-intervention.

The Court then went on to consider the exact content of the principle as far as was relevant to the resolution of the dispute:

The principle forbids all states or groups of states to intervene directly or indirectly in internal or external affairs of other states. A prohibited intervention must accordingly be one bearing on matters in which each state is permitted, by the principle of state sovereignty, to decide freely. One of these is the choice of a political, economic, social and cultural system, and the formulation of foreign policy. Intervention is wrongful when it uses methods of coercion in regard to such choices, which must remain free ones. The element of coercion, which defines, and indeed forms the very essence of, prohibited intervention, is particularly obvious in the case of an intervention which uses force, whether in the direct form of military action, or in the indirect form of support for subversive or terrorist armed activities within another state. General Assembly resolution 2625 (XXV) equates assistance of this kind with the use of force by the assisting state when the acts committed in another state involve a threat or use of force. These forms of action are therefore wrongful in the light of both the principle of the non-use of force and that of non-intervention.[15]

The *Nicaragua* case thus made clear the considerable overlap between the rules on forcible intervention and the customary law codified in Article 2(4).

After its statement of the general prohibition of forcible intervention the Court had to consider whether any fundamental modification of the principle of non-intervention had taken place. Significantly, the USA did not itself put forward any argument that there had been such a fundamental shift in the law. It did not advance the argument that it had a legal right to help the opposition *contras* to use force to overthrow a government; it based its right to use force on collective self-defence. Nevertheless, the Court examined the possible argument that the USA was justified in using force against Nicaragua to help the *contras* in their forcible opposition to the government. The International Court of Justice said that a government may invite outside help, but a third state may not forcibly help the opposition to overthrow the government. Although there had been in recent years a number of instances of foreign intervention for the benefit of

---

[13] *Nicaragua* case para 191.　　[14] Ibid. para 202.　　[15] Ibid. para 205.

forces opposed to the government of another state this did not in itself change the law. The Court had to consider whether there were indications of a practice illustrative of a belief in a kind of general right for states to intervene in support of internal opposition in another state, whose cause appeared particularly worthy by reason of the political and moral values with which it was identified. For such a general right to come into existence would involve a fundamental modification of the customary principle of non-intervention.

The Court, in considering whether there was *opinio juris* to support such a change, said it had to take account of the grounds offered by states to justify their interventions in support of opposition; states had not in fact justified their conduct by reference to a new right of intervention or a new exception to the principle of its prohibition. The United States authorities had on some occasions stated their grounds for intervening in the affairs of a foreign state for reasons connected with the domestic policies of that country or its ideology, the level of its armaments or the direction of its foreign policy. But these were statements of international policy and not an assertion of rules of existing international law. Accordingly, 'The Court therefore finds that no such general right of intervention in support of an opposition within another State exists in contemporary international law. The Court concludes that acts constituting a breach of the customary principle of non-intervention will also, if they directly or indirectly involve the use of force, constitute a breach of the principle of non-use of force in international relations.'[16] It later said that the principle of non-intervention would certainly lose its effectiveness as a principle of law if intervention 'which is already allowable at the request of the government of a State' were also to be allowed at the request of the opposition. This would permit any state to intervene at any moment in the internal affairs of another state.[17]

On the facts of the case the Court found that the US aid to the *contras* in Nicaragua in 'recruiting, training, arming, equipping, financing, supplying and otherwise encouraging, supporting, aiding and directing military and paramilitary actions in and against Nicaragua' was a breach of the prohibition of the use of force. The Court found that the USA had committed a *prima facie* violation of the principle of the non-use of force by 'organizing or encouraging the organization of irregular forces or armed bands . . . for incursion into the territory of another state' and 'participating in acts of civil strife in another state' in the terms of General Assembly Resolution 2625. The arming and training of the *contras* could be said to

---

[16] *Nicaragua* case para 206–9. The ICJ deliberately left on one side the question of the use of force by national liberation movements. Judge Schwebel, in his Dissenting Opinion, para 179–80, was critical of this in so far as it indicated an exception to the principle of non-intervention.   [17] *Nicaragua* case para 246.

involve the threat or use of force against Nicaragua, but the mere supply of funds to the *contras*, while undoubtedly an act of intervention in the internal affairs of Nicaragua, did not in itself amount to a use of force.[18]

THE RIGHT OF A GOVERNMENT TO INVITE OUTSIDE INTERVENTION

The reference by the Court in the *Nicaragua* case to the legality of intervention in response to an invitation by the government was very brief; this brevity masks the complexity that may arise in the interpretation and application of this rule. The basic principle of the right of a government to invite a third state to use force and the absence of any such right for an opposition may be accepted in theory, but its application in practice has not been simple. The previous chapter examined the debates as to humanitarian intervention, national liberation movements, and pro-democratic intervention; the law on all these may affect the legality of help to the opposition in a state. Various other limits on the right of a government to seek and receive outside assistance have been suggested as evolving through practice since the inception of the UN. The duty of nonintervention and the inalienable right of every state to choose its political, economic, social, and cultural systems have brought with them the duty not to intervene to help a government in a civil war. However, if there has been outside subversion against the government, then help to the government becomes permissible, whether or not there is a preexisting treaty provision for this. And if the conflict is limited, then it will not be characterized as a civil war but merely as domestic unrest, and so help will be permissible.

This generally agreed position was put forward by the UK in a *Foreign Policy Document* in 1984 which set out the general prohibition of forcible intervention and the possible exceptions to this.[19] It said that normally if one state requested assistance from another, then clearly that intervention could not be dictatorial and therefore unlawful. But a major restriction on the lawfulness of states providing outside assistance to other states was that any form of interference or assistance was prohibited when a civil war was taking place and control of the state's territory was divided between warring parties.[20] However, it was widely accepted that outside

---

[18] Ibid. para 228.

[19] 'UK Materials on International Law', 57 BYIL (1986) 614.

[20] This relatively narrow conception of a civil war requires that the opposing forces control territory; this mirrors the provision in the laws of armed conflict set out in the 1977 *Additional Protocol II to the 1949 Geneva Conventions Relating to the Protection of Victims of Non-International Armed Conflicts*. Article 1 sets the threshold for the existence of a non-international armed conflict and the application of the Protocol at a high level, requiring that dissident armed forces or other organized armed groups exercise such control over part of

interference in favour of one party to the struggle permitted counter-intervention on behalf of the other.[21]

CLASSIFICATION OF CONFLICTS

The categorization of a conflict may therefore be crucial in the determination of the legality of forcible intervention. The question arises first as to whether a conflict is actually a civil war or whether it is merely limited local unrest. Are opposition forces in control of territory? This line between unrest and civil war has proved controversial. States have not on the whole been willing to admit that the threshold of a civil war has been reached; they see such an acknowledgement as legitimating opposition forces.[22] This has proved a fundamental obstacle to the effective implementation of humanitarian law on non-international armed conflicts. Second, if the conflict is a civil war, is it a purely civil war or has there been outside intervention? What has been the scope of the outside intervention: does it amount to an armed attack allowing collective self-defence or is it merely a lesser intervention allowing aid short of collective self-defence to the government? Is the government using force against a people with the right of self-determination? All these issues affect the rights of third states to intervene to assist the government.

Even the determination as to whether a conflict is an inter-state conflict or a civil war may be far from straightforward. Questions as to classification—is the conflict civil or international—may be decisive as to the applicable law and as to the legality of the use of force. In the past this issue came up dramatically over the 1961–75 war in Vietnam. The competing parties fundamentally disagreed as to the nature of the conflict. The USA and South Vietnam argued that the conflict was an inter-state war begun by the invasion of South Vietnam by North Vietnam, a Cold War conflict in which the USA was operating in collective self-defence of its ally against a Chinese-aided invasion by North Vietnam, and later also against forces in Cambodia and Laos. North Vietnam argued that the conflict was one of decolonization; the people of the whole of Vietnam were resisting

---

its territory as to enable them to carry out sustained and concerted military operations and to implement this Protocol. The Protocol does not apply to internal disturbances and tensions such as riots, isolated and sporadic acts of violence, and other acts of a similar nature. This threshold is higher than that set in Common Article 3 of the 1949 *Geneva Conventions*. Article 1(4) of the *Additional Protocol I* has established that conflicts involving national liberation movements should be categorized as international. See Fleck, *The Handbook of Humanitarian Law in Armed Conflicts* (1995), 48; Green, *The Contemporary Law of Armed Conflict* (2nd edn, 2000), 54.

[21] The UK cited Angola as an example of this; see below at page 77.
[22] Above note 20.

the perpetuation of colonial rule.[23] If the former was accurate, then the rules applicable were those in Article 51 on inter-state conflict; if the latter view was correct, then the conflict was one in which the USA was intervening in a struggle for decolonization by the people of the whole of Vietnam. The Security Council did not play an active role in this conflict and did not pronounce on the issue.[24] Conflicts in other divided states such as Korea, Yemen, and Ireland have given rise to similar issues of classification.

More recently the question of classification came up in the 1991–95 conflict in Bosnia-Herzegovina.[25] The states involved took radically opposing views on the nature of the conflict; Bosnia-Herzegovina said that it was the victim of aggression by Yugoslavia (Serbia and Montenegro) whereas Yugoslavia claimed that the conflict in Bosnia was a civil war. This issue of classification arose in many different contexts; it was central to the case brought by Bosnia against Yugoslavia before the International Court of Justice; it affected Yugoslavia's claim to be treated as the successor state to the former Yugoslavia; it was important in the debate over the lifting of the arms embargo on Bosnia and on Bosnia's right to self-defence. The issue of classification was also central to the application of the laws of war. This question had arisen earlier in the *Nicaragua* case when the Court said that the conflict between the *contras'* forces and those of the government of Nicaragua was an armed conflict which was not of an international character and the acts of the *contras* towards the Nicaraguan government were therefore governed by the law applicable to conflicts of that character, whereas the actions of the USA in and against Nicaragua fell under the legal rules relating to international conflicts.[26] In Yugoslavia this question came up in several cases before the International Tribunal for the Former Yugoslavia with regard to the scope of the jurisdiction of the Tribunal and as to the availability of charges of 'grave breaches' of the laws of war in international armed conflict.[27]

---

[23] See Wright, 'Legal Aspects of the Viet-Nam Situation', 60 AJIL (1966) 750; Falk (ed.), *The Vietnam War and International Law*, 4 volumes (1968, 1969, 1972, 1978).

[24] 1965 UNYB 185. The UN Secretary-General said:

The escalation of the conflict in Viet-Nam was perhaps the most important of developments on the international scene which had repercussions on the UN. Paradoxically the problem was one in regard to which the Organisation had not been able to take any constructive action, as was to some extent understandable since the settlement reached at Geneva in 1954 prescribed no role for the UN. Moreover, neither North Viet-Nam nor South Viet-Nam was a Member of the UN and parties directly interested in the conflict had openly voiced the view that the UN as such had no place in the search for a solution to the problem. This, of course, could not in itself prevent the UN from discussing the problem, but it did militate against the Organisation being able to play a constructive role at the present stage.

[25] See Gray, 'Bosnia and Herzegovina: Civil War or Inter-State Conflict?', 67 BYIL (1996) 155.   [26] *Nicaragua* case para 216, 219.

[27] This issue has arisen in *Tadic Jurisdiction*, 35 ILM (1996) 132; *Judgment*, 36 ILM (1997) 908; *Appeal*, 38 ILM (1999); *Celebici*, 38 ILM (1999) 57; *Rajic*, 91 AJIL (1997) 523.

INVITATION BY GOVERNMENTS IN PRACTICE

Many states have relied on an invitation by a government to justify their use of force; they have claimed that their intervention was lawful because they were merely dealing with limited internal unrest or, at the other end of the spectrum, because they were helping the government respond to prior intervention by other states. In many cases a government has been maintained in power not by the actual use of force by foreign troops, but by less dramatic means. A foreign government may provide financial support or arms or training for the armed forces or police. Foreign military bases or other forms of foreign military presence may also provide stability.[28] During the Cold War the superpowers and other states used these means to help maintain friendly governments in power. USA support for the governments that it helped to instal by coups in Guatemala (1954), Chile (1973), and Iran (1953) and for pro-Western governments all over the world and USSR support for governments such as those of Cuba, Angola, Vietnam, and Ethiopia was well known. Similarly France supported certain regimes in Africa in order to maintain its influence; it concluded defence treaties and retained bases in many of its former colonies. Also its aid and support for rulers in francophone Africa such as President Mobutu in Zaire, Emperor Bokassa in the Central African Republic, the Hutu regime in Rwanda, and President Eyadema in Togo helped them to remain in power for many years.[29]

The right of a third state actually to use force at the invitation of a government in order to keep that government in power or to maintain domestic order has apparently been taken for granted by states since 1945 if the domestic unrest falls below the threshold of civil war. It is commonly said that the *Definition of Aggression* implicitly acknowledges the right of a state to invite a foreign army because it spells out that failure of that foreign army to leave or actions in excess of the invitation will constitute aggression.[30] Interventions limited to action to help governments

---

[28] The impact of such facilities was indicated by the General Assembly in, for example, Resolution 51/427 (1996) on Bases and Installations on Non-Self Governing Territories, passed by 109–47–5. This expressed its strong conviction that military bases and installations in the territories could constitute an obstacle to the exercise by the people of those territories of their right to self-determination.

[29] Moisi, 'Intervention in French Foreign Policy', in Bull (ed.), *Intervention in World Politics* (1984), 67.

[30] Article 3(e) includes in the *Definition of Aggression* 'the use of armed forces of one state which are within the territory of another state with the agreement of the receiving state, in contravention of the conditions provided for in the agreement or any extension of their presence in such territory beyond the termination of the agreement'. The delay by Russia in withdrawing their forces from the Baltic states (1994 UNYB 58, 576); by the UK in leaving Egypt (1947 UNYB 356); and by France in leaving Tunisia (1961 UNYB 101) were all the subject of complaint on this basis.

to repress local protests or army mutinies have generally attracted relatively little international attention. Thus France intervened at the request
of the government of Gabon to protect it against an army mutiny in 1964;
it invoked a defence treaty which allowed force not only against external
attack but also against domestic unrest, and sent extra troops to supplement those French forces already in Gabon.[31] Its justification was that it
had been invited to re-establish the elected government and to prevent
disorder. There was no discussion in the UN. France also used this justification in 1968 when its troops in Chad were strengthened by rein-
forcements from outside to 're-establish order' at the request of the
government under a 1960 defence treaty. Its troops remained until 1972.[32]
Again when the French intervened to overthrow Emperor Bokassa in the
Central African Republic in 1979 they claimed that they had been invited
in by the new ruler to ensure order; in fact the French forces and the new
President arrived together.[33] The UK provision of troops to use force in
support of the governments of Tanganyika, Uganda, and Kenya against
army mutinies in 1964 similarly did not meet with any adverse response.[34]
A more recent example is the intervention by Senegal when it sent troops
into Guinea-Bissau in 1998 to protect the government against an army
rebellion.[35]

The case of Sri Lanka demonstrates the reluctance of states to acknowledge the existence of a civil war; states may continue to claim that a conflict is mere internal unrest even when rebels have in fact gained control
of territory.[36] The Tamil Tigers sought a separate state for the minority
Tamil population; the government of Sri Lanka regarded the Tamil Tigers
as a terrorist force without legitimacy. India, which has a large Tamil population in Tamil Nadu, and which was accused of allowing support to the
Tamil Tigers from its territory, put pressure on Sri Lanka to negotiate a
political settlement with the Tamil Tigers. But in 1987 Sri Lankan government troops responded to the increasing attacks by the Tamil Tigers by
resorting to large-scale force against them; the government attempted to
reassert control of the Jaffna peninsula from which the Tigers operated
and which they effectively controlled. India then intervened. It sent
humanitarian supplies to Sri Lanka destined for the Tamils; the ships
–carrying this were turned back by the Sri Lankan navy. India then made
air-drops over Sri Lanka; Sri Lanka protested.[37] Under pressure from
India the government of Sri Lanka entered into negotiations with the

---

[31] Keesings (1964) 20024.   [32] 1969 RGDIP 469.   [33] 1979 AFDI 908.
[34] Keesings (1964) 19963.
[35] Keesings (1998) 42323. It was subsequently replaced by a regional force established by
ECOWAS, see Chapter 7 below.
[36] Alam, 'Indian intervention in Sri Lanka and International Law', 38 Netherlands International Law Review (1991) 346.   [37] Keesings (1987) 35315.

Tamil Tigers and with India and arranged a far-reaching cease-fire agreement. This agreement included a provision that Sri Lanka could request
India to send troops to police the cease-fire.[38] Sri Lanka immediately made
such a request.

Both states insisted on the legality of the Indian presence. When Turkey,
in a Security Council debate, drew a parallel between the Indian intervention and its own intervention in Cyprus, India rejected the comparison
and argued that its position in Sri Lanka was quite different from that of
Turkey in North Cyprus; it was there at the specific request of the government.[39] Sri Lanka also insisted that India was there at its invitation and
would leave when requested.[40] The cease-fire agreement broke down and
India sent a total of 65,000 troops to try to stop the disorder; they operated
against the Tamil Tigers in the north. Just as there was room for doubt
about the free nature of the original invitation to India to intervene, so the
voluntary nature of the continuation of that consent was also doubtful.
India proved reluctant to withdraw its troops even when asked to do so
by Sri Lanka in June 1989. The Indian forces finally left in March 1990. The
Indian intervention did not meet with any UN response.

Another example of a state denying intervention in a civil war can be
seen in the US insistence that it is not interfering in the long-running civil
war in Colombia but is merely helping the government to fight the drugs
trade. The USA has funded and trained a Colombian anti-narcotics army
battalion and shares intelligence with the Colombian army, but denies any
intent to intervene militarily in the conflict. The theoretical distinction that
the USA draws between the anti-drugs efforts and involvement in the
civil war is difficult to maintain in practice.[41]

In contrast to the above examples of intervention which have escaped
international condemnation, there have been dramatic abuses of the right
to assist a government. The USSR intervention in Hungary in 1956 to
repress the move away from one-party rule was justified by the USSR as
a response to a request from the former Prime Minister. It was 'an internal matter' for Hungary to invite the Soviet forces already present in
Hungary to suppress an armed rebellion by a 'reactionary underground
movement'. This intervention was condemned by the General Assembly
by 50–8–15, and condemnation by the Security Council was avoided only
by a USSR veto.[42] It is striking that when the USSR later intervened in
Czechoslovakia in 1968 to deal with a similar attempt to move away
from one-party rule it did not again base its justification on an invitation
to deal with internal unrest; rather, it sought to portray the events in

---

[38] 26 ILM (1987) 1175.   [39] 1987 UNYB 246.
[40] India S/19354, Sri Lanka S/19355.   [41] The *Guardian*, 15 September 1999.
[42] 1956 UNYB 67. The only states defending the USSR were from the socialist bloc.

Czechoslovakia as an international conflict. The move for change in Czechoslovakia was portrayed as the result of foreign subversion which justified intervention to assist the government.[43]

The maintenance of order was also one of the justifications that was claimed by Iraq for its invasion of Kuwait in August 1991; it said that its forces had responded to a request from the Free Provisional Government of Kuwait to assist it 'to establish security and order so that Kuwaitis would not have to suffer'. Iraqi troops would withdraw as soon as order had been restored.[44] This specious claim was unanimously rejected by the Security Council in Resolution 660, which condemned the invasion and called for the immediate and unconditional withdrawal of Iraqi forces. In both these cases claims to be using force to help a government maintain order were mere pretexts for much more far-reaching intervention and as such were rejected by the Security Council in the case of Kuwait and by the General Assembly in the case of Hungary.

INTERVENTION AND PROTECTION OF NATIONALS

Because intervention to prop up unpopular governments has often proved controversial, foreign states in some instances have not openly said that they were using force to quell unrest at the request of the government. Rather, they have chosen to say that their role was limited to the protection of foreign nationals with the consent of the government, or to claim this as an additional justification to strengthen the other.[45] The USA in particular has sometimes chosen to offer a variety of legal arguments in justification of its interventions. In 1964 US and Belgian forces went into the Congo at the request of President Tshombe, who was faced with rebel seizure of Stanleyville; they reported to the Security Council that they had been invited by the government and were also acting to protect US nationals. Twenty-two states called for a meeting of the Security Council and condemned the intervention; they said that the intervention was a dangerous precedent which might threaten the independence of African states. They also questioned the legality of the government. The USSR claimed that President Tshombe had not taken the initiative in requesting the Stanleyville operation, but had rather given his agreement only after such an agreement had been sought from him. The Congo in turn accused Algeria, Sudan, Ghana, UAR, China, and the USSR of assisting the rebels. The Security Council passed Resolution 199 in general

---

[43] 1968 UNYB 298. [44] S/PV 2932.
[45] See Chapter 4 below on the use of force in protection of nationals abroad *without* the consent of the territorial state.

terms requesting all states to refrain from intervention and appealing for a cease-fire.[46]

Again France (with logistic support from the USA) and Belgium used force in Zaire in 1978 when rebels threatened to bring down President Mobutu; Belgium was careful to emphasize that its action was limited to the evacuation of nationals, whereas the mission of France was also to re-establish security.[47] In other cases France claimed that its action was limited, but in Mauritania in 1977 and in Gabon in 1990 there were doubts as to whether the French intervention was really just to protect nationals.[48] In the Central African Republic in 1996 France used force ostensibly to protect its nationals but in fact to prop up the government.[49] A further mutiny was defeated by French troops protecting the palace. But when yet another mutiny occurred in 1997 French troops left and were replaced by an African force (MISAB) and then a UN force (MINURCA). France's intervention in Chad in 1992 was similarly claimed to be limited to the protection of nationals, although in fact it seems to have gone beyond this to protect the government.[50] Again the intervention by France, Belgium, and Zaire in Rwanda in 1990 was in fact to protect the Hutu government threatened by a Tutsi invasion rather than merely to protect nationals as claimed.[51] Most recently the UK intervention in Sierra Leone in 2000 was initially claimed to be to allow its nationals to leave the country, but it was clear that there was also an intention to prop up the government against rebel forces at a critical time.[52]

More attention has been paid to the instances when the USA used force claiming to be acting both at the invitation of a government and in protection of nationals. The USA, in its forcible interventions in the Dominican Republic (1965) and Grenada (1983), used the justification that it was invited by the legitimate government as part of a regional peacekeeping operation and also that it was acting to protect US nationals in self-defence; in both operations it actually overthrew the old government and installed new governments. Controversy about the existence of the invitation and its constitutional propriety was strong in both cases; in the former the invitation came from unspecified 'government officials' and in the latter from the Governor-General, a post without executive powers. The intervention in the Dominican Republic was the first overt military

---

[46] 1964 UNYB 95; see Virally, 'Les Nations Unies et L'Affaire du Congo', 1960 AFDI 557; Abi-Saab, *The United Nations Operation in the Congo 1960–1964* (1978).

[47] Keesings (1978) 29125.   [48] Keesings (1977) 28573, (1990) 37444.

[49] Keesings (1996) 41080, 41353. France also put pressure on the government; when a settlement was negotiated after the army mutinies had been suppressed France secured the appointment of a new Prime Minister of its choice.   [50] Keesings (1992) 38710.

[51] Keesings (1990) 37766.

[52] Statement by the Secretary of State for Defence in the House of Commons, 15 May 2000; UN Press Release SC/6857.

intervention by the USA after the Second World War, designed to prevent the establishment of another communist government in the western hemisphere; its legality was supported in the Security Council only by the UK. There was also criticism in the General Assembly, but no condemnation by either body.[53] The intervention in Grenada was condemned by the UN General Assembly; it said it 'deeply deplores the armed intervention in Grenada, which constitutes a flagrant violation of international law and of the independence, sovereignty and territorial integrity of that state'.[54]

It is significant that when the USA intervened in Panama in 1989 it chose not to rely on invitation by a government. Although it noted that Endara (who had a clear claim to the presidency because he had been elected to replace Noriega, but had been prevented by him from taking power[55]) had welcomed the intervention, the US legal justification as reported to the Security Council was self-defence in protection of its nationals and defence of the Panama Canal under the 1977 Canal Treaty. This reluctance to rely on invitation may indicate a new caution about using invitation by a 'legitimate' rather than an effective government. The Security Council resolution denouncing the US intervention was vetoed by the USA, the UK, and France because it was unbalanced in that it did not address the illegal nature of the Noriega regime. The General Assembly condemned the intervention in Resolution 44/240 by 75–20–40. This less than overwhelming vote is usually explained as attributable to the hostility to Noriega and the special relation of the USA to Panama. The OAS, however, overwhelmingly condemned the intervention.[56]

In all these cases of US intervention the defence of nationals was used to mask the use of force to overthrow the government; the motive of the USA was to install a new government more ideologically appealing to it. The claim of invitation was controversial in the case of the Dominican Republic, was not accepted as a justification in the case of Grenada, and was abandoned in Panama. The US interventions clearly went beyond the protection of nationals that was claimed as one of the justifications for the intervention and the invitation was not enough to legitimate the intervention as far as a majority of states were concerned.[57]

[53] 1965 UNYB 140; Meeker, 'The Dominican Situation in the Perspective of International Law', 53 Department of State Bulletin (1965) 60.

[54] The GA condemned the intervention in GA Res 38/7 (108–9–27). The condemnation by the Security Council was vetoed by the USA: 1983 UNYB 211. See Gilmore, *The Grenada Intervention* (1984).   [55] 1989 UNYB 172.

[56] Keesings (1989) 37113; D'Amato, 'The Invasion of Panama was a Lawful Response to Tyranny', 84 AJIL (1990) 516; Henkin, 'The Invasion of Panama under International Law: A Gross Violation', 29 Columbia Journal of Transnational Law (1991) 293.

[57] On the regional peacekeeping justification also used in the Dominican Republic and Grenada, see Chapter 7 below.

INTERVENTION IN RESPONSE TO PRIOR FOREIGN INTERVENTION

If there is a civil war rather than mere internal unrest, it has come to be accepted that there is a duty not to intervene, even at the request of the government, in the absence of UN or regional authorization. But even if there is a civil war states may justify forcible intervention at the request of the government on the ground that there has been prior foreign intervention against the government. This is the best established exception to the prohibition of intervention and possibly the most abused. The USSR interventions in Czechoslovakia (1968) and Afghanistan (1979) are the most infamous examples of abuse of the doctrine that prior foreign intervention justifies counter-intervention at the request of the government.[58] In both the invitation was a fiction. In the former the USSR first claimed invitation by the existing government, but Czechoslovakia appeared before the Security Council to deny this.[59] In Afghanistan the USSR installed a new government and then said that it had invited in their forces.

The intervention in Czechoslovakia was explained by the USSR in terms of the 'Brezhnev doctrine' of limited sovereignty for socialist bloc states: this portrayed the movement away from one-party socialism in Czechoslovakia as necessarily the result of foreign subversion and thus as justifying a forcible response by the USSR in collective self-defence.[60] Inconsistently with this, the USSR also argued that the matter was a purely internal affair for Czechoslovakia and so not appropriate for discussion in the Security Council.[61] Under Gorbachev the USSR later expressly disavowed the Brezhnev doctrine; the USSR and the four other Warsaw Pact states which had participated in the invasion and occupation made a statement condemning the invasion of Czechoslovakia as an unlawful interference in an internal dispute and an intervention in a friendly state. They also acknowledged that the intervention in Hungary had been unjustified.[62] The 75,000 Soviet troops remaining in Czechoslovakia were withdrawn by May 1991. The USSR and Czechoslovakia, and later Russia and Czechoslovakia, concluded Friendship Treaties confirming the denunciation of the 1968 invasion.[63]

---

[58] Both these episodes show the absence of a clear line between helping a government to deal with outside subversion and collective self-defence; it was not always obvious which argument the government was relying on. But the distinction does not affect the right to send troops into the state to help the government; it only affects the scope of the right to use force. See Chapter 5 on collective self-defence.

[59] SC 1441st meeting, para 133; 1968 UNYB 299.

[60] On the relationship between the Brezhnev doctrine and earlier US justification for its intervention in the Dominican Republic, see Franck and Weisband, *Word Politics* (1972).

[61] 1968 UNYB 299.   [62] Keesings (1991) 38687.

[63] Keesings (1989) 36982; see Gray, 'Self-Determination and the Break-Up of the Soviet Union', 12 European Yearbook of International Law (1992) 465.

In Afghanistan the new government installed by the USSR said that it had requested Soviet military aid because of foreign threats. The USSR claimed that it was responding to a request from the government to repel armed intervention from outside on the basis of a treaty of December 1978. In the Security Council debate the USSR said that it was responding to US and other Western intervention and China's intervention in Afghanistan's internal affairs to foment counter-revolution; in the General Assembly it invoked instead collective self-defence.[64] This intervention, unlike that in Czechoslovakia, was condemned by a resolution of the General Assembly.[65] The Soviet forces remained until 1989.[66] In both these cases, Czechoslovakia and Afghanistan, the claim of an invitation masked an invasion to overthrow the government.

Turkey also invoked a prior intervention to justify its invasion of Cyprus in 1974 and again this justification was overwhelmingly rejected by the UN. In July 1974 a coup was instigated against the President of Cyprus, apparently with the support of the government of Greece, in order to destroy the constitution created for Cyprus on independence and to secure the union of Greece and Cyprus. The constitution had been designed to protect the interests of both Greek Cypriot and Turkish Cypriot communities. Turkey argued that this was equivalent to a Greek intervention in Cyprus and therefore that it was justified in using force under the 1960 *Treaty of Guarantee* to secure the independence and constitution of Cyprus. Article IV provided that, 'In the event of a breach of the provisions of the present Treaty, Greece, Turkey and the United Kingdom undertake to consult together with respect to the representations or measures necessary to ensure observance of those provisions. In so far as common or concerted action may not prove possible, each of the three guaranteeing powers reserves the right to take action with the sole aim of re-establishing the state of affairs created by the present Treaty.' Turkey seized control of about a third of Cyprus and in 1983 Turkish Cyprus proclaimed itself a state.[67]

The Security Council passed a series of resolutions at first deeply deploring the outbreak of violence and calling for a cease-fire and an immediate end to foreign military intervention in Cyprus; Resolution 360 expressed formal disapproval of the unilateral military actions against Cyprus and the withdrawal of foreign military personnel.[68] The General Assembly also condemned the intervention in Resolution 3213 by 117–0.

---

[64] 1980 UNYB 296 at 298, 299.   [65] GA Res 35/37 (111–22–12), 1980 UNYB 296, 308.

[66] Keesings (1991) 38437, (1992) 38725.

[67] For a discussion of the Cyprus intervention and the interpretation of the Treaty of Guarantee, see Ronzitti, *Rescuing Nationals Abroad* (1985) at 117–34; Necatigil, *The Cyprus Question and the Turkish Position in International Law* (1989); 1974 UNYB 256.

[68] SC Res 351, 353, 355, 356, 358, 359, 360, 361, etc.

The Turkish use of the *Treaty of Guarantee* was apparently not accepted as justifying unilateral forcible intervention, although there was no extended discussion of this in 1974.

Other states making forcible interventions in civil wars have almost invariably argued that they did so in response to a prior outside intervention against the government. Those rejecting these claims have denied the existence of such prior intervention, or denied that there was any invitation from the government. Intervention in response to government request has met with protest when it was seen as support for an unacceptable government or for an outdated monarchy. In the 1950s and 1960s the UK in the Middle East claimed to be responding to government requests to deal with outside subversion or even threatened armed attacks, but it encountered criticism that it was hiding its true motives. The Security Council in these cases was called on to take a view as to whether an intervention was a lawful response to an invitation by a ruler to an outside threat, even amounting to collective self-defence, or whether it was an interference with a popular movement to overthrow a hereditary ruler, an attempt to keep in power a ruler sympathetic to a former colonial power. As with the USA in Vietnam, the UK description of its role as support at the invitation of a government to resist outside subversion or attack was rejected by others who saw it as the perpetuation of colonial rule.

Thus, when the UK forcibly intervened in 1958 to protect the ruler of Jordan it argued that its intervention was lawful because it was in response to an invitation and was a response to external subversion by the UAR. Jordan invoked Article 51 of the UN Charter and called a meeting of the Security Council. This intervention met with criticism by the USSR that the UK was intervening in an internal struggle; it cast doubt on the free nature of the invitation by pointing out that the invitation by Jordan and the UK response took place on the same day.[69] In the debate in the Security Council states who were opposed to the continued British presence denied that there had really been outside intervention. The intervention took place against the background of the rise of Arab nationalism and a successful revolution in Iraq overthrowing the royal family; it was claimed that the true motive of the UK was to repress the rise of Arab nationalism.[70] The General Assembly unanimously passed a resolution calling for the withdrawal of all foreign forces from Jordan.[71]

Again in Oman from 1957 to 1962 the UK said that it was helping the Sultan against rebels from outside; others said that it was a purely civil conflict and the UK was intervening to maintain the Sultan in power and

[69] SC 831st meeting, para 3; 1958 UNYB 41.   [70] SC 831st meeting, para 32, 33; S/4082.
[71] 1958 UNYB 36, 41.

to perpetuate its influence in the region. They called on the UK to give independence to Oman, although the UK said that it was already independent. The Arab League referred the question to the Security Council, but the item was not included on its agenda.[72] Also from 1965 to 1976 there was civil war in Oman when rebels rose against the Sultan and subsequently his son; the UK provided help to the rulers and said that the rebels were helped by South Yemen and the USSR.[73] And in North Yemen when the UAR organized a republican coup against the monarchist rulers in 1962 the UK and Saudi Arabia supported the royalist government.[74] In all these cases the legality of the UK intervention was challenged by those who were suspicious of its motives.

Chad

The problems with the application of the doctrine that a government may invite outside intervention in a civil war if there has been foreign interference were also apparent in the civil war in Chad. Thus when France and Libya intervened in the prolonged civil war each supported a different faction and claimed that it was the true government of Chad.[75] The complexities of the long civil war in which leaders repeatedly shifted allegiance made any objective assessment of the validity of these claims problematic at times. France maintained a military presence in Chad almost continuously from its independence in 1960; the French position when it actually used force was that it was helping the government against Libyan intervention. In 1978 France was accused of sending combat troops to Chad to intervene in the civil war, but it denied this, saying that its soldiers were there only to ensure the safety of French nationals and to train the army of Chad.[76] In 1983 and 1986–7 French troops intervened on the basis that they were helping the government because of prior Libyan intervention. In some of these episodes the French response was expressed to be collective self-defence, in others it was said to be a response to foreign intervention and Article 51 was not invoked. Libya generally denied intervention; it said that the conflict in Chad was internal. When it occupied the Aouzou strip on the border of Libya and Chad in 1973 it claimed that this was part of its own territory. It also denied the legitimacy of the government which had invited France.

When a pro-Libyan government came to power in Chad in 1979 the positions were reversed and Libya claimed invitation by the government.[77]

---

[72] 1957 UNYB 57, 1960 UNYB 194, 1961 UNYB 149.
[73] Weisburd, *Use of Force* (1997), 187.   [74] Ibid. 184.
[75] For a general account of the conflict in Chad, see Weisburd, *Use of Force* (1997), 188; Alibert, 'L'affaire du Tchad', 90 RGDIP (1986) 368.   [76] Keesings (1978) 28976.
[77] 1981 UNYB 222.

The OAU expressed concern when Libya subsequently announced a union with Chad. Libyan troops withdrew in 1981 and were replaced by an OAU peacekeeping force in 1981–2, but the civil war continued. By 1988 all parties were ready for peace; Libya recognized the Habré government against which it had been fighting for much of the past ten years. Libya and Chad agreed to submit the dispute about sovereignty over the Aouzou strip to the International Court of Justice. But France finally ended its support for Habré, and when there was a coup against him in 1990 the French troops stationed in Chad did not intervene; in 1991, when Habré supporters attacked the capital, France sent more troops to protect the new government. Again in 1992 French troops intervened in response to repeated incursions by rebels; France claimed that it was acting merely to protect its nationals, but it was actually seen to be helping the government.[78] The new government remained in power and maintained good relations with France and Libya. Libya accepted the judgment of the International Court of Justice when it determined that Chad had title to the Aouzou strip and withdrew its troops. In 1997 the first multi-party elections were held and in 1999 precarious peace continued.

Generally the international response to foreign intervention in Chad was limited. In 1978 Chad made a complaint about Libyan aggression; Libya denied that it was involved in the internal struggle in Chad and said that any frontier dispute should be handled within the OAU.[79] When a cease-fire was agreed Chad withdrew its complaint to the Security Council. Again in 1983 Chad took two complaints of Libyan intervention to the Security Council in March and August. Libya again denied unlawful intervention in the affairs of Chad; it underlined that it did not recognize the Habré government of Chad and said that it had been invited to send its army to help the legitimate government of Oueddei. Few states spoke in favour of Libya, but equally it was condemned only by those who were hostile to it. The split was clearly on Cold War lines. A significant number of states limited themselves to calling for peaceful settlement or, like the Netherlands, for an end to all foreign intervention. The Security Council issued a statement simply expressing concern and calling for peaceful settlement.[80]

In its second complaint in August 1983 Chad accused Libya of escalating aggression. Libya again denied intervention and said that the cause of instability was the intervention by the USA, France, Sudan, and Zaire to help Habré; they were intervening in a civil war. Zaire and France replied that their forces were in Chad at the request of the legitimate government because there had been external aggression. France said that it was pur-

---

[78] Keesings (1992) 38710.   [79] 1978 UNYB 235.
[80] SC 2419th meeting, 2428–30th meetings; 1983 UNYB 180.

suing no other goal but that of allowing Chad to exercise fully its right of self-defence as enshrined in Article 51 of the Charter. Some states called for an end to all external involvement, but the Netherlands now said that it was necessary to distinguish between the provision at the request of the legitimate government of military assistance to a country acting in self-defence on the one hand and an instance of armed intervention in the affairs of a neighbouring state, in clear violation of the Charter on the other hand. The UK took the same line. Sudan argued that no dispute over the legitimacy of governments could serve as a pretext for occupation or aggression. Despite the calls for Security Council action or at least condemnation of Libyan intervention, the Council was not able to agree on a resolution; the NAM member states were not willing to pass a resolution to condemn Libya.[81] Again in 1986–7 the parties characterized the dispute in radically different ways. Chad and France accused Libya of intervention and invoked collective self-defence; Libya maintained that the dispute was a civil war going back to 1965, and an internal problem arising from French colonialism. It had withdrawn when requested by the legitimate government and had returned to assist that government when requested. It called on other states to end their intervention. It also claimed that it was acting in self-defence of the Aouzou strip, under attack from Chad and France.[82]

As well as its long involvement in Chad, France repeatedly justified its interventions in other African states by claiming that it was responding to prior foreign intervention. For example, it used force to help the government of Tunisia in 1980, saying that it was threatened by insurgents supported by Libya.[83] In 1986 it helped Togo to keep the dictator Eyadema in power, saying that Ghana and Burkina Faso had intervened against the government.[84] It helped the government of Djibouti in 1991 against an alleged Ethiopian intervention; the defence treaty between France and Djibouti did not allow intervention to restore domestic order but did allow the use of force if there was a foreign threat.[85] Other states have also used this justification. Senegal helped the government of Gambia against alleged Libyan opposition in 1981 under their 1965 mutual defence agreement.[86] From 1986 Tanzania and Zimbabwe used force to help the government of Mozambique in its battle against subversion by South African-backed RENAMO rebels.[87]

---

[81] SC 2462–3, 2465, 2467, 2469th meetings; 1983 UNYB 184.
[82] 1986 UNYB 168; 1987 UNYB 176.   [83] Keesings (1980) 30261.
[84] Keesings (1987) 35110.   [85] Keesings (1991) 38564, (1992) 38755.
[86] Keesings (1981) 30687, 31165.
[87] The United Nations Blue Book Series, Vol V, *The United Nations and Mozambique 1992–1995* (1995), 11.

It is apparent that in many of these cases there has been controversy as to the right of the government to invite outside intervention. This question as to who may invite outside help does not arise only in this context of civil wars but also with regard to collective self-defence, invitation to UN and regional peacekeeping forces, and rescue of foreign nationals. Academic debates about effectiveness and legitimacy have been common; writers have divided on the question whether an invitation can only justify intervention if it comes from the effective government or whether it is the legitimate government that has the right to invite assistance to maintain itself in power or to restore it to power when it has been overthrown. Such academic debate has been inconclusive in the light of the diversity of state practice. Roth's exhaustive study demonstrates persuasively that state practice has not produced uniform doctrine as to who counts as the government with the right to invite outside intervention in this context. Cold War divisions meant that, although there was agreement as to the principles governing non-intervention, states often divided on political lines in their determination of who was the government or whether there was a government, whether there actually was an invitation and, if so, whether it was freely given.[88] The disagreements as to who was the government in Chad and Angola are among the most dramatic examples of splits along Cold War lines; the question also arose with regard to Hungary, Afghanistan, Czechoslovakia, the Dominican Republic, and Grenada. In all these cases the claims of invitation were not accepted as a justification for the use of force and the intervention led to condemnation. But in Security Council and General Assembly debates on the use of force, although there has been discussion of the reality of the invitation and of the effectiveness or legitimacy of the government concerned, the main focus has been on the substantial issue of whether the invitation was a mere pretext for intervention.[89]

In contrast, the Syrian intervention in Lebanon since 1976 and India's intervention in Sri Lanka in 1987 met with no General Assembly or Security Council condemnation. In both cases the conflict was serious and the government did not control the whole of its territory. In both cases the voluntary nature of the invitation by the government and the motives of the intervening state were at least open to doubt. Syria has had a presence in Lebanon since 1976; it maintains that it has a special 'fraternal' relation with Lebanon, deriving from their early unity under the Ottoman Empire until the territory was divided by France during the mandate. The need

---

[88] See Roth, *Governmental Illegitimacy in International Law* (1998).

[89] Doswald Beck, 'The Legal Validity of Military Intervention by Invitation of the Government', 56 BYIL (1985) 189; Mullerson, 'Intervention by Invitation', in Damrosch and Scheffer (eds), *Law and Force in the New International Order* (1991), 13.

to balance Muslim and Christian interests has led to instability and Lebanon has been further destabilized by its involvement in the conflict between Palestinians and Israel, and between Syria and Israel. In 1976 civil war broke out between the Maronite Christians on one side and the Muslims and Palestinians on the other.[90] Israel secretly supplied weapons to the Christians[91] and for the first time Syria sent troops to Lebanon, apparently at the invitation of President Franjieh.[92] Israel and the USA acquiesced in the Syrian intervention; Iraq and Libya protested. But in June 1976 the Syrian intervention acquired greater legitimacy through its official absorption into a regional peacekeeping force of the Arab League, the Arab Security Force, later to become the Arab Deterrent Force of about 30,000 soldiers. This remained in Lebanon until 1983, and was dominated by the Syrians. From 1979 this force was intermittently involved in clashes with Israeli forces in Lebanon. The legality of its presence was not challenged in the UN.

But after 1982 the USA and Israel took a different line. The invasion of Lebanon by Israel and its siege of Beirut brought changes in the political situation; a multinational force of Western states was established in Beirut and remained until February 1984. Elements of this force became involved in the civil war and in clashes with Syrian forces. In September 1982 the President of Lebanon requested an end to the ADF mandate and in March 1983 he formally dissolved it, but he did not ask the Syrian forces to leave.[93] From 1984 (after the peace treaty negotiated in May 1983 between Israel and Lebanon was rejected by Lebanon) Israel and the USA protested at the Syrian presence. They complained of double standards in Security Council debates on Israel and the Lebanon; they said that, in contrast to the repeated calls for Israeli troops to leave the 'security zone' that they occupied in south Lebanon, not much had been said by other states about the presence of 50,000 Syrian troops in Lebanon.[94] The USA vetoed resolutions calling for Israeli withdrawal, saying that it was necessary that all foreign forces should leave. Syria replied that its presence was based on a legitimate Lebanese request; Israel tried to give the impression that the Syrian presence was an occupation imposed on Lebanon, but in fact it was there at the request of the legitimate Lebanon government. The Arab League said that whatever might have been the circumstances of the Syrian presence it could not be equated with that of Israel.[95] In December 1985 the position was formalized in the 1985 *Damascus Accord*; Lebanon and Syria both referred to this as an invitation justifying the continued

---

[90] For an account of the conflict in Lebanon, see Weisburd, *Use of Force* (1997), 155.
[91] Bregman and El-Tahri, *The Fifty Years War* (1998), 157–60.
[92] Keesings (1976) 27765.   [93] Keesings (1983) 31905.   [94] 1984 UNYB 285.
[95] 1984 UNYB 285; S/PV 2556, S/17694.

Syrian presence. Israel challenged this, saying that the agreement simply formalized Syrian control of Lebanon.[96]

There were occasional challenges from Lebanon to the presence or activity of the Syrian troops; in 1987 the Lebanese President challenged the constitutionality of 7,000 Syrian troops going into Beirut, but he later reversed his position. In 1989 the Maronite commander, General Aoun, with some backing from France, called for the Syrians to leave and tried to drive them out, but the Arab League negotiated a cease-fire and a new constitutional settlement was accepted by all but Aoun. The Syrians supported the new government and helped it to reassert control over its territory and to ensure stability against the militias. In 1991 Lebanon and Syria concluded two treaties. The first in May was on coordination and cooperation; Lebanon would not allow forces hostile to Syria to operate from its territory and joint councils would coordinate policy. The second agreement in September was a mutual defence treaty. These agreements formally recognized the special position of Syria.[97] Lebanon gradually returned to peace, apart from the repeated confrontations arising out of the continued occupation of the southern 'security zone' by Israel.[98] That is, there have in the last twenty years been occasions when the Syrian presence in Lebanon has been challenged, but on the whole it has been only Israel and the USA which have done so with no support from other states.

FORCIBLE INTERVENTION TO ASSIST THE OPPOSITION

It is apparent from all the above cases that states will seek to invoke an invitation by a government to justify their invasion where this is even remotely plausible. They do not generally claim a legal right to use force to help the opposition forcibly to overthrow the government except in cases of national liberation movements seeking decolonization, as the International Court of Justice made clear in the *Nicaragua* case. Some writers have doubted the legal force of the prohibition of intervention to assist the opposition against the government because practice since the Second World War shows such extensive intervention to help oppositions.[99] But

---

[96] S/PV 2640.   [97] 1991 Annual Register 215.

[98] In April 2000 Israel notified the UN Security Council of its intent to withdraw from Lebanon (S/PRST/2000/13). The Secretary-General put forward the requirements for the implementation of SC Res 425 (1978) regarding withdrawal (S/2000/460), and this was endorsed by the Security Council (UN Press Release SC/6865). In June 2000 the Security Council endorsed the Secretary-General's conclusion that Israel had withdrawn in accordance with SC Res 425 (SC 4160th meeting, UN Press Release SC/6878).

[99] Lowe, 'The Principle of Non-intervention: Use of Force' in Lowe and Warbrick (eds), *The United Nations and the Principles of International Law* (1994), 66; Weisburd, *Use of Force* (1997), 1–27. See *contra*, Mullerson, 'Sources of International Law: New Tendencies in Soviet Thinking', 83 AJIL (1989) 494.

they acknowledge that in fact those states helping the opposition have generally done so without direct use of their own troops. Nor have they openly assisted opposition forces to operate from their territory; often a civil war is internationalized when opposition forces operate from a neighbouring state against their government. If the neighbouring state supports this action, then it is intervening in the civil war. Such support could constitute aggression, use of force or armed attack. But almost invariably states deny any such support for the rebels on their territory for fear of a forceful response.

The open use of a state's own troops against a foreign government involved in civil conflict was rare. Covert action was much more common even in cases where the intervening state challenged the legitimacy of the government of the state involved in civil war. The US intervention in Laos illustrates this clearly. From 1958 to 1960 the USA was trying to secure the removal of a government it saw as ideologically unsound; its intervention was covert. But when a government friendly to the USA came to power in 1961 the USA was willing to use force openly in its support. It undertook bombing against opposition forces which it said were supported from outside.[100]

The USA, although it gave support to opposition groups in Angola, Cambodia, and Afghanistan, did not openly go beyond this to direct forcible intervention. Any direct use of force was generally, as in the *Nicaragua* case, carried out covertly through the CIA. The supply of arms or training to opposition forces was generally covert and thus did not involve a need for legal justification. But it was in the massive financial support for opposition groups in Angola, Cambodia, Afghanistan, and Nicaragua under President Reagan that the USA seemed to come close to blatant disregard, if not rejection, of the legal principle of non-intervention. The President's development of the 'Reagan doctrine' for the containment of the spread of socialism, with its rhetoric of the duty to help 'freedom fighters' against socialist governments, seemed to indicate that the USA was applying a new doctrine of national liberation; it was apparently adopting the doctrine developed by former colonies and socialist states during decolonization, the doctrine that it was legal for national liberation movements to use force in self-determination, to justify intervention in civil wars.[101] But the Reagan doctrine was, like the

---

[100] Weisburd, *Use of Force* (1997), 179.

[101] Reisman, 'Old Wine in New Bottles: The Reagan and Brezhnev Doctrines in Contemporary International Law and Practice', 13 Yale Journal of International Law (1988) 171; Reisman, 'The Resistance in Afghanistan is Engaged in a War of National Liberation', 81 AJIL (1987) 906 and 82 AJ1L (1988) 459. Reisman seems to go further than the US government in his argument. Vertzberger, *Risk Taking and Decisionmaking; Foreign Military Intervention Decisions* (1998), demonstrates that despite the belligerent rhetoric President Reagan's administration in fact took a cautious attitude to intervention.

Brezhnev doctrine, not put forward as a legal justification of the use of force; the right to use force was still based on self-defence.[102] The aid was ostensibly limited to financial assistance, sometimes portrayed as 'non-lethal' or 'humanitarian' aid.[103]

In the case of Cambodia after the Vietnamese invasion of 1978 the government installed by the Vietnamese forces was not accepted in the UN as the legitimate representative of the state and the invasion was repeatedly condemned by the General Assembly by increasing majorities.[104] But even though the General Assembly deplored the foreign armed intervention and occupation and noted 'the continued and effective struggle waged against foreign occupation by the Kampuchean forces' under the leadership of Sihanouk, it did not expressly call for aid to the Sihanouk forces in the way that it called for assistance to Angola against South Africa.[105] However, the repeated accusations by Vietnam that China, Thailand, and the USA were helping Pol Pot opposition forces against the government of Cambodia did not meet any Security Council action or General Assembly response. In all these cases the USA challenged the legitimacy of the government it was attempting to subvert. Even in the middle of the Reagan era, however, the USA was not willing to try to justify its support for the *contras* in Nicaragua as based on the right to support oppositions forcibly to overthrow the government. In the *Nicaragua* case, as was discussed above, the USA did not rely on a legal right to intervene for 'freedom fighters', but rather on collective self-defence; this was clearly regarded as important by the Court.

Exceptionally, the USA went further in the 1998 Iraq Liberation Act. Congress passed this measure after the USA had determined that Iraq was in material breach of its international obligations imposed under the cease-fire regime in Security Council Resolution 687 passed after Iraq's invasion of Kuwait. The Act said that 'It should be the policy of the United States to seek to remove the regime headed by Saddam Hussein from power in Iraq and to promote the emergence of a democratic government to replace that regime.' It went on to authorize the President to provide designated Iraqi 'democratic opposition organizations' with military assistance comprising

---

[102] Kirkpatrick and Gerson, 'The Reagan Doctrine, Human Rights and International Law', in Henkin (ed.), *Right v Might* (1991), 19. D'Amato also was insistent that the doctrine did not involve the forcible overthrow of the government: 'The Secret War in Central America and the Future of World Order', 80 AJIL (1986) 43 at 111.

[103] Keesings (1986) 34426; (1987) 35121, 35174; (1988) 35896. This pretence seems to have come near to being abandoned in 1987 with reports of the *direct* supply of Stinger missiles to the opposition forces in Angola and Afghanistan: Keesings (1987) 34864; (1988) 35786. Some of these weapons ended up in the hands of the Iranian opposition and of Qatar: Keesings (1998) 36220, 36313.

[104] UN Publications, Blue Book Series, Vol II, *The United Nations and Cambodia 1991–1995* (1995).   [105] GA Res 43/19 (1988).

defence articles, defence services, and military education and training of up to US $97 million in value. This provision for arming and training opposition forces, if implemented, could amount to the use of force against Iraq by the USA. Although the President reluctantly signed the Act into law, the US government has not in fact used its powers to assign military assistance, thus confirming the doubts as to the legality of the provisions.[106] The UK, which had supported US military action against Iraq in response to breach of Security Council Resolution 687, did not support this measure; it said that 'It would not be right for the British Government to play a part in attempts . . . to overthrow the Iraqi regime. We have always made it clear that we cannot provide military support as envisaged by the Iraq Liberation Act.'[107]

INTERVENTION AND COUNTER-INTERVENTION IN ANGOLA AND MOZAMBIQUE

The civil war in Angola was fuelled by outside intervention; states divided on Cold War lines.[108] But all were in agreement as to the governing principle that forcible assistance to opposition forces is illegal. When South Africa intervened in Angola it did not openly claim the right to use force to help the opposition against the government, even though it did challenge the legitimacy of the government. In the period leading to independence in Angola (before Portugal finally abandoned its long opposition to independence for its colonies) there was conflict between the different liberation movements in Angola. Both the MPLA and the FNLA had been recognized by the UN as representatives of the people of Angola.[109] Portugal recognized the MPLA, the FNLA, and UNITA as the sole and legitimate representatives of the people of Angola.[110] All received support from other states; the FNLA received aid from the USA, China, and Zaire, the USSR supported the MPLA, and South Africa supported UNITA.

At the start of 1975 the three movements made an agreement to form a coalition government, but on the day after it was formed fighting broke out again. South Africa provided training and leaders to UNITA; Cuba sent military advisers to assist the MPLA. In August 1975 South African

---

[106] 'Contemporary Practice of the United States Relating to International Law', 93 AJIL (1999) at 479.

[107] Letter from FCO Minister of State, 16 March 1999, to President of the 'Iraqi National Congress' (http://www.inc.org.uk).

[108] For a general account of the conflict in Angola, see Brogan *World Conflicts* (1998), 13; UN Publications, *The Blue Helmets: A Review of UN Peace-Keeping* (3rd edn, 1996) at 231.

[109] 1974 UNYB 820.   [110] 1975 UNYB 863.

forces went into Angola in support of UNITA and the FNLA; the justification that it put forward was that it had acted to protect a hydro-electric project. It claimed that it had expressed a readiness to withdraw from Angolan soil in September 1975, long before the date set for independence. However, because of the Portuguese government's inability to provide the necessary protection South Africa had no choice but to protect the project. South Africa claimed that Portugal had said that it would like its troops to stay until the takeover of the next government; Portugal denied this claim.[111] In November Cuba sent armed forces, airlifted in by the USSR, and with their help the MPLA repelled the attack and drove the South African forces out. Some states in the UN General Assembly expressed concern over the direct intervention by South African forces in Angola.[112] The USA accused the USSR of expansionism and said that Angola had been invaded by two other countries as well as South Africa.[113]

The MPLA gained control of most of the territory of Angola and was accepted by the OAU as the government of Angola when it came to independence on 11 November 1975. In 1976 Angola became a member of the UN even though the USA and China wanted to defer this because of the presence of Cuban troops in Angola. The MPLA government answered that the troops were present at the request of the government and would be withdrawn when Angola could defend itself.[114]

The Security Council debates in 1976 set the pattern that was to be followed for the next twelve years. Western states like the USA and the UK said that all foreign intervention should end, but did not actually challenge the *legality* of the Cuban presence. Other states expressly affirmed the right of the MPLA government to invite outside help; they rejected any linkage between the withdrawal of South African forces illegally in Angola and those of Cuba present at the invitation of the government.[115] The Security Council passed Resolution 387 by 9–0–5; this condemned South Africa's acts of aggression against Angola. The USA, France, Italy, Japan, and the UK abstained because, while the intervention of South Africa was condemned, they would also have liked to have seen that condemnation extended to all foreign military intervention in Angola. Later Security Council resolutions, when not vetoed as one-sided by the USA, condemned South African incursions into Angola and also warned South Africa against destabilization of independent African states. For example, Resolution 581 (1986) deplored any form of assistance which could be used to destabilize states in southern Africa.

---

[111] 1976 UNYB 175.   [112] 1975 UNYB 147.   [113] Ibid.   [114] 1976 UNYB 305.
[115] The Security Council later rejected linkage in SC Res 539 (1983).

In 1975 the US Congress passed the Clark Amendment barring covert aid to UNITA by the US government, but South Africa continued to support UNITA and to deny the legitimacy of the government.[116] It said that it did not recognize the government because it did not control the whole territory and was incapable of maintaining itself without foreign troops.[117] But when South Africa made incursions into Angola after independence it invoked self-defence of Namibia against SWAPO guerrillas operating from Angola. In fact its aim was not limited to this; it was dedicated to the destabilization of Angola and the overthrow of the government. Accordingly it helped UNITA covertly, but also intervened with its own forces to help UNITA in 1985 and 1987. Even so, when Angola then accused it of aggression, South Africa continued to use self-defence as the main justification of this use of force; it said that the sources of the conflict were the civil war in Angola between the MPLA and UNITA and the presence of Cuban forces and SWAPO. South Africa claimed to be protecting the people of Namibia against incursions from Angola.[118]

South Africa also referred to the support by the USA for UNITA to back its claim of the lack of legitimacy of the government. Under President Reagan Congress had repealed the Clark Amendment in 1985 and the government gave massive aid to UNITA.[119] The NAM expressed concern at this as the repeal indicated that the USA was contemplating assistance to rebels in Angola. The Security Council passed several resolutions condemning South Africa for its acts of aggression against Angola in 1985; Resolutions 574 and 577 affirmed the right of Angola to self-defence under Article 51. The USA was critical of this as it 'incorrectly implies' that outside intervention was the main cause of destabilization in Angola.[120] The USA went on covertly assisting UNITA, mainly through Zaire with the assistance of the government of President Mobutu.

Even after the tripartite agreement between Angola, Cuba, and South Africa in 1988 whereby South Africa would leave Namibia and Cuban forces would leave Angola, the USA went on helping UNITA, although South Africa terminated its aid.[121] After peace was agreed between the MPLA government and UNITA in 1991, the USA later ended its aid in 1993 when it finally recognized the MPLA government of Angola in response to UNITA's failure to comply with the peace agreement.[122] Thus from the moment of Angola's independence the USA and South Africa challenged the legitimacy of its government, but even so they did not claim a legal right forcibly to overthrow that government.

---

[116] 1985 UNYB 178.   [117] 1985 UNYB 180.   [118] 1985 UNYB 181, 1987 UNYB 167.
[119] 1985 UNYB 183, 1986 UNYB 162.   [120] S/PV 2662.
[121] Keesings (1989) 36388, 36453.   [122] Keesings (1992) 38752, (1993) 39447.

South Africa played a similar role in Mozambique, and here again it did not openly claim a right to help the opposition RENAMO forces.[123] The Frelimo government came to power in Mozambique on its independence from Portugal in 1975; Frelimo had been supported in its struggle for independence by the USSR and Cuba. On achieving independence it supported the opposition to the white minority government in Rhodesia; Rhodesia responded by fighting against the government of Mozambique through RENAMO. When Rhodesia reached majority rule and came to independence as Zimbabwe in 1980, South Africa took over the support for RENAMO. Malawi also allowed RENAMO to operate from its territory. But South Africa denied that it was aiding RENAMO. It justified its incursions into Mozambique as self-defence against ANC forces; it did not claim a legal right to support an opposition to overthrow a government. Nevertheless, it concluded the *Nkomati Accord* with Mozambique in 1984: Mozambique would end its support for the ANC and South Africa would not support RENAMO.[124] This may be seen as an implicit admission of intervention in that both parties undertook not to allow their territory to be used to launch acts of aggression against the other. Mozambique made repeated complaints that South Africa did not comply with this commitment and that it continued to help RENAMO.[125] Mozambique turned to Zimbabwe for assistance; its forces remained until 1993.[126] The UN General Assembly condemned covert and overt aggression aimed at the destabilization of the front-line states.[127] In 1986 the Security Council also condemned the destabilization in general terms in Resolution 581. After the reactivation of the *Nkomati Accord* in 1988 South Africa claimed that the continued fighting in Mozambique was between Frelimo and RENAMO when Mozambique accused it of further attacks.[128]

THE END OF THE COLD WAR

The end of the Cold War brought an end to many of these conflicts as the USSR and the USA abandoned their expensive support for sympathetic governments or opposition forces. South Africa left Namibia and Cuba pulled out of Angola; Vietnam left Cambodia; France has repeatedly announced an end to its intervention in Africa. Agreements were made

---

[123] The United Nations Blue Book Series, Vol V, *The United Nations and Mozambique 1992–1995* (1995).   [124] 1984 UNYB 178.
[125] 1985 UNYB 178, 196; 1986 UNYB 156. In 1985 South Africa admitted involvement but only a technical violation of the accord.
[126] The United Nations Blue Book Series, Vol V, *The United Nations and Mozambique 1992–1995* (1995) at 11.   [127] 1984 UNYB 180; also GA Res 39/17, 39/43, 39/72.
[128] 1988 UNYB 161.

to end the conflicts in Angola, Namibia, Mozambique, Cambodia, Afghanistan, and Central America with UN help. Some of these agreements clearly reflected the foreign involvement that had occurred in the conflicts.[129] As regards Afghanistan, a series of four *Agreements on the Settlement of the Situation Relating to Afghanistan* were concluded on 14 April 1988. First, a bilateral agreement between Afghanistan and Pakistan on the principles of mutual relations, in particular on non-interference and non-intervention. This expressly referred to the obligations in the *Declaration on Friendly Relations* and the 1981 *Declaration on the Inadmissibility of Intervention*. Second, a declaration on international guarantees was agreed between the USA and the USSR; in this the parties agreed to refrain from any form of interference in Afghanistan or Pakistan internal affairs. Third, a bilateral agreement between Afghanistan and Pakistan on the return of refugees and, fourth, an agreement between all four states providing for the withdrawal of Soviet forces.[130]

The agreement to end the conflict in Angola was tripartite; Angola, Cuba, and South Africa made an agreement on 22 December 1988 after South Africa agreed to accept the implementation of Security Council Resolution 435 (1987) on Namibia; Angola and Cuba accordingly agreed on the withdrawal of Cuban troops.[131] South Africa ended its support for UNITA. At first the USA did not follow suit, but when UNITA did not cooperate with the UN peace process the USA finally terminated its aid in 1993.[132]

In contrast, the Mozambique peace agreement was bilateral, although intervention by South Africa directly and through RENAMO had profoundly destabilized Mozambique.[133] In 1990 there was a partial cease-fire and in October 1992 a *General Peace Agreement*, a bilateral agreement between the government and RENAMO. But the UN account said that regional dimension was a crucial factor in the peace process: 'A key element in this success was the active participation of governments in the region in bringing peace negotiations to a fruitful conclusion.'[134]

In Cambodia Vietnam withdrew the last of its forces in 1988.[135] The *Paris Peace Agreements* followed in October 1991; the peace conference was attended by nineteen states and the four Cambodian factions. There were nineteen signatory states to the peace agreements, a symbol of the manifold ramifications of the conflict.[136] Article 10 of the UN-sponsored

---

[129] But contrary to the reasoning in the *Tadic Appeal*, 38 ILM (1999) 1518 at para 157, such agreements do not necessarily demonstrate control or responsibility by the intervening state for all the acts of the opposition forces.   [130] 1988 UNYB 184; 27 ILM (1988) 577.

[131] 1988 UNYB 159.   [132] Keesings (1993) 39447.   [133] 1988 UNYB 158.

[134] 1992 UNYB 193; UN Publications, Blue Book Series, Vol V, *The United Nations and Mozambique 1992–1995* (1995).   [135] 1988 UNYB 179.

[136] UN Publications, Blue Book Series, Vol II, *The United Nations and Cambodia 1991–1995* (1995) 5–8. The parties were Cambodia (represented by a coalition government, the Supreme

peace agreement provided that 'Upon entry into force of this Agreement, there shall be an immediate cessation of all outside military assistance to all Cambodian parties.' Thailand and China claimed to end their support for the Khmer Rouge and they gradually lost influence, but it was not until 1990 that the USA ended its aid to the opposition.[137]

However, some of the conflicts continued, despite the peace settlements; in Angola, Afghanistan, and Cambodia fighting broke out again. The massive assistance that the parties had received during the Cold War helped them to continue the conflict. Thus in Afghanistan the withdrawal of Soviet troops did not end the conflict; Afghanistan accused the USA and Pakistan of continuing to help the rebels. In 1991 the USA and the USSR agreed to halt arms supplies to Afghanistan from 1 January 1992; they also called on Saudi Arabia and Pakistan to follow suit.[138] But intervention from Pakistan in support of Taliban opposition forces has continued. The government of Afghanistan has complained to the Security Council, saying that the objective of Pakistan was strategic, to be secured through a subservient Taliban government. Pakistan said that the Taliban believed that they were being unjustly treated by the international community, despite the fact that they controlled 90 per cent of the territory, including the capital.[139] The Security Council had repeatedly called for an end to foreign intervention, directed at Pakistan.[140]

The Cold War conflicts demonstrated irreconcilable divisions between states on the question as to who was the legitimate government, but they also show an impressive uniformity among states as to the law on intervention. States did not claim the legal right forcibly to overthrow a government; when they did aid the opposition they challenged the legitimacy of the government. The end of the Cold War has not brought an end to foreign intervention in civil wars, but it has made it easier for the UN to play a much greater role in this area. The Security Council may now find it easier to pronounce on who is the government, partly because the UN increasingly plays a role in monitoring or supervising the conduct of elec-

---

National Council formed in 1990 by the warring parties), the five permanent members of the Security Council, the six members of ASEAN, Laos and Vietnam, Australia, Canada, India, Japan, and Yugoslavia.

[137] Keesings (1990) 37598. Other civil wars also ended. In Central America settlements were reached in Nicaragua in 1988, El Salvador in 1992, and Guatemala in 1996 when an *Agreement on a Firm and Lasting Peace* was concluded (1995 UNYB 419, 1996 UNYB 152). With regard to the thirty-year civil war in Guatemala, President Clinton acknowledged in 1999 that the USA had been wrong to interfere (Keesings (1999) 42828). In Chad Libya pulled out of the Aouzou strip which it had occupied since 1973 after the decision of the ICJ in 1994; France has not significantly intervened since the new government came to power in 1990, except for 1992.   [138] Keesings (1991) 38437; 1991 UNYB 161.

[139] SC 4039th meeting, 27 August 1999, UN Press Release SC/6718.

[140] S/PRST/1996/6 and 40; 1995 UNYB 472. The Security Council has called for an end to intervention in a series of resolutions: SC Res 1076, 1193, 1214.

tions as part of post-conflict peace-building. In recent years when the Security Council has imposed an arms embargo on a state on the outbreak of civil war it has sometimes subsequently made an express exception for the supply of arms to the government it regards as legitimate and also to states assisting that government.[141]

[141] See Chapter 6 below at page 155.

4
Self-defence

INTRODUCTION

The law on self-defence is the subject of the most fundamental disagreement between states and between writers. The divisions over the scope of the right of self-defence, especially as to whether anticipatory or 'preventive' self-defence and protection of nationals are lawful, are much discussed and date back to the creation of the United Nations.[1] Other divisions centre on the right to use force in self-defence in response to colonial occupation and to terrorism. Differences over the scope of self-defence prevented any substantive provision on this being included in General Assembly resolutions designed to codify the law on the use of force. States negotiating the 1970 *Declaration on Friendly Relations* and the 1974 *Definition of Aggression* did not include any provision on self-defence; in the 1987 *Declaration on the Non-Use of Force* they could not go beyond the statement that 'States have the inherent right of individual or collective self-defence if an armed attack occurs, as set forth in the Charter of the United Nations.'[2]

However, in practice these fundamental doctrinal differences have not proved to be of decisive significance as to the legality of the use of force except in a few isolated, though much discussed, instances. States using force against another state almost invariably invoke self-defence; in the vast majority of such claims this has not given rise to any doctrinal issues or to any divisions between states as to the applicable law. Whether the use of force is a one-off minor incident (either involving an attack on a state's territory or on its land, sea or air forces outside its territorial limits[3]) or an ongoing conflict, typically one or both states involved asserts that it has been the victim of an armed attack and claims the right to self-defence; the controversy centres on the questions of fact as to

---

[1] Cot and Pellet, *La Charte des Nations Unies* (1991), 771; Simma, *The Charter of the United Nations: a Commentary* (1994), 661; Alexandrov, *Self-Defense Against the Use of Force in International Law* (1996); Bowett, *Self-Defence in International Law* (1958); Brownlie, *International Law and the Use of Force by States* (1963); Zourek, 'La notion de légitime défense en droit international', 56 AIDI (1975) 1.

[2] See Treves, 'La Déclaration des Nations Unies sur le renforcement de l'efficacité du principe du non recours à la force', 1987 AFDI 379. Gray, 'The Principle of Non-use of Force', in Lowe and Warbrick (eds), *The United Nations and the Principles of International Law* (1994), 33 at 38.

[3] On the inclusion of such attacks as self-defence, see Simma, *The Charter of the United Nations: a Commentary* (1994), 670.

whether there has been an armed attack and, if so, which state was the victim. In theory it should always be possible to determine whether there was an armed attack and who is acting in self-defence. But in practice the situation is more complex. The issue is left unresolved in the vast majority of cases; certainly the Security Council does not generally make express pronouncements determining this crucial legal issue. The parties may register their positions with the Security Council, but often there may be no debate and no resolution or statement. Even if there is a resolution or statement, it is far more common for this to take the form of a call for a cease-fire rather than any attribution of responsibility. This can be seen in the recent conflict between Ethiopia and Eritrea; the Security Council has not condemned one or the other of the two states involved in the conflict which broke out in 1998, but has repeatedly called for an end to the hostilities and peaceful settlement of the territorial dispute which is at the root of what the Secretary-General has called an 'incomprehensible war'.[4]

The 1980–8 Iran/Iraq conflict was unusual in that the Security Council asked the UN Secretary-General to investigate responsibility for the conflict and the latter did make an express finding on the facts of the case after the conflict had ended. Iran persistently claimed that Iraq bore responsibility for initiation of the conflict and eventually secured an inquiry into the origin of the conflict by the UN Secretary-General and vindication of its position. The Secretary-General reported that the conflict was begun in contravention of international law through the illegal use of force and disregard for a state's territorial integrity; Iraq was responsible for the conflict because of its armed attack against Iran on 22 September 1980.[5] This willingness to identify the outbreak of a conflict and to determine responsibility was more common in the early days of the UN.[6] It is rare for the Security Council today to enter into this question; members clearly see its role as the promotion of the restoration of peace rather than as the assignment of responsibility. The 1990 Iraq/Kuwait conflict was another exceptional case, seen by many as marking a new role for the Security Council and the start of a new legal order; in this case the Security Council did explicitly uphold the right of Kuwait to self-defence.[7] But more typical have been the many, relatively minor, limited conflicts where the Security Council did not involve itself in any pronouncements on self-defence. There is a striking contrast

---

[4] UN Press Release SG/SM/7410; SC Res 1171, 1226, 1297.

[5] 1991 UNYB 165; S/23273.

[6] For example, Greece 1947–8 UNYB 63, 337; 1948–9 UNYB 238; Indonesia/Netherlands 1947–8 UNYB 369; 1948–9 UNYB 212; Korea 1950 UNYB 245, 251–1; Laos 1959 UNYB 62; Cambodia/Thailand 1959 UNYB 80. On the early practice of the UN in establishing responsibility, see Higgins, *The Development of International Law through the Political Organs of the United Nations* (1963), 166.   [7] SC Res 661 (13–0–2).

between the hundreds of communications to the Security Council in which states claim to be the victims of armed attacks and the few conflicts discussed by the Council. The vast mass of use of force passes unmarked by any debate or resolution, let alone by any formal finding as to who was the victim. And in the vast mass of cases there is no controversy as to the applicable law.

Thus the natural focus of writers on controversial cases where states invoke self-defence, in protection of nationals, anticipatory self defence and response to terrorism inevitably gives an unbalanced picture and distorts our perception of state practice; it helps to give the impression that the far-reaching claims of states like the USA and Israel are normal rather than exceptional.

THE ACADEMIC DEBATE

As far as writers are concerned, the disagreement as to the scope of self-defence generally turns on the interpretation of Article 51. This provides:

Nothing in the present Charter shall impair the inherent right of individual or collective self-defence if an armed attack occurs against a Member of the United Nations, until the Security Council has taken measures necessary to maintain international peace and security. Measures taken by Members in the exercise of the right of self-defence shall be immediately reported to the Security Council and shall not in any way affect the authority and responsibility of the Security Council under the present Charter to take at any time such action as it deems necessary to maintain or restore international peace and security.

There is no need here to do more than set out the basic arguments of the two main groups of writers whose opposing positions have become well entrenched in the last fifty years. Those who support a wide right of self-defence going beyond the right to respond to an armed attack on a state's territory argue, first, that Article 51 of the UN Charter, through its reference to 'inherent' right of self-defence, preserves the earlier customary international law right to self-defence. The Charter does not take away pre-existing rights of states without express provision. Second, they argue that at the time of the conclusion of the Charter there was a wide customary international law right of self-defence, allowing the protection of nationals and anticipatory self-defence.[8] The opposing side argues that the meaning of Article 51 is clear; the right of self-defence arises only if an armed attack (French: *agression armée*) occurs. This right is an exception to

---

[8] For example, Bowett, *Self-Defence in International Law* (1958); Schwebel, 'Aggression, Intervention and Self-Defense in Modern International Law' 136 RCADI (1972–II) 463; McDougal and Feliciano, *Law and Minimum World Public Order* (1961).

the prohibition of the use of force in Article 2(4) and therefore should be narrowly construed. The limits imposed on self-defence in Article 51 would be meaningless if a wider customary law right to self-defence survives unfettered by these restrictions. Moreover, they claim that by the time of the Charter customary law allowed only a narrow right of self-defence.[9] These early arguments turned, first, on treaty interpretation and, second, on an assessment of the state of customary international law in 1945. Policy considerations as to the realism of taking a wide or narrow view also played a crucial role.

Those still supporting the wide right of self-defence today discount the rejection of their position by the large majority of states in practice since 1945; for these writers the Charter preserves customary law as it allegedly was in 1945. Thus the term 'inherent right of self-defence' in Article 51 is not for them a dynamic term capable of shifting in meaning over time; the scope of the right was fixed in customary international law in 1945 and is apparently not susceptible of restriction in the light of subsequent state practice. An alternative approach invokes the breakdown of the UN collective security system during the Cold War in order to justify a wide right to self-defence in the same way that some argue for a narrow interpretation of the prohibition of the use of force in Article 2(4). Again this argument is at variance with the mass of state practice and has to discount the views of the vast majority of states.[10]

In practice, states making their claims to self-defence try to put forward arguments that will avoid doctrinal controversy and appeal to the widest possible range of states. Especially since the *Nicaragua* case, states have taken care to invoke Article 51 to justify their use of force. They do so even when this seems entirely implausible and to involve the stretching of Article 51 beyond all measure. Even when relying on a wide right of self-defence in the absence of an armed attack on their territory, or on their armed forces outside their territory, states invoke Article 51. Either this is just ritual incantation of a magic formula, not expected to be taken seriously, or their case is implicitly that Article 51 allows a wider customary right, including anticipatory self-defence or forcible response to terrorism.

States, in making their own justification or in responding to the claims of others, on the whole and not surprisingly do not enter into extended doctrinal debate in their communications to the Security Council. And even in Security Council debates or in negotiation of General Assembly 'law-making' resolutions on the use of force, they tend simply to assert a

---

[9] For example, Brownlie, *International Law and the Use of Force by States* (1963); Rifaat, *International Aggression: A Study of the Legal Concept* (1979).

[10] This argument was adopted by Judge Jennings in his Dissenting Opinion in the *Nicaragua* case, at 543–4.

wide or narrow view of self-defence without going into the theoretical justifications for their view. Generally more time is devoted to expounding their own version of the facts and their political justifications. It is only in the most controversial cases where there is a doctrinal division that states do enter into protracted legal justification. Israel's arguments in defence of its 1976 rescue operation at Entebbe and of its attack on the Iraqi nuclear reactor in 1981 are unusual in that they are protracted.[11] There was a similarly protracted discussion of the US 1983 intervention in Grenada and its 1986 bombing of Tripoli.[12]

THE ROLE OF THE SECURITY COUNCIL

Article 51 assigns a central role to the Security Council: states are under a duty to report measures taken in the exercise of the right of self-defence to the Security Council and the right to self-defence is temporary until the Security Council 'takes measures necessary to maintain international peace and security'. The USA in the *Nicaragua* case argued that the International Court of Justice should not pronounce on claims of self-defence because Article 51 provides a role in such matters only for the Security Council.[13]

Although Article 51 envisages a crucial role for the Security Council, it does not necessarily require the Council to pronounce on the legality of any claim to self-defence. In practice the Security Council has generally not made such express pronouncements. Some French writers have therefore claimed that it has not done enough to give self-defence a clear content or indeed any real meaning: the right of self-defence is 'indeterminate' or even obsolescent.[14] Thus Combacau takes a rather formalistic approach. He argues that the Security Council can only contribute to the crystallization of the law in this area when a state *expressly* makes a claim

---

[11] On Entebbe, see SC 1939th–1943rd meetings; on the Iraqi nuclear reactor, see 1981 UNYB 275.

[12] On Grenada, S/PV 2677; on Tripoli, 1986 UNYB 247. In contrast, there was little discussion in the Security Council of the US action against sites in Afghanistan and Sudan in response to the terrorist attacks on its embassies in Kenya and Ethiopia in August 1998: 'Contemporary Practice of the US', 93 AJIL (1999) 161.

[13] *Nicaragua case, Jurisdiction and Admissibility*, ICJ Reports (1984) 551 para 92–3; the Court rejected this argument, saying that the USA was attempting to transfer municipal law concepts of separation of powers to the international plane, whereas these concepts are not applicable to the relations among international institutions for the settlement of disputes. Also the fact that a matter is before the Security Council should not prevent it being dealt with by the Court.

[14] Combacau, 'The Exception of Self-defence in UN practice', in Cassese (ed.), *The Current Legal Regulation of the Use of Force* (1986) Chapter 13; Delivanis, *La légitime défense en droit international public moderne* (1971).

to be acting in self-defence to the Council and the Council makes an express response; on the basis of the *Repertoire of the Practice of the Security Council* up to 1974 Combacau claimed that states rarely made such claims. First, this approach seems too rigid. Security Council resolutions and statements may be of significance in the development of the law if in substance they deal with state behaviour and implicitly or expressly accept or reject claims of self-defence. Second, his argument was based on the *Repertoire of the Practice of the Security Council* up to 1974. This does not give a complete picture and, moreover, is based on practice before the decision in the *Nicaragua* case which led to a clear change in state behaviour.

It is true that only a very few Security Council resolutions have made express reference to Article 51. Typically these assert in general terms the right of a particular state to take action in self-defence. Such resolutions have generally not been passed in recent years. They were passed in response to South Africa's attacks on the front-line states during the apartheid era, and in response to the use of force by Portugal and Israel. For example, Angola's right to take measures in accordance with Article 51 when it had been subject to attacks by South Africa was affirmed by the Security Council; these resolutions also condemned South Africa's use of force.[15] More recently, and exceptionally, Kuwait's right to self-defence was affirmed by the Security Council after the Iraqi invasion.[16]

Other resolutions respond to the use of force by states; in so far as they condemn particular actions they may be taken as rejections of a state's claim to self-defence even if this is not express in the resolution. Thus the attempt to deny any clear content to the right of self-defence because of the nature of the decision-making of the Security Council underestimates the significance of the vast mass of state practice, and especially of the many state communications to the Security Council. The core content of self-defence is universally accepted.[17]

However, the approach of Combacau and Delivanis, although formalistic, has some justification. The Security Council resolutions and statements, although they may be authoritative as to the legality of particular uses of force, cannot do much to resolve the doctrinal controversies as to the scope of the right of self-defence. Any condemnation of controversial use of force such as protection of nationals, anticipatory self-defence, and action against irregulars and terrorists may be limited to the particular facts. Rather than condemn protection of nationals or anticipatory self-defence in general, the Security Council condemns the particular use of

[15] SC Res 546 (1984 UNYB 180–3), SC Res 574 (1985 UNYB 178 at 187), GA Res 38/39 (1983 UNYB 173 at 174).   [16] See below at page 93.
[17] Schacter, 'Self-Defense and the Rule of Law', 83 AJIL (1989) 259.

force. The Security Council debates will usually reveal the doctrinal divisions between states; it is clear that in order to secure agreement on a resolution the Security Council may have to avoid any pronouncement on the underlying doctrine. Therefore the resolutions may provide only indirect evidence as to the state of the law. They do not contain general statements of the law. Pronouncements on individual breaches may do no more than make it possible to argue, for example, that the fact that almost all uses of anticipatory self-defence have been condemned suggests the weakness of such a doctrine.

The duty to report to the Security Council

Since the judgment in the *Nicaragua* case it is noticeable that states on the whole do comply with the Article 51 obligation to report actions in self-defence to the Security Council; it is clear that states have taken seriously the Court's message that failure to do this will weaken any claim to be acting in self-defence. The Court held that 'the absence of a report may be one of the factors indicating whether the State in question was itself convinced that it was acting in self-defence'.[18] Judge Schwebel, in his Dissenting Opinion, strongly criticized this as unacceptable in the case of covert self-defence.[19] But any attempt to attack this finding by the Court as an objectionable innovation is fundamentally misconceived.

The argument that failure to report was evidence against a claim to self-defence had been made many times even before the case. For example, the UK during the Vietnam conflict said that the fact that the USA had reported to the Security Council in 1964 its actions in response to alleged attacks by North Vietnamese naval vessels in the Gulf of Tonkin was an indication that it was actually acting in self-defence.[20] And after the USSR intervention in Afghanistan the UK asked in the General Assembly debate why, if there had really been attacks on Afghanistan, it had not raised the matter before the Security Council.[21] Failure to report was also used as a sign of bad faith by the USA itself. After the clashes between the USA and Libya in the Gulf of Sirte in March and April 1986 (that is, during the *Nicaragua* case proceedings) the USA used the argument that Libya had not reported its actions to the Security Council as evidence that it was not acting in self-defence. Conversely, the UK said that the US report of these episodes to the Security Council under Article 51 was as a sign of good

---

[18] *Nicaragua* case, ICJ Reports (1986) 14, para 200.
[19] Dissenting Opinion, paras 7, 221–30.   [20] 1964 UNYB 147.
[21] 1980 UNYB 296 at 300; see also Higgins, *Development of International Law through the Political Organs of the United Nations* (1963) at 207.

faith.[22] However, it is clear that the reporting requirement is merely procedural; failure to comply does not of itself invalidate a claim to self-defence.[23]

Before the *Nicaragua* case the reporting requirement was not always strictly observed in cases of individual self-defence (in marked contrast to the practice with regard to collective self-defence). But, even before the *Nicaragua* decision, reporting by states was more common than the *Repertoire of the Practice of the Security Council* indicates; a study of the communications of states to the Security Council gives a fuller picture of state practice in this regard.[24] After *Nicaragua* it can no longer be maintained that the reporting requirement is rarely observed.[25]

Indeed, there is now a tendency to over-report claims to individual self-defence, if anything. It seems clear that a state involved in a one-off episode should report if relying on self-defence. Also states parties to a prolonged conflict should, if relying on self-defence, go to the Security Council at the start of that conflict. However, when there is a prolonged conflict the states parties tend not simply to make their claims to self-defence at the start of the conflict, but often to report each episode separately. That is, they apparently interpret the reporting requirement in Article 51 that 'Measures taken by Members in the exercise of this right of self-defence shall be immediately reported to the Security Council' as requiring continuing reports. This may significantly increase the burden on the state claiming self-defence in that it has to show that each episode in isolation constitutes necessary and proportionate self-defence, rather than simply the campaign taken as a whole. This repeated reporting was marked in the practice of Iran and Iraq during their 1980–8 conflict and in the practice of the UK and Argentina in the Falklands conflict. It was also the practice of the USA with regard to its involvement in the 1980–8

[22] S/PV 2671; S/17938; S/PV 2668. Here again self-defence is being invoked with regard to the protection of armed forces outside a state's territory.

[23] Greig, 'Self-Defence and the Security Council: What does Article 51 require?', 40 ICLQ (1991) 366.

[24] There was, however, some genuine concern about the issue; the UN Secretary-General in *The Report of the Special Committee on Enhancing the Effectiveness of the Principle of the Non-Use of Force in International Relations* (1986), A/41/41, called for consideration of the possibility that the Security Council might inquire into episodes when the states involved had not reported.

[25] A misleading impression has been given by writers who rely on an earlier, pre-*Nicaragua* account: Simma, *The Charter of the United Nations: A Commentary* (1994), 677, note 148, Schacter, 'Self-Defense and the Rule of Law', 83 AJIL (1989) 259, and Greig, 'Self-Defence and the Security Council', 40 ICLQ (1991) 366, all rely on Combacau's earlier, pre-*Nicaragua* account based on *The Repertoire of Practice of the Security Council* up to 1974. Combacau, 'The Exception of Self-defence in UN practice', in Cassese (ed.), *The Current Legal Regulation of the Use of Force* (1986), Chapter 13, also took a formalistic approach in that he distinguished between a special report and ordinary communications to the Security Council or statements in debates. Thus there is a danger that a misleading myth of non-reporting will be perpetuated.

Iran/Iraq conflict, when the US navy was providing convoys for US-flagged ships through the Gulf to protect them against attack by the belligerent parties. Instead of making a blanket statement at the start of its involvement, the USA sought to justify each episode of the use of force against Iran.[26] Here we see self-defence being invoked with reference to the protection of US ships and aircraft; this is sometimes referred to as 'unit self-defence' as opposed to 'national self-defence' of a state's territory. This choice to report individual episodes led the USA into some difficulties when it had to justify its actions against Iranian oil platforms and its shooting down of the Iran Airbus in 1988 as self-defence.[27]

Such repeated reporting may seem to play partly a propaganda role.[28] Given that the Security Council does not usually pronounce on the legality of a claim to self-defence at the start of a conflict, it may be understandable that the states refer each individual episode to the Security Council in an attempt to portray themselves as victims, as in the Iran/Iraq conflict when Iran and Iraq repeatedly reported particular incidents to the Security Council. Because the Security Council made no initial determination that Iraq was the aggressor, it could seek to portray itself as the victim, especially when Iran later refused to accept the 1987 mandatory cease-fire resolution. Also controversially, such reporting of individual episodes as self-defence may represent an attempt to rely on Article 51 rather than the laws of war where an action's legality is doubtful as a matter of international humanitarian law. Thus in the Vietnam war the USA justified its use of force generally as collective self-defence of South Vietnam. It also subsequently reported individual episodes such as its mining of the ports of North Vietnam and its bombing of neutral Cambodia as constituting self-defence.[29] Again in the Falklands conflict the UK reporting of individual episodes as self-defence may reflect its doubts as to the adequacy of the laws of war at sea.[30]

Self-defence as a temporary right

The Security Council also has a role in the control of the right of self-defence through the stipulation in Article 51 that the right of self-defence

---

[26] S/19149, S/19194, S/19219, S/19791, S/19989.

[27] See below at 96, 113. Iran took both these cases to the ICJ. In the first, the *Case concerning Oil Platforms*, ICJ Reports (1996) 803, the ICJ found jurisdiction; the second case, *Aerial Incident of 3 July 1988*, was withdrawn in 1996 after a settlement between the parties and the payment by the USA of *ex gratia* compensation.

[28] Combacau, 'The Exception of Self-defence in the Practice of the United Nations', in Cassese (ed.), *The Current Legal Regulation of the Use of Force* (1986), 21.

[29] On the USA mining see 1972 UNYB 153; on the US actions in Cambodia, see Falk (ed.), *The Vietnam War and International Law*, Vol 3 (1972), 23–148.

[30] 1982 UNYB 1320 at 1325; see also Gray, 'The British Position in regard to the Gulf Conflict, Part 1', 37 ICLQ (1988) 420.

continues 'until the Security Council has taken measures necessary to maintain international peace and security'. Given that the UN Charter aims not only to limit but also to centralize the use of force under UN control, it seems clear that the intention was to give the Security Council itself the right to decide whether such measures terminating the right to self-defence had been taken. But, in the absence of express determination of the existence or continuation of the right to self-defence, this provision has in the past given rise to some controversy.[31] The Falklands (Malvinas) conflict is a famous example; after the Argentine invasion of the UK colonial territory in 1982 the Security Council, in Resolution 502 (10–1–4), determined that there had been a breach of the peace, demanded an immediate cessation of hostilities, demanded an immediate withdrawal of all Argentine forces, and called on the governments of Argentina and the UK to seek a diplomatic solution to their difficulties. Did this amount to 'necessary measures to maintain international peace and security' which terminated any UK right to use force in defence of the Falklands? The UK argued that it did not, since Argentina, the aggressor, remained in occupation of the islands.[32] The question came up again in the 1980–8 Iran/Iraq conflict. After the mandatory Security Council Resolution 598 (1987) calling for a cease-fire, was Iran subsequently exceeding its right to self-defence in its refusal to accept the cease-fire, given that it had already by mid-1982 recovered the territory earlier occupied by Iraq? Although the USA and the UK did not expressly make this argument in the Security Council, they came close to it.[33]

The UK apparently learned its lesson from the controversy over the Falklands. When the Security Council responded to Iraq's 1990 invasion of Kuwait it imposed sanctions on Iraq; in the same resolution it included an affirmation of 'the inherent right of individual or collective self-defence, in response to the armed attack by Iraq against Kuwait, in accordance with Article 51 of the Charter'.Thus no problem could arise as to whether the imposition of economic sanctions by the Security Council had terminated any right of states to use collective self-defence to help

[31] Higgins, *The Development of International Law through the Political Organs of the United Nations* (1963) at 198, 206; Waldock, 'The Regulation of the Use of Force by Individual States in International Law', 81 RCADI (1952–II) 496. On drafting history, see M. Halberstam, 'The Right to Self-Defense once the Security Council takes action', 17 MJIL (1995–6) 229; see also Chayes, Reisman, and Schacter in Damrosch and Fisher (eds), *Law and Force in the New International Order* (1991), 1, 26, 65; Franck and Patel, 'UN Police Action in Lieu of War', 85 AJIL (1991) 63; Rostow, 'Until What? Enforcement Action or Collective Self-Defense?', 85 AJIL (1991) 506.
[32] 1982 UNYB 1320; SC 2360th meeting, SC 2362nd meeting.
[33] See De Guttry and Ronzitti (eds), *The Iran–Iraq War (1980–1988) and the Law of Naval Warfare* (1993) at 219, 226; Gray, 'The British Position with regard to the Gulf Conflict', 37 ICLQ (1988) 420 at 427, 40 ICLQ (1991) 464 at 466.

Kuwait. The USA and the UK could act in collective self-defence of Kuwait even before specific authorization for the interception of ships and aircraft bound for Iraq and Kuwait was given by the Security Council.[34]

Security Council measures and self-defence

The question has also arisen of the relationship between the state's right to self-defence and the powers of the Security Council: are the powers of the Security Council under Chapter VII of the Charter limited by the require- ment that such measures do not undermine the right of self-defence under Article 51? This question came up first in 1977 when France argued that an arms embargo on South Africa might violate its right to self-defence. How- ever, France said, the intention here, in the aftermath of the recent crack- down by the South African government, was to protest against the stockpiling of weapons intended for purposes of internal repression; there- fore it had decided to vote in favour of a mandatory arms embargo on South Africa.[35] This issue arose again in the debate over the compatibility of the arms embargo on the whole of the former Yugoslavia with the right of self-defence under Article 51.[36] At the outbreak of the conflict in Yugoslavia in 1991 the Security Council imposed an arms embargo on the whole of Yugoslavia. Resolution 713 was passed unanimously and the arms embargo was imposed with the consent of the federal government of Yugoslavia. When Yugoslavia split up and Bosnia-Herzegovina became a member state of the UN in May 1992 it argued that the arms embargo should not be applied to it. It sought the lifting of the embargo by the Security Council from September 1992. It claimed that its inherent right to self-defence under Article 51 took priority over the embargo, and that in order to exercise this right against Yugoslavia (Serbia and Montenegro) the embargo must be lifted. In the Security Council debates those in favour of lifting the embargo argued either that Resolution 713 had been superseded when Bosnia became a member of the United Nations or that the resolu- tion should be interpreted as not applying to Bosnia or, more radically, that if the resolution did impose an embargo on it, then the resolution was invalid as outside the powers of the Security Council because it violated

[34] SC Res 661. Greenwood, 'New World Order or Old?, 55 MLR (1992) 153; Warbrick, 'The Invasion of Kuwait by Iraq', 40 ICLQ (1991) 482.

[35] *Repertoire of Practice of the Security Council 1975–1980*, 311. This question also came up over Sierra Leone when those who wanted to defend the supply of arms to the legitimate government claimed that the arms embargo applied only to those who had seized power in a coup. However, this was not express in the resolution. See UK *Parliamentary Report of the Sierra Leone Arms Investigation* (1998).

[36] Gray, 'Bosnia and Herzegovina: Civil War or Inter-State Conflict? Characterization and Consequences', 67 BYIL (1996) 155; Report of the Secretary-General pursuant to GA Resolu- tion 53/35 (1998), *'Srebrenica' report*.

Bosnia's inherent right to self-defence. The Security Council refused to accept this argument and did not lift the embargo even though the General Assembly repeatedly urged it to consider this.[37]

It is clear that there are strong arguments against a claim that an arms embargo violates Article 51 of the UN Charter. If every arms embargo is automatically inconsistent with Article 51 this would restrict the Security Council's discretion to take measures under Article 41 and deprive it of a useful tool to put pressure on a wrongdoing state or to try to limit the escalation of a conflict. All states subject to an arms embargo could claim that their rights under the Charter prevailed over the arms embargo. It seems unlikely that Bosnia-Herzegovina, in putting its claim for the lifting of the embargo, was really making the argument that every arms embargo violated Article 51.

Even if Bosnia-Herzegovina was putting forward a less fundamental argument and was claiming merely that in the particular circumstances the arms embargo in Resolution 713 violated its right to self-defence, this seems a dangerous precedent and one that would undermine the freedom of the Security Council to maintain an arms embargo. States suffering civil wars and subject to arms embargoes could make plausible cases that they were under outside threat and needed to exercise their rights to self-defence. The better position is that an arms embargo may affect the right to self-defence but does not actually deny that right.

This question came up again with regard to Rwanda.[38] The Security Council imposed an arms embargo in 1994, against the wishes of the government then in power, to try to prevent the escalation of violence. Following Bosnia's claims, Rwanda pursued a similar line of argument, that the arms embargo imposed on it after large-scale massacres in 1994 should be lifted because there was a threat to it from outside. This time the Security Council did respond, noting with concern the reports of military preparations and incursions into Rwanda by supporters of the former government. It recalled that the original prohibition on the delivery of arms was aimed at preventing their use in the massacre of innocent citizens. The embargo was lifted as far as arms destined for the government were concerned, but otherwise remained in place.[39] This precedent may

---

[37] The International Court of Justice, in *Application of the Convention on the Prevention and Punishment of the Crime of Genocide (Provisional Measures)* ICJ Reports 1993, 3, 325, was also faced with a claim by Bosnia for the lifting of the arms embargo, but it decided that this was not within its jurisdiction; see Gray, 43 ICLQ (1994) 704; Report of the Secretary-General pursuant to GA Resolution 53/35 (1998), *'Srebrenica' report* para 99–102.

[38] Rwanda successfully campaigned for the lifting of the arms embargo imposed on it because of the internal conflict on the grounds that this made it vulnerable to outside interference: 1995 UNYB 347.

[39] 1994 UNYB 281; 1995 UNYB 370 at 380; SC Res 1011; UN Publications Blue Book Series, Vol 10, *The United Nations and Rwanda 1993–1996* (1996).

have made it more difficult for the Security Council to keep in place against the wishes of the government of the state concerned an arms embargo imposed during a civil war. The modification of the total arms embargo on Sierra Leone to allow arms to be supplied to the government and those supporting it reinforces this view.[40]

THE SCOPE OF SELF-DEFENCE

Armed attack

All states agree that if there is an armed attack the right to self-defence arises, but there are disagreements as to what constitutes an armed attack. Some of these disagreements centre on cross-border activity by irregular forces. Other questions concerning the definition of the concept and the identification of the start of an armed attack arise out of the special characteristics of particular weapons.[41] The concept of armed attack was

---

[40] SC Res 1132, 1171, 1299. See Chapter 6 on regional action.

[41] The question of what is an armed attack arises because of the characteristics of certain weapons. On the special question of nuclear weapons, see Boisson de Chazounes and Sands (eds), *International Law, the International Court of Justice and Nuclear Weapons* (1999). Naval mines and modern missiles have also given rise to special questions in recent years. For an early discussion of these issues see, O'Connell, *The Influence of Law on Sea Power* (1975), 70. As regards modern radar-guided missiles, some states argue that an armed attack begins when the radar guiding the missile is locked on ready to fire. The rules of engagement of their armed forces reflect this approach. For example, in 1998 US aircraft in the no-fly zone over Iraq fired at a missile battery when its radar had locked on to planes patrolling the zone. There was controversy over whether the radar had actually locked on (and over the right of the planes to fly over Iraq), but the idea that an armed attack started when the radar locked on was apparently accepted by Iraq and other states: Keesings (1998) 42368. This contrasts with the hostile reaction that the USA and the UK met later when they further extended their rules of engagement to allow a wider range of targets (see below).

With regard to naval mines, the difficulty of fitting these into the traditional conception of self-defence became apparent during the Iran/Iraq war. Iranian minelaying led to conflict with the USA in 1987–8. First, the USA responded when US flagged vessels were damaged by mines. After this occurred the *Iran Ajr* was detected laying mines. The USA boarded and seized the Iranian vessel. Because the USA chose to justify its actions in protection of US flagged vessels incident by incident rather than invoke self-defence once to cover its entire operation, it had to explain its actions against Iranian minelayers in terms of Article 51 rather than the laws of war. Accordingly it argued that its actions taken to intercept minelaying vessels were in self-defence. See Gray, 'The British Position in Regard to the Gulf Conflict', 37 ICLQ (1988) 420 at 427; Thorpe, 'Mine Warfare at Sea', 18 Ocean Development and International Law (1987) 255; Nordquist and Wachenfeld, 'Legal Aspects of Reflagging Kuwaiti Tankers and the Laying of Mines in the Persian Gulf', 31 German Yearbook of International Law (1988) 138. More controversially, in response to mine damage to the *USS Samuel B. Roberts* in 1988 the USA attacked and destroyed Iranian oil platforms which it said had been used as a base for Iranian operations. The legality of the US action is now before the International Court of Justice in the *Case Concerning Oil Platforms*. The USA reported its actions to the Security Council under Article 51 as self-defence, but the justification that it offered made the action appear more like a reprisal; it said that its actions were designed to deter

central to the International Court of Justice's judgment on collective self-defence in the *Nicaragua* case; the USA claimed that its use of force against Nicaragua was justified as collective self-defence of Costa Rica, Honduras, and El Salvador in response to armed attacks on those states by Nicaragua, but the Court rejected this as it found that there was no armed attack by Nicaragua. The Court's view of armed attack has been severely attacked, especially by US writers.[42] However, the Court's description of the scope of armed attack is consistent with state practice and with the practice of the Security Council.

The Court first considered whether an armed attack had to be by a regular army. It used the *Definition of Aggression* to support its view that 'the sending by or on behalf of a state of armed bands, groups, irregulars or mercenaries, which carry out acts of armed force against another state of such gravity as to amount to (inter alia) an actual armed attack conducted by regular forces, or its substantial involvement therein' could be an armed attack. This limited reliance on the *Definition of Aggression* (stopping short of a complete identification of the two concepts) to elucidate the meaning of armed attack seems justified in the light of state practice.[43] States do not today challenge the view that actions by irregulars can constitute armed attack; the controversy centres on the degree of state involvement that is necessary to make the actions attributable to the state and to justify action in self-defence in particular cases.

The Court then held that assistance to rebels in the form of the provision of weapons or logistical or other support did not amount to an armed attack, although it could be illegal intervention.[44] This was strongly criticized by Judges Schwebel (USA) and Jennings (UK) in their Dissenting Opinions. Judge Schwebel said that the reference in the *Definition of Aggression* to 'substantial involvement' in the sending of armed bands meant that an armed attack could include financial and logistical support for armed bands. However, the drafting history of the resolution does not

---

further unlawful use of force against the USA: Gray, 'The British Position in Regard to the Gulf Conflict, Part II', 40 ICLQ (1991) 464; 1987 UNYB 235, S/19149; see also De Guttry and Ronzitti (eds), *The Iran–Iraq War (1980–1988) and the Law of Naval Warfare* (1993) at 195–7, 222–3.

[42] For example, Franck, 'Some Observations on the ICJ's Procedural and Substantive Innovations', 81 AJIL (1987) 116; Norton Moore, 'The *Nicaragua* case and the Deterioration of World Order', 81 AJIL (1987) 151; Macdonald, 'The Nicaragua case: New Answers to Old Questions', 1986 Canadian Yearbook of International Law 127; Higgins, *Problems and Process* (1994) 251.

[43] Judge Ago, in his Separate Opinion, 181 para 7, expressed reservations about the legal significance of General Assembly resolutions. In contrast, Judge Schwebel was prepared to accept the *Definition of Aggression* as reflecting customary international law (Dissenting Opinion para 168). See Gray, 'The Principle of Non-Use of Force', in Lowe and Warbrick (eds), *The United Nations and the Principles of International Law* (1994) 33.

[44] *Nicaragua* case para 195.

support this construction and it is not consistent with Schwebel's own earlier recognition of a distinction between the wider conception of aggression and the narrower conception of armed attack.[45] Schwebel argued that the Court's narrow definition of armed attack and consequent limit of the right of self-defence offered a prescription for overthrow of weaker governments by predatory governments while denying potential victims what in some cases may be their only hope of survival.

Judge Jennings similarly argued that the Court's approach was not realistic, given that power struggles are in every continent carried on by destabilization, interference in civil strife, comfort, aid and encouragement to rebels, and the like. Because Chapter VII of the UN Charter was not working it was dangerous to define unnecessarily strictly the conditions for lawful self-defence.[46] The converse argument could equally well be made; because Chapter VII was not working it was important not to allow the abuse of the right of self-defence. Jennings said that 'It may readily be agreed that the mere provision of arms cannot be said to amount to an armed attack. But the provision of arms may nevertheless be an important element in what might be thought to amount to an armed attack where it is coupled with other kinds of involvement.'[47]

The focus for both dissenting judges was on the question of fact: did the particular actions of Nicaragua taken as a whole amount to an armed attack? They also were making policy arguments as to what the law ought to be. Neither Schwebel nor Jennings adduced any evidence that in state practice mere provision of weapons and logistical support in isolation had been treated as armed attack (as opposed to unlawful intervention) in cases of self-defence.

A few commentators accepted the arguments of the dissenting judges on the facts, but also went further and made strong criticisms of the Court's conception of armed attack. That is, they did not just reject the Court's interpretation of the facts, they also said that it was mistaken on the law.[48] They did not go so far as to say that a mere supply of arms could alone amount to an armed attack, but they argued that arms supply combined with financial and logistical support could in principle be an armed attack. However, their criticisms were based on policy considerations; they did not give any examples of state practice or Security Council prac-

[45] Schwebel, 'Aggression, Intervention and Self-Defense in Modern International Law', 136 RCADI (1972–II) 463.

[46] Dissenting Opinion 543–4; Jennings' argument echoes that of Reisman, 'Coercion and Self-determination: construing Charter Article 2(4)', and is open to the rebuttal by Schacter, 'The legality of pro-democratic invasion', 78 AJIL (1984) 642, 646.

[47] Jennings, Dissenting Opinion 543.

[48] Franck, 'Some Observations on the ICJ's Procedural and Substantive Innovations', 81 AJIL (1987) 116 at 120; Norton Moore, 'The *Nicaragua* case and the deterioration of World Order', 81 AJIL (1987) 151 at 154.

tice to support their arguments. Nor do they apply such principles to US interventions. In contrast, the Court's judgment is consistent with state practice. The Security Council, in its many calls for an end to the supply of arms or other outside support to opposition forces in situations such as those in Afghanistan, Yugoslavia, and Rwanda, has never identified such interventions as an armed attack.

The issue of cross-border action by irregular forces has given rise to much difficulty. If these forces are acting on behalf of the state from whose territory they are operating and their actions are of such gravity as to amount to an armed attack, the situation is clear.[49] However, the question of what degree of state involvement is necessary to allow the use of force against the territory of the host state in self-defence has proved an intractable issue. In the *Nicaragua* case the Court treated the *Definition of Aggression* with its provision 'sending by or on behalf of a state' as definitive as to what amounted to an armed attack. It did not expressly go into the issue of whether a lesser degree of state involvement, such as acquiescence or even inability to control armed bands operating on its territory, could ever be enough to constitute an armed attack, but it seems implicit in its judgment that armed attack is narrower than this.[50]

'Victim' states have tended to blame the host state for incursions by armed bands operating from their territory and to hold it responsible in order to justify their invocation of self-defence; that is, they seem implicitly to take the view that if there is no state involvement in the actions of the irregular forces there can be no self-defence against that state but only lesser action not going beyond the territory of the victim state. The best known practice is that of Israel, South Africa, and Portugal: they all took extensive action against irregular forces in neighbouring states.

Portugal's reluctance to give up its colonial possessions in Africa led it into conflict with national liberation movements and newly independent African states. In the 1960s and 1970s Guinea, Senegal, and Zambia repeatedly complained of armed invasions by Portugal from its colonies. Portugal argued in response that it was acting in self-defence because

---

[49] Brownlie, 'International Law and the Activities of Armed Bands', 7 ICLQ (1958) 731; Cot and Pellet (eds), *La Charte des Nations Unies* (1991) 780; Rifaat, *International Aggression: A Study of the Legal Concept* (1979), Chapter 15; Lamberti-Zanardi, 'Indirect Military Aggression', in Cassese (ed.), *Current Legal Regulation of the Use of Force* (1986), 111.

[50] This question of involvement in irregular actions has been discussed in several different contexts: the definition of intervention, aggression, armed attack, and use of force. It also arises with regard to the degree of state involvement necessary for the acts of armed bands to give rise to state responsibility. The drafting of the GA resolutions on *Friendly Relations, Definition of Aggression,* and *Non-Use of Force* reflect differences between states on these issues. Related questions about state responsibility for the actions of irregular forces and the international nature of a conflict arose before the ICTY; see Meron, 'Classification of Armed Conflict in the former Yugoslavia: Nicaragua's Fallout', 92 AJIL (1998) 236; *Tadic Appeal*, 38 ILM (1999) 1518.

these states were responsible for the acts of terrorists operating from their territories against its colonies.[51] Similarly South Africa's apartheid regime and illegal occupation of Namibia led to conflict; also on the independence of Angola and Mozambique, South Africa intervened in the Cold War-fuelled conflicts in those states. It said in justification of its invasions of the front-line states, Angola, Botswana, Mozambique, and Zambia, that these states had been supporting terrorist operations by the ANC and SWAPO, or acquiescing in their operations, or allowing their territory to be used by them.[52] Israel had been involved in cross-border actions against irregular forces operating from neighbouring states since 1948; in particular, it undertook operations against forces in Lebanon from 1967. It held Lebanon responsible for not preventing armed action against Israel and claimed the right to take action in self-defence.[53] The precise degree of host state involvement alleged has varied, but Portugal and Israel seemed to feel the need to assert some degree of state involvement in the cross-border activities of the armed bands. At the widest, failure to prevent, or mere acquiescence in, the activities of armed bands was claimed not only to cause state responsibility but also to justify self-defence.

In contrast, South Africa sometimes did not allege state complicity to justify its use of force, but rather relied on a novel doctrine of 'hot pursuit'. This is a law of the sea doctrine whereby coastal states have the right to pursue ships guilty of offences in territorial waters into areas of the sea beyond national jurisdiction; by analogy with this, South Africa claimed the right to pursue alleged terrorists into neighbouring states.[54] But this doctrine was not well received; in Resolution 568 (1985) the Security Council said that it 'denounces and rejects racist South Africa's practice of "hot pursuit" to terrorize and destabilize Botswana and other countries in southern Africa'. South Africa later abandoned this argument and returned to asserting the responsibility of the state from whose territory the guerrillas were operating.[55]

---

[51] For example, 1966 UNYB 117, 122; 1967 UNYB 123, 131; 1968 UNYB 159; 1969 UNYB 135, 137, 140; 1970 UNYB 187, 191, 192; 1971 UNYB 113, 116, 119, 121; 1972 UNYB 136; 1973 UNYB 109. See Alexandrov, *Self-Defense against the Use of Force in International Law* (1996), 179.

[52] For example, South Africa argued host state support by Angola: 1981 UNYB 217, Mozambique, 1981 UNYB 228, Botswana, 1985 UNYB 189, Zambia, 1980 UNYB 263. See Alexandrov, *Self-Defense against the Use of Force in International Law* (1996), 180.

[53] For example, 1969 UNYB 200, 1970 UNYB 227, 1978 UNYB 295, 1982 UNYB 428 at 431. See Alexandrov, *Self-Defense against the Use of Force in International Law* (1996), 174.

[54] SC 1944th meeting (1976).

[55] SC 1944th meeting; 1985 UNYB 180 at 184. Hot pursuit was rejected by India and Nigeria (S/PV 2606), by Trinidad (S/PV 2607). In S/PV 2616 Mozambique says South Africa has abandoned hot pursuit. See Kwakwa, 'South Africa's May 1985 Military Incursions into Neighbouring African States', 12 Yale JIL (1987) 421. The white minority government in Rhodesia also espoused hot pursuit; see Luttig, 'The legality of the Rhodesian military operations inside Mozambique—the problem of hot pursuit on land', 1977 SA Yearbook 136.

The Court in the *Nicaragua* case, in its discussions as to whether the actions of irregular forces could constitute an armed attack, said that customary international law required that the actions be of such gravity that they would amount to an armed attack if committed by regular troops. This distinction between armed attack and acts of lesser gravity was later elaborated on by the Court and will be discussed in the next chapter in the context of collective self-defence.

Although, as the Court recognized in the *Nicaragua* case, in principle self-defence is permissible against attacks by irregular forces, in practice the claims by Portugal, South Africa and Israel to be acting in self-defence were generally not accepted by the Security Council. These claims to self-defence were undermined by the fact that the states invoking self-defence were regarded as being in illegal occupation of the territory they were purporting to defend. Portugal's defence of its colonial possessions in Africa led it into conflict with forces fighting for decolonization; its attacks on states such as Guinea, Zambia and Senegal were condemned by the Security Council. Many of the states arguing for condemnation did so because Portugal was using force to maintain its illegal colonial power. The right of self-defence could not be invoked to perpetuate colonialism and to flout the right to self-determination and independence.[56] South Africa was in illegal occupation of Namibia and therefore many states were not willing to accept that it could use force in self-defence to protect the regime in Namibia.[57] South Africa's claims to be acting in self-defence against incursions by SWAPO fighters seeking the liberation of Namibia were not valid. South African territory was not in danger; the cause of the dangerous situation was the illegal presence of South Africa in Namibia. Even France and the USA sometimes took this line; they continued to make this argument even when they later vetoed condemnations of South Africa in pursuit of their policy of constructive engagement or seeking a negotiated solution.[58] Very unusually, in its resolutions rejecting South Africa's justifications for its use of force against Angola and condemning this use of force the Security Council expressly asserted the right of Angola to self-defence under Article 51 of the UN Charter in Resolutions 546 and 574. Again the mere fact that many states regarded Israel's occupation of the West Bank and Gaza, the Golan, and (until 2000) areas of South Lebanon as illegal was enough for them to condemn Israel's use of force against cross-border attacks by irregulars. They say that Israel has no right to be in these territories and so no right to invoke self-defence against attacks on their forces in these territories or against attacks on

---

[56] 1969 UNYB 137, 140, 143.   [57] *Namibia* Advisory Opinion, ICJ Reports (1971) 16.
[58] 1980 UNYB 252; 1981 UNYB 220; S/PV 2607.

Israel designed to secure its withdrawal from the territories it occupied illegally.[59]

The use of force against neighbouring states by Portugal, South Africa, and Israel was condemned on many different grounds. States in the Security Council debates on the use of force by these states mentioned many factors as contributing to the illegality of their actions in different cases: the neighbouring states were not responsible for any armed attack; the response to cross-border incursions was disproportionate; the use of force was not necessary. All three grounds for condemnation were invoked in the responses to the massive invasions and lengthy occupations of Lebanon by Israel in 1978 and 1982, and the South African operations in Angola from 1981.[60] Also in some cases actions by South Africa and Israel were seen as unlawful reprisals rather than self-defence; the states using force regularly said that their aim was to prevent future attacks.[61] And for many states the use of force by Portugal, South Africa and Israel was illegal because it was directed against the legitimate struggle of a people with the right to self-determination.

Even when Western states on the Security Council abstained or vetoed a resolution condemning the use of force by Portugal, South Africa, and Israel, they did not necessarily do so because they defended the legality of the actions of those states. In the early days of the decolonization struggle against Portugal the USA and the UK sometimes abstained on the grounds that the facts of the particular case had not been properly established or there were extenuating circumstances.[62] As regards South Africa, the USA and the UK sometimes abstained as part of their policy of seeking a negotiated solution.[63] Occasionally they said that they regarded the resolution as one-sided because they wanted an end to all foreign intervention in Angola.[64] They used the veto to prevent the imposition of

---

[59] Barsotti, 'Armed Reprisals', in Cassese (ed.), *The Current Legal Regulation of the Use of Force* (1986), 79.   [60] 1978 UNYB 295, 1981 UNYB 217, 1982 UNYB 312, 428.

[61] On pre-emptive action by South Africa against the ANC, see, for example, S/PV 2598; against SWAPO, S/PV 2606, Botha, 'Anticipatory Self-Defence and Reprisals Re-examined', 11 South African Yearbook of International Law (1985–86) 138. On pre-emptive action by Israel, see, for example, S/1997/740, 1982 UNYB 428 at 435, O'Brien, 'Reprisals, Deterrence and Self-Defense in Counterterror Operations', 30 Virginia Journal of International Law (1990) 421, Alexandrov, *Self-Defense against the Use of Force in International Law* (1996), 174, 180.   [62] 1969 UNYB 134, 137, 140; 1971 UNYB 116; 1972 UNYB 136.

[63] SC Res 447 and 454 on Angola, 1979 UNYB 225; SC Res 475, 1980 UNYB 252; SC Res 545, 1983 UNYB 169; SC Res 546, 1984 UNYB 177.

[64] SC Res 387, 1976 UNYB 171. Most extreme was the US statement in 1981 when it vetoed a draft resolution condemning the large scale invasion by South Africa into Angola. The USA said that the draft blamed South Africa alone for the escalation of violence, but the presence of Cuban troops and USSR military advisers in Angola had fuelled the explosive atmosphere: 1981 UNYB 217. The USA made a similar statement in 1987, but was nevertheless prepared to vote for the resolution condemning South Africa's invasion of Angola: 1987 UNYB 167.

mandatory economic sanctions. As regards Israel, they sometimes said that they would abstain or veto a resolution because it was one-sided in that it did not condemn terrorist attacks against Israel.[65] But for the most part, Portugal, South Africa, and Israel were regarded as not able to invoke self-defence because of their illegal occupation of territory. Issues of the precise involvement of states in the actions of armed bands thus did not have to be determined.

Other more straightforward claims to self-defence against irregular forces operating from neighbouring states have also been made. These have generally been more limited operations than the long-term and extensive action by the three states discussed above. For example, Thailand pursued guerrillas into Burma in 1995 after warning Burma to control the cross-border attacks by the guerrillas.[66] Senegal similarly went into Guinea-Bissau in operations against opposition forces based in Guinea-Bissau in 1992 and 1995. In the latter case it is interesting that in 1992, when Guinea-Bissau protested that it had not supported the rebel incursions into Senegal, Senegal apologized for its action.[67] Recently, Tajikistan was involved in more extensive actions against irregular forces operating from Afghanistan. On attaining independence in 1991 Tajikistan became involved in a civil war which continued until the 1997 *General Agreement on the Establishment of Peace and National Accord in Tajikistan;* forces opposing the government made cross-border attacks from Afghanistan. Tajikistan blamed Afghanistan for supporting the opposition forces and claimed the right to act in self-defence against the armed bands in Afghanistan.[68]

Special problems over responses to cross-border attacks by irregular forces arose with regard to Turkey's actions against the Kurds in Iraq. As part of its domestic campaign against the Kurdistan Workers Party (PKK), a Kurdish separatist organization involved in terrorism since the 1970s, Turkey has undertaken cross-border operations against Kurdish bases in northern Iraq. These operations escalated after the Iraqi invasion of Kuwait in 1990, the imposition of the cease-fire on Iraq under Resolution 687, and the creation of 'safe havens' for the Iraqi Kurds in northern Iraq patrolled by US and British aircraft operating from Turkey. As long as Iraq acquiesced or even formally consented to Turkey's operations on its territory, and in the absence of any international support for the right of the Kurds to independent statehood, Turkey at first offered

---

[65] 1984 UNYB 289, 1985 UNYB 299, 1986 UNYB 286, 1988 UNYB 218; see Patil, *The UN Veto in World Affairs* (1992), 287.   [66] Keesings (1995) 40554.

[67] Keesings (1992) 39228; (1995) 40396.

[68] 1993 UNYB 382. Tajikistan said that *mujahedin* and sub-units under the Ministry of Defence of Afghanistan were responsible for a major incursion into Tajikistan on 13 July 1993: Russia S/26110; Tajikistan S/26092; Afghanistan S/1994/310.

little in the way of legal justification for its cross-border operations against Kurds.[69]

Since 1991 Iraq has repeatedly protested at Turkey's incursions. It complained of the penetration by Turkish armed forces inside Iraqi territory on the pretext that they were in pursuit of separatist terrorists; this was a violation of the UN Charter and of international law.[70] Like Turkey, Iran has also occasionally pursued Kurds over the border into Iraq; when it did so, it did not directly accuse Iraq of supporting the 'bands of armed and organised terrorist mercenaries' engaged in trans-border military attacks against and sabotage in Iranian border provinces. However, Iran did expressly invoke self-defence as a justification for its operations. It said that 'in response to these armed attacks from inside Iraq and in accordance with Article 51 of the Charter of the United Nations, the fighter jets of the Islamic Republic Air Force carried out a brief, necessary and proportionate operation against the military bases of the terrorist group where the recent armed attacks had originated.'[71]

In contrast, Turkey has not expressly invoked Article 51; it did not itself report its operations in Iraq to the Security Council. It normally only responded (usually belatedly) to Iraq's allegations; even then it did not clearly rely on self-defence. Thus Turkey avoided the issue as to how far Iraq was responsible for the actions of the Kurds and whether it was guilty of an armed attack, but left the legal basis for Turkey's actions unclear. After a major operation in 1995 Turkey said:

As Iraq has not been able to exercise its authority over the northern part of its country since 1991 for reasons well known, Turkey cannot ask the Government of Iraq to fulfil its obligation, under international law, to prevent the use of its territory for the staging of terrorist acts against Turkey. Under these circumstances, Turkey's resorting to legitimate measures which are imperative to its own security cannot be regarded as a violation of Iraq's sovereignty. No country could be expected to stand idle when its own territorial integrity is incessantly threatened by blatant cross-border attacks of a terrorist organization based and operating from a neighbouring country, if that country is unable to put an end to such attacks. The recent operations of limited time and scope were carried out within this framework.[72]

It is very striking that the USA in defending the Turkish action, apparently took the view that it was acting in self-defence,[73] whereas Turkey itself did not make this claim. And in other letters to the Security Council, in response to Iraqi protests about its cross-border actions in 1996 and

---

[69] Bothe and Lohmann, 'Der türkische Einmarsch im Nordirak', 5 *Schweizerische Zeitschrift für internationales und europäisches Recht* (1995) 441.
[70] For example, S/23141, S/23152.   [71] S/25843.   [72] S/1995/605.
[73] S/1995/566.

1997, Turkey again did not mention Article 51 or self-defence; it referred to the duty in the *Friendly Relations Resolution* to refrain from acquiescing in organized activities within its territory directed towards the commission of terrorist acts in another state. It relied on the principles of necessity and self-preservation. It also referred to its determination to take measures to safeguard its legitimate security interests, defending its borders and protecting its people against terrorism.[74] This may come nearer to the language of self-defence, but it falls short of an express claim. Nor has Turkey offered a clear legal justification of its occupation of a 'buffer zone' in northern Iraq.[75]

Iraq claims, with some plausibility, that there is a double standard: while the UN claims that it is protecting the Kurds in Iraq against the Iraqi government, it closes its eyes to persecution by Turkey of its own Kurds. Iraq says that it could not be held responsible for the incursions by Kurds from its territory into Turkey because of the abnormal situation in northern Iraq, created particularly by the USA. It said that the US policy of interference and the deployment of US and British forces in Turkey in order to intervene militarily in northern Iraq prevented Iraq from exercising its sovereignty there. Iraq complained of the inaction of the Security Council.[76] For, in spite of the absence of a clear legal justification for its use of force, Turkey has avoided condemnation by the Security Council; the apparent support of the USA helped it to escape discussion of its actions. But condemnation was expressed by the Arab League, the Gulf Cooperation Council, and the NAM.[77]

Necessity and proportionality

As part of the basic core of self-defence all states agree that self-defence must be necessary and proportionate.[78] The requirements of necessity and proportionality are often traced back to the 1837 *Caroline* incident, involving a pre-emptive attack by the British forces in Canada on a ship manned by Canadian rebels, planning an attack from the USA.[79] This episode has attained a mythical authority. States and writers still refer to it, generally to support their own wide claims to self-defence, but also to support the necessity and proportionality limitation.[80] Others challenge the authority

---

[74] S/1996/479, S/1997/7, S/1997/552.   [75] S/1996/731, S/1996/796.
[76] S/1995/566, S/1997/393, S/1997/420; Keesings (1997) 41652.   [77] S/1997/461.
[78] Some writers have rejected these limits on self-defence as not established in customary international law: Kunz, 'Individual and Collective Self-defence in Article 51 of the Charter of the UN', 41 AJIL (1947) 872; Delivanis, *La légitime défense en droit international public moderne* (1971), Chapter 2. See also on proportionality in general, Gardam, 'Proportionality and Force in International law', 87 AJIL (1993) 391.
[79] See Jennings, 'The Caroline and McLeod cases', 32 AJIL (1938) 86.
[80] For example, the UAE referred to the *Caroline* case in S/PV 2616; the GDR invoked it over the clashes between the USA and Libya (S/PV 2677).

of this episode for the modern doctrine of self-defence, seeing it rather as an episode of self-help pre-dating the modern law on the use of force and as a one-off episode of pre-emptive action not of relevance to the conduct of wider-scale conflict.[81] But, irrespective of the status of the *Caroline* incident as a precedent, necessity and proportionality have played a crucial role in state justification of the use of force in self-defence and in international response.

The *Nicaragua* case and the Advisory Opinion on the *Legality of the Threat or Use of Nuclear Weapons*[82] reaffirmed that necessity and proportionality are limits on all self-defence, individual and collective. These requirements are not express in the UN Charter, but are part of customary international law. There has been relatively little general academic discussion of these essential characteristics of self-defence, as opposed to discussion in application to particular incidents; this is because the question whether self-defence lives up to these requirements is inevitably almost exclusively one of fact. Commentators agree on a few basic uncontroversial principles: necessity and proportionality mean that self-defence must not be retaliatory or punitive; the aim should be to halt and repel an attack. This does not mean that the defending state is restricted to the same weapons or the same numbers of armed forces as the attacking state; nor is it necessarily limited to action on its own territory.

In the *Nicaragua* case the Court treated these limitations as marginal considerations. That is, the use of force by the USA was first held not to qualify as lawful self-defence on other grounds, then its illegality was confirmed because the actions were not necessary or proportionate. Even if the supply of arms from Nicaragua to opposition forces in El Salvador had amounted to an armed attack, the measures taken by the USA against Nicaragua were not necessary because they were taken months after the

---

[81] Cot and Pellet (eds), *La Charte des Nations Unies* (1991), 772; Brownlie in Butler (ed.), *The Non-Use of Force in International Law* (1989), 17; Schwebel in *Nicaragua* case, Dissenting Opinion, para 200, argued that the narrow criteria of the *Caroline* case concerned anticipatory self-defence only.

[82] ICJ Reports (1996) 226, para 141; the Court went on at para 143 to refuse to decide the issue whether the effects of any use of nuclear weapons would be so serious that it could not constitute a necessary and proportionate measure. It said:

Certain states have in their written and oral pleadings suggested that in the case of nuclear weapons, the condition of proportionality must be evaluated in the light of still further factors. They contend that the very nature of nuclear weapons, and the high probability of an escalation of nuclear exchanges, mean that there is an extremely strong risk of devastation. The risk factor is said to negate the possibility of the condition of proportionality being complied with. The Court does not find it necessary to embark upon the quantification of such risks; nor does it need to enquire into the question whether tactical nuclear weapons exist which are sufficiently precise to limit those risks: it suffices for the Court to note that the very nature of all nuclear weapons and the profound risks associated therewith are further considerations to be borne in mind by States believing they can exercise a nuclear response in self-defence in accordance with the requirements of proportionality.

major offensive of the opposition against the government of El Salvador had been completely repulsed. Nor were the US activities relating to the mining of the Nicaraguan ports and attacking oil installations proportionate to the aid received by the Salvadorian opposition from Nicaragua.[83] Thus the questions of necessity and proportionality are dependent on the facts of the particular case.

The inquiry into necessity and proportionality in the *Nicaragua* case was not necessary for the Court's judgment on the merits; the US use of force had already been found to be illegal on other grounds. These criteria of necessity and proportionality were said by the Court to be an additional ground of wrongfulness. This may seem a logical approach, but in state practice generally these factors of necessity and proportionality are often the *only* factors relied on in deciding the legality of particular actions. They constitute a minimum test by which to determine that a use of force does not constitute self-defence. In Security Council debates states have thus been able to avoid going into doctrinal disputes as to whether self-defence is wide or narrow; they can simply say that the use of force was not necessary or proportionate and therefore illegal. Those states which maintain a controversially wide view of self-defence allowing protection of nationals or anticipatory self-defence are thus able to make an argument rejecting wide claims to self-defence by other states without undermining their doctrinal position. For example, condemnation of Israel and South Africa for pre-emptive action was possible for states supporting the legality of anticipatory self-defence on the basis that the use of force was not necessary or proportionate on the particular facts.[84]

Questions of necessity and proportionality also help states to distinguish unlawful reprisals from lawful self-defence. In cases of repeated cross-border incursions commentators have spoken of the 'accumulation of events' or 'pin-prick' theory of armed attack in order to justify otherwise disproportionate response.[85] That is, they claim that states may use force not in response to each incursion in isolation but to the whole series of incursions as collectively amounting to an armed attack. Such arguments were made by the USA with regard to Vietnam and by

[83] *Nicaragua* case para 237.
[84] See, for example, the US statement with regard to South Africa's pre-emptive action against Angola in 1985, that there is no inherent right to engage in military activity across one's border on the basis that it is a pre-emptive strike. The question is whether it is self-defence, a necessary, reasonable, and proportionate response to the danger posed. In this instance the USA said that it was not: S/PV 2616.
[85] Feder, 'Reading the UN Charter connotatively: toward a new definition of armed attack', 19 New York University Journal of International Law and Politics (1987) 395; Higgins, *The Development of International Law through the Political Organs of the United Nations* (1963), 201.

Israel, South Africa, and Portugal. Some have claimed that the Security Council has rejected this doctrine of accumulation of events and have criticized it for this.[86] In fact the Security Council has not gone so far. It has certainly condemned disproportionate responses by Israel, Portugal, and South Africa, but as usual the condemnation did not address the doctrinal issue of the scope of self-defence; it could be interpreted as based strictly on the special facts of these cases.[87] The International Court of Justice in the *Nicaragua* case actually seemed to accept the possibility of an accumulation of events amounting to an armed attack when it said of the trans-border incursions into Honduras and Costa Rica that 'Very little information is available to the Court as to the circumstances of these incursions or their possible motivations, which renders it difficult to decide whether they may be treated for legal purposes as amounting, singly or collectively, to an armed attack by Nicaragua on either or both States.'[88] Thus everything depends on the particular circumstances.

Necessity and proportionality are also crucial in the rejection by states of the legality of prolonged occupation of territory in the name of self-defence. Thus Israel's presence in South Lebanon from 1978 to 2000 and South Africa's occupation of a buffer zone in Angola from 1981 to 1988 were both claimed to be justified as self-defence and both repeatedly and universally condemned as not necessary or proportionate self-defence.[89] And similarly the use of force in self-defence has not been accepted as a valid root of title to territory.[90]

Protection of nationals

The use of force to rescue nationals in a foreign state without the consent of that state is uncommon and has been practised by only a few states since the Second World War.[91] Nevertheless, it has attracted a vast amount of academic debate. The interventions in Suez (1956), Lebanon (1958), Congo (1960), Dominican Republic (1965), in the *Mayaguez* incident (1975), Entebbe (1976), Iran (1980), Grenada (1983), and Panama (1989)

---

[86] Levenfeld, 'Israeli Counter-fedayeen Tactics in Lebanon: Self-Defense and Reprisal under Modern International Law', 21 Columbia Journal of Transnational Law (1982–3) 1.

[87] Higginbottom, 'International Law and the Use of Force in Self-defence and the Southern Africa Conflict', 25 Columbia Journal of Transnational Law (1986–7) 529.

[88] *Nicaragua* case para 231.

[89] On Israel, see 1978 UNYB 295, 306; the Security Council called for Israel to end its occupation in SC Res 425. On South Africa, see 1982 UNYB 312; the Security Council called for it to withdraw in SC Res 545; the General Assembly also called for this in GA Res 36/9.

[90] Jennings, The *Acquisition of Territory in International Law* (1963) 55; Korman, *The Right of Conquest* (1996), 203; Gerson, *Israel, the West Bank and International Law* (1978).

[91] See Chapter 3 above for further practice where the state using force in protection of nationals claimed consent by the territorial state.

have all been exhaustively discussed.[92] In these episodes all the states using force invoked self-defence as at least a partial justification for their action. For the most part they have expressly referred to Article 51 as covering their operation.[93] That is, these states and those who expressly support them interpret the Charter as allowing the forcible protection not only of a state's territory but also of its nationals abroad. The UK view is typical; it says that 'the better view' is that the justification comes from Article 51 as a form of self-defence: 'An alternative, less satisfactory view is to seek to derive from customary international law a right of intervention to protect nationals.'[94]

The international response to these interventions shows a clear division between states, with few states accepting a legal right to protect nationals abroad. The legal arguments of Belgium, the USA, Israel, and the UK in favour of such a wide right to self-defence have attracted few adherents.[95] The Security Council has generally not taken a collective view or has been prevented by the veto from condemnation.[96] Its debates show the radical divisions between states on the doctrinal issue of the permissibility of the use of force to protect nationals. In the most recent cases the General Assembly condemned the US interventions in Grenada and Panama, but these condemnations were not unequivocal. First, in these particular episodes the US action went far beyond the protection of nationals and the USA offered other justifications for its intervention. In Grenada the US

[92] For early practice on protection of nationals, see Bowett, 'The Use of Force for the Protection of Nationals Abroad', in Cassese (ed.), *The Current Legal Regulation of the Use of Force* (1986), 39; Schweisfurth, 'Operations to Rescue Nationals in Third States', 23 German Yearbook of International Law (1980); Ronzitti, *Rescuing Nationals Abroad* (1985). On Suez, see Marston, 'Armed Intervention in the 1956 Suez Canal Crisis: the Legal Advice tendered to the British Government', 37 ICLQ (1988) 773; on Entebbe, see *Repertoire of Practice of the Security Council 1975–80*, 286; on the attempted rescue of the Iranian hostages, see Stein, 'Contempt, Crisis and the Court', 76 AJIL (1982) 499; on Grenada, Contemporary Practice of the US, 78 AJIL (1984) 200; on Panama, 'Contemporary Practice of the US', 84 AJIL (1990) 545.

[93] With regard to Iran, the USA reported its action to the Security Council under Article 51, *Case concerning United States Diplomatic and Consular Staff in Tehran*, ICJ Reports 1979, at 18. The ICJ did not pronounce on the legality of the US action; Judges Morozov and Tarazi, in their Dissenting Opinions, ICJ Reports 1980, 57, 64, said that the US action was not lawful self-defence. With regard to Grenada, the USA invoked Article 51 (S/16076). With regard to Panama, it invoked Article 51 as giving an inherent right of self-defence to protect American lives (S/21035).

[94] 'UK Materials on International Law', 57 BYIL (1986) 614.

[95] The statements by certain Russian government ministers after the break-up of the former Soviet Union that Russia would intervene using force in the former republics to protect ethnic Russians gave rise to concern rather than support, even from the states that have themselves used force to protect their nationals. It led to concern in the Baltic states and the claim has not been publicly pursued: Keesings (1993), 40513.

[96] On Grenada the draft resolution was defeated by 11–1 (USA) –3 (France, Canada, UK), 1983 UNYB 211. On Panama the draft resolution was defeated by 10–4 (France, UK, USA, Canada) –1, 1989 UNYB 172 at 174.

forces argued that US nationals were in danger after a socialist coup, but there was considerable controversy as to the reality of this danger. Moreover, the US forces did not simply rescue the nationals; they remained and oversaw the installation of a new government. To justify its intervention the USA used not only protection of nationals but also relied on an invitation by the Governor-General of Grenada and the claim that its action was regional peacekeeping under Chapter VIII of the Charter.[97] In justification of its use of force in Panama the USA put more stress on protection of nationals than it had with regard to Grenada, but its actions clearly went far beyond this. The US forces again installed a new government. Moreover, just as in Grenada, there was controversy as to the existence of actual danger to US nationals. Its other main legal argument was that it was acting to defend the integrity of the Panama Canal Treaties. Therefore the grounds for condemnation of the US use of force were not necessarily based on the rejection of a wide doctrine of self-defence that covered protection of nationals.[98] Second, the condemnations by the General Assembly in these two cases, especially in the case of Panama, were less than overwhelming.[99]

Some writers who seek to justify the use of force in protection of nationals seize on this failure to condemn by the Security Council and the failure to take any action against the state using force.[100] They discount the General Assembly votes and the rejection by a majority of states of such a doctrine. There is a clear division between writers on this question; some see intervention as furthering the purposes of the United Nations and attempt to derive from state practice conditions under which the right may be exercised.[101] Essentially these are all variations on the early version offered by the UK over its intervention in Suez in 1956. It said that the relevant conditions were: (a) whether there is an imminent threat of injury to nationals; (b) whether there is a failure or inability on the part of the territorial sovereign to protect the nationals in question; and (c)

---

[97] For the USA justification for Grenada, see 1983 UNYB 211, S/16076; SC 2487th, 2489th, 2491st meetings. Gilmore, *The Grenada Intervention* (1984); Weiler, 'Armed Intervention in a Dichotomized World: The Case of Grenada', in Cassese (ed.), *Current Legal Regulation of the Use of Force* (1986), 241.

[98] For the USA justification for Panama, see S/21035; 84 AJIL (1990) 545. Contrasting assessments of the intervention are given by Henkin, 'The Invasion of Panama under International Law: a Gross Violation', 29 Columbia Journal of Transnational Law (1991) 293, and D'Amato, 'The Invasion of Panama was a Lawful Response to Tyranny', 84 AJIL (1990) 516.

[99] GA Res 38/7 on Grenada was passed by 108–9–27, 1983 UNYB at 214; GA Res 44/240 on Panama was passed by 75–20–40, 1989 UNYB 175.

[100] Arend and Beck, *International Law and the Use of Force: Beyond the UN Charter Paradigm* (1993), 107–10.

[101] Bowett, 'The Use of Force for the Protection of Nationals Abroad', in Cassese (ed.), *The Current Legal Regulation of the Use of Force* (1986), 39; Dinstein, *War, Aggression and Self-Defense* (2nd edn, 1994), 226.

whether the measures of protection are strictly confined to the object of protecting them against injury.[102] On the other side are those writers who regard intervention to protect nationals as of doubtful value in furthering the purposes of the United Nations as it may be a pretext for intervention and cause more harm than it prevents.[103]

Irrespective of the doctrinal divide, most of the above interventions clearly could not be justified as protection of nationals because the action was not necessary or proportionate and was really a pretext for intervention. Only the rescue operation of the *Mayaguez*, and those in Iran and Entebbe were limited actions; in Suez, the Dominican Republic, Grenada, and Panama the interventions were prolonged and the states using force added further justifications.

In recent practice there have been various instances of states sending in troops to extract nationals and others from dangerous situations where a state was involved in a civil war or domestic unrest. The USA sent troops into Liberia in 1990,[104] the Central African Republic in 1996,[105] and Sierra Leone in 1997,[106] France and Belgium intervened in Rwanda in 1990, 1993, and 1994.[107] However, with regard to these recent episodes issues of legality have not been raised in the United Nations. The state using force has not reported it to the Security Council under Article 51 and the state where the intervention took place did not raise the matter. Nor did other states protest about the use of force. These can therefore be seen as cases of consent or perhaps implied consent by the government to the rescue operation. But many of these cases occurred when there was no effective government; the previous government had been overthrown and the state was in confusion. It seems that third states were willing to acquiesce in the forcible evacuation of nationals; their concern is roused only with regard to those rescue missions where the territorial state objects to the intervention or where the protection of the nationals was just a pretext for an invasion with wider objectives.

Anticipatory self-defence

The same states that claim a right under Article 51 to protect their nationals abroad also claim or defend the right to use force even before

---

[102] Marston, 'Armed Intervention in the 1956 Suez Canal Crisis: the Legal Advice tendered to the British Government', 37 ICLQ (1988) 773 at 795, 800.

[103] Brownlie, *International Law and the Use of Force by States* (1963), 432; Akehurst, 'Humanitarian Intervention', in Bull (ed.), *Intervention in World Politics* (1984), 95; Ronzitti, *Rescuing Nationals Abroad* (1985).

[104] Lillich, 'Forcible Protection of Nationals Abroad: the Liberian Incident of 1990', 35 German YIL (1992) 205; Weller, *Regional Peacekeeping and International Enforcement: The Liberian Crisis* (1994), 63–5, 85.   [105] Keesings (1996) 41080.

[106] Keesings (1997) 41626.   [107] Keesings (1990) 37765–6, (1993) 39304, (1994) 39943–4.

their territory or units of their armed forces abroad are attacked; the majority of states reject anticipatory self-defence in both cases. The divisions between states as to the scope of the right of self-defence meant that no detailed provisions on self-defence could be included in General Assembly resolutions such as the *Declaration on Friendly Relations*, the *Definition of Aggression*, and the *Declaration on the Non-Use of Force*. It is interesting that those states which argued that self-defence was permissible only against an armed attack made this argument expressly, whereas those states who took a wider view of self-defence adopted a low profile and simply resisted the inclusion of any detailed provisions.[108] Also in the ILC work on state responsibility when self-defence was considered as a circumstance precluding wrongfulness, those states who have in the past defended anticipatory self-defence said only that the ILC should not try to define the scope of self-defence; they did not actually send in comments in favour of anticipatory self-defence.[109]

Moreover, the actual invocation of the right to anticipatory self-defence in practice is rare. States clearly prefer to rely on self-defence in response to an armed attack if they possibly can. In practice they prefer to take a wide view of armed attack rather than openly claim anticipatory self-defence. It is only where no conceivable case can be made for this that they resort to anticipatory self-defence. This reluctance expressly to invoke anticipatory self-defence is in itself a clear indication of the doubtful status of this justification for the use of force. States take care to try to secure the widest possible support; they do not invoke a doctrine that they know will be unacceptable to the vast majority of states. Certain writers, however, ignore this choice by states and argue that if states in fact act in anticipation of an armed attack this should count as anticipatory self-defence in state practice. This is another example of certain writers going beyond what states themselves say in justification of their action in order to try to argue for a wide right of self-defence.[110]

Thus in 1967 Israel launched what was apparently a pre-emptive strike against Egypt, Jordan, and Syria, but it did not seek to rely on anticipatory self-defence. It argued that the actions of the Arab states in fact amounted

[108] Ferencz, 'Defining Aggression: Where it stands and where it's going', 66 AJIL (1972) 491; Gray, 'The Principle of Non-Use of Force', in Lowe and Warbrick (eds), *The United Nations and the Principles of International Law* (1994), 33.
[109] Cot and Pellet (eds), *La Charte des Nations Unies* (1991), 779.
[110] Both Alexandrov, *Self-Defense against the Use of Force in International Law* (1996) and Arend and Beck, *International Law and the Use of Force: Beyond the UN Charter Paradigm* (1993), include a very wide range of incidents under the heading Collective self-defence; they do not restrict themselves to those episodes where states actually invoked the doctrine. The latter make the unusual argument that a great many states are for anticipatory self-defence. They base this on the states using force and are extremely selective in their choice of practice; they do not refer to all the statements of states against their position.

to prior armed attack. For example, in the Security Council debates Israel claimed that the blocking by Egypt of the Straits of Tiran to passage by Israeli vessels amounted to an act of war; it was an armed attack justifying self-defence under Article 51. Some states rejected this claim and ruled out the legality of anticipatory use of force; some said that it was not productive to apportion blame; even those supporting the Israeli action did not expressly give their backing to its claim that it had been the victim of a prior attack.[111] But, whatever position is taken on the facts of the outbreak of the Six Day War, the point of importance here is that Israel did not rely on anticipatory self-defence to justify its actions.

Again in the 1962 Cuban missile crisis, when Cuba was proposing to import nuclear missiles from the USSR, the USA did not rely on anticipatory self-defence to justify its forcible interception of the missiles on the high seas; rather, it relied on regional peacekeeping under Chapter VIII of the UN Charter.[112] And in the Iran/Iraq war Iraq first began its justification for its invasion of Iran in 1980 by relying on preventive self-defence, but quickly shifted its position and claimed to be acting in response to a prior armed attack by Iran; this remained its position and this was the view that it put in response to the Secretary-General's report on the responsibility for the conflict.[113]

The USA, in its attempt to justify the shooting down by the *USS Vincennes* of the civilian Iran Airbus in July 1988 during the Iran/Iraq war, made elaborate argument that its action had been part of an ongoing battle and that it was engaged in a response to an armed attack by Iran. It said that its forces had exercised self-defence under international law by responding to an attack by Iran: Iranian aircraft had fired on a helicopter from the *USS Vincennes*, then Iranian patrol boats had closed in. In the course of exercising its right to self-defence the *USS Vincennes* fired at what it believed to be a hostile Iranian military aircraft after sending repeated warnings. It is very striking that the USA did not expressly rely on anticipatory self-defence even though its rules of engagement had been altered to allow its forces to take action against enemy ships and aircraft displaying 'hostile intent'. In the debate Iran argued that Article 51 does not allow pre-emptive self-defence and that the US action amounted to aggression. Many other states also took this approach. The UK offered

---

[111] 1967 UNYB 166, 174, 196; Pogany, *The Security Council and the Arab-Israeli Conflict* (1984), Chapter 5.

[112] Alexandrov, *Self-Defense against the Use of Force in International Law* (1996) at 154 uses these as examples of anticipatory self-defence despite the choice of the USA and Israel not to invoke this doctrine. Chayes, 'Law and the Quarantine of Cuba', 41 Foreign Affairs (1963) 550.

[113] 1980 UNYB 312. For Iraq's reaction to the Secretary-General's report, see 1991 UNYB 165.

support for the US action in general terms, but did not expressly support anticipatory self-defence.[114]

The USA and the UK (and France until 1996), in patrolling the 'no-fly' zones over Iraq, claim the right to use force in self-defence. Since the establishment of the northern zone in 1991 and the southern zone in 1993 there have been many clashes between US and UK aircraft and Iraqi aircraft and ground defences. Iraq denies the legality of the 'no-fly' zones; in this it is supported by Russia and China and other states who say that the USA and the UK acted unilaterally and without Security Council authorization in establishing the zones. In 1999 the USA and the UK significantly extended the rules of engagement for their aircraft; they were now to take pre-emptive action against Iraq's air defences. Not only the direct source of an attack, such as a missile site, but any threat to aircraft, such as a command centre, could be targeted.[115] However, the USA and the UK continued to insist that their actions were purely defensive. Their legal position remains that the military actions were taken to ensure the safety of aircraft patrolling the zone in support of Security Council Resolution 688; once a no-fly zone is authorized in accordance with international law it is entirely appropriate to act in self-defence to ensure the safety of those who are imposing the no-fly zone.[116] In Security Council debates on Iraq discussion has focused on the legality of the no-fly zones; Russia, China, and Iraq have condemned the US and UK actions on the fundamental basis that there is no legal basis for the no-fly zones and therefore no justification for the presence of US and UK aircraft and no right for them to act in self-defence.[117]

Very occasionally states have expressly used anticipatory self-defence. As was mentioned above, Israel and South Africa both claimed the right to take 'pre-emptive action' against incursions from neighbouring states. These claims were expressly rejected by some states on the ground that anticipatory self-defence was unlawful. Other states used other grounds for condemnation. Therefore authoritative pronouncements on the issue of principle—the legality of anticipatory self-defence—were avoided in these cases by the Security Council and the General Assembly.

Israel, in its 1981 attack on the Iraqi nuclear reactor, claimed anticipatory self-defence. It said that it had acted to remove a nuclear threat to its existence; the Iraqi reactor under construction was designed to produce

---

[114] Vincennes, S/PV 2818; S/19989 US justification and Article 51 report; 1988 UNYB 199; see Gray, 'The British Position with regard to the Gulf Conflict', 37 ICLQ (1988) 464.

[115] Keesings (1999) 42754, 42811, 42866, 42917, 42972, 43036, (2000) 43492, 43542.

[116] For an early statement of this position, see 'UK Materials on International Law', 64 BYIL (1993) 728; more recently, 'Contemporary Practice of the United States Relating to International Law', 94 AJIL (2000) 102; The *Guardian*, 5 March, 1999.

[117] S/PV 4084 (1999).

nuclear bombs whose target would have been Israel. Under no circumstances would Israel allow an enemy to develop weapons of mass
destruction against it. In the Security Council debate it relied on a series
of writers to support its position that anticipatory defence was lawful. But
significantly Israel was not able to rely on any clear state practice to support its position.[118] In none of these cases did the Security Council make
any pronouncement on doctrine; the debates again revealed the divisions
between states on the law in this area. The USA, in allowing the condemnation of Israel by the Security Council, said that its judgment that Israel's
actions violated the Charter was based solely on the conviction that Israel
had failed to exhaust peaceful means for the resolution of the dispute.
Others said that the action was not justified on the particular facts, given
that the IAEA said that there was no evidence that Iraq was planning to
use the reactor for the development of nuclear weapons. Other states
rejected anticipatory self-defence in principle.[119]

This reluctance to rely on anticipatory self-defence even by the USA
and Israel is not conclusive that they do not believe that it is legal, as it is
natural for states to choose the strongest grounds to justify their claims,
but it is strong evidence of the controversial status of this justification for
the use of force, as is the deliberate avoidance of the issue of the legality
of anticipatory self-defence by the International Court of Justice in the
Nicaragua case.[120] States prefer to argue for an extended interpretation of
armed attack and to avoid the fundamental doctrinal debate. The clear
trend in state practice is to try to bring the action within Article 51 and to
claim the existence of an armed attack rather than to expressly argue for
a wider right under customary international law.

Further extensions of self-defence: the use of force against terrorism

The most extensive use of self-defence, by states invoking Article 51 but
in reality going far beyond the bounds of this provision, has been by the
USA and Israel in response to terrorist attacks on nationals abroad. These
actions combine the protection of nationals and anticipatory self-defence.
They were taken by Israel in 1968 against Beirut and in 1985 against Tunis
and by the USA against Libya in 1986, Iraq in 1993, and Sudan and

---

[118] 1981 UNYB 275; Israel explained its action in S/14510; in the Security Council debates
Israel referred to writers in support of the doctrine of anticipatory self-defence: SC 2280th
meeting at para 98, 99, 100; SC 2288th meeting at para 38. The General Assembly voted to
condemn Israel's action as a premeditated and unprecedented act of aggression in GA Res
36/27 (109–2–34). Many of those who abstained said that they did so because it was for the
Security Council rather than the General Assembly to act. D'Amato defended the legality of
the use of force: 'Israel's Air Strike upon the Iraqi Nuclear Reactor', 77 AJIL (1983) 584.
[119] SC 2288th meeting para 156.   [120] *Nicaragua* case para 194.

Afghanistan in 1998. In all these episodes force was used, in response to past terrorist attacks, against the state allegedly harbouring the terrorist organization responsible; Israel and the USA used language that combined claims to be acting in response to past attacks and to deter future attacks.[121]

The first instance was the attack by the Israeli air force on Beirut airport in December 1968; Israel attempted to justify this action as a response to the earlier terrorist attack on an Israeli plane in Athens airport. It said that Lebanon had permitted Arab terrorist organizations to set up their headquarters in Beirut and to maintain training bases in Lebanon, thus officially encouraging warfare by terror against Israel. The Lebanese government had assumed responsibility for the activities of terror organizations. The attack on the Israeli civil aircraft at Athens airport had violated the cease-fire between Israel and Lebanon, and Israel was entitled to exercise its right of self-defence. The Security Council unanimously condemned the Israeli action in Resolution 262. It is striking that although the USA joined in the condemnation it made a point of explaining that it did so only because Lebanon had not in fact been responsible for the terrorist attack on Athens airport and the Israeli action was not proportionate; it accepted the principle on which the Israeli action was based. A state subject to continuing terrorist attacks may respond by appropriate use of force to defend itself against further attacks; this is an aspect of the inherent right of self-defence recognized in the UN Charter.[122]

This was not the view of the other states in the Security Council in 1968 but it has been repeated by the USA and Israel in later episodes. Israel, in its 1985 attack on Tunis claimed that it was acting against the PLO headquarters in response to terrorist attacks on Israelis abroad by Palestinians. Tunisia had a duty to prevent such attacks being carried out from its territory. Israel said that it was acting in self-defence and the USA in the Security Council debate accepted this argument. But the other member states did not agree and the action was vigorously condemned as an act of armed aggression against Tunisia's territory in flagrant violation of the UN Charter by 14–0–1 in Resolution 573 (1985). For the other member states the Israeli conception of self-defence was very far from that in international law.[123]

The USA itself undertook this type of action in 1986 against Libya. In response to terrorist attacks against US citizens abroad for which it said

---

[121] Alexandrov, *Self-Defense against the Use of Force in International Law* (1996) at 182; Arend and Beck, *International Law and the Use of Force: Beyond the UN Charter Paradigm* (1993) at 138; O'Brien, 'Reprisals, Deterrence and Self-Defense in Counterterror Operations', 30 Virginia Journal of International Law (1990) 421.

[122] 1968 UNYB 228. See Falk, 'The Beirut Raid and the International Law of Retaliation', 63 AJIL (1969) 415; Blum, 'The Beirut Raid and the International Double Standard', 64 AJIL (1970) 73.   [123] 1985 UNYB 285; S/PV 2610, 2615.

Libya was responsible, US aircraft, flying from bases in the UK with the support of the UK government, attacked targets in Tripoli. The USA reported the action to the Security Council as self-defence under Article 51; its action was a response to past terrorist attacks on nationals and also taken to deter such attacks in the future. Most states rejected this claim, saying that self-defence should be narrowly interpreted and could not be pre-emptive. However, the UK and France joined the USA in vetoing the resolution condemning its action.[124] The UK accepted that 'the right of self-defence is not an entirely passive right'; it was within the inherent right of self-defence to try to turn the tide of terrorism and to discourage further attacks.[125]

Recently the USA used the same wide doctrine of self-defence to justify its action in its response to the alleged assassination attempt on ex-President Bush by Iraqi agents in Kuwait in April 1993. The USA responded in June 1993 by firing missiles at the Iraqi Intelligence Headquarters in Baghdad. It again invoked Article 51 in its letter to the Security Council. The response of the Security Council showed considerable sympathy with the USA and some commentators have tried to argue that this marks the emergence of a new rule of international law allowing such actions in response to terrorism. But in the Security Council it was only Russia and the UK which offered express support for the USA *legal* argument. The UK took a fairly cautious line; it said that force may be used in self-defence against threats to one's nationals if the target continues to be used in support of terrorist acts against one's nationals and there is no other way to respond.[126] Several states expressed concern, although only China actually condemned the US action. Other states generally said that they understood the US action.[127]

Similarly, when the USA responded to terrorist attacks on its embassies in Kenya and Ethiopia in August 1998 by missile attacks on a terrorist

---

[124] 1986 UNYB 247; the USA reported to the Security Council in S/17990; SC Debate S/PV 2677, 2679, 2680; see, 'Contemporary Practice of the US', 80 AJIL (1986) 632; on the UK position, see, 'UK Materials on International Law', 57 BYIL (1986) 641. Greenwood, 'International Law and the United States Air Operation Against Libya', 89 West Virginia Law Review (1987) 933.

[125] The USA denied that there was any parallel between the South African attacks on Zambia, Zimbabwe, and Botswana and its own acts against Libya; the UK apparently accepted this ('UK Materials on International Law', 57 BYIL (1986) 621), but other states said there was such a parallel between the actions of the USA and those of South Africa (S/PV 2684, 2686).   [126] 'UK Materials on International Law', 64 BYIL (1993) 732.

[127] 1993 UNYB 431; US to the Security Council S/26003; Kritsiotis, 'The legality of the 1993 US Missile Strike on Iraq and the right of self-defence in international law', 45 ICLQ (1996) 162; Gray, 'After the Cease-fire: Iraq, the Security Council and the Use of Force', 65 BYIL (1994) 135; Reisman, 'The Raid on Baghdad: some reflections on its lawfulness and implications', 5 EJIL (1994) 120; Condorelli, 'A propos de l'attaque américaine contre l'Iraq du 26 juin 1993', 5 EJIL (1994) 134.

training camp in Afghanistan and a pharmaceutical plant in Sudan, the response of the rest of the world was generally muted. The USA said that the camp had been used by the Osama Bin Laden organization to support terrorism and that the pharmaceutical plant also produced chemical weapons for terrorist activities. It reported its actions to the Security Council under Article 51; it wished to report that the USA had exercised its right of self-defence in responding to a series of armed attacks against US embassies and nationals. It said that it was acting in response to those terrorist attacks and to prevent and deter their continuation. Its attacks were carried out after repeated efforts to convince Sudan and the Taliban regime in Afghanistan to shut down the terrorist facilities. The targets struck and the timing and method of attack used were designed to comply with rules of international law, including the rules of necessity and proportionality.[128] Sudan requested a meeting of the Security Council, but the issue was not put on the agenda and there was only a very brief meeting, with no action taken. There were condemnations by Arab states, Pakistan, and Russia. As before, those who refrained from condemnation or expressed support were careful not to adopt the US doctrine of self-defence.[129]

All these episodes were justified by the states using force as self-defence, but on the basis of the explanations given by Israel and the USA themselves the actions look more like reprisals, because they were punitive rather than defensive. Even if the actions were aimed at those actually responsible for the terrorist attacks, and even if the response could be accepted as proportionate, it is difficult to see how the use of force was necessary, given that the attacks on the nationals had already taken place. The USA and Israel aimed to retaliate and deter and said that their actions were pre-emptive. The problem for the USA and Israel is that all states agree that in principle forcible reprisals are unlawful.[130] The General

---

[128] S/1998/780.

[129] 'Contemporary Practice of the United States relating to International Law', 93 AJIL (1999) 161. There was considerable doubt as to whether the plant in Sudan was really a chemical weapons factory linked to international terrorism, Keesings (1999) 42766. The UK position showed some uncertainty; the Prime Minister defended the legality of the US action, but the Foreign Secretary took a much more cautious line. It is noteworthy that the UK Materials on International Law for BYIL (1998), prepared with the help of the UK Foreign and Commonwealth Office, do not include any materials on the UK reaction.

[130] Once again writers have gone further than states in claiming that it is unrealistic to outlaw reprisals. Some have tried to argue that certain reprisals may be legitimate, although technically illegal. Bowett was the first to make this claim with regard to Israel. He said that failure to condemn by the Security Council was an indication that the action was permissible: Bowett, 'Reprisals involving Recourse to Armed Force', 66 AJIL (1972) 31. O'Brien followed this line and updated it, O'Brien, 'Reprisals, Deterrence and Self-Defense in Counterterror Operations', 30 Virginia Journal of International Law (1990) 421. But this argument was forcefully and successfully refuted by Barsotti, 'Armed Reprisals', in Cassese (ed.), *Current Legal Regulation of the Use of Force* (1986) 79.

Assembly made this clear in the *Declaration on Friendly Relations* and the *Resolution on the Inadmissibility of Intervention*. The Security Council also passed Resolution 188 in 1964, in response to a British attack on Yemen, but declaring in absolute terms that it condemned reprisals as incompatible with the purposes and principles of the UN. This universal agreement that reprisals are not lawful led Israel and the USA to try to stretch the meaning of Article 51; although other states were not prepared to condemn the USA for its attacks on Baghdad, Afghanistan, and Sudan, nor did they accept the legal argument. Only Russia and the UK were prepared openly to support the legality of the US action in 1993. Russia has since abandoned its brief moment of enthusiasm and returned to a critical approach; even the UK, so often the main supporter of the USA, took an ambivalent position in 1998. Failure to condemn the USA should be taken to indicate sympathy and understanding rather than acceptance of a legal doctrine which destroys the distinction between reprisals and self-defence and which the USA would never contemplate being used against itself.

CONCLUSION

The picture that emerges is one of polarization. A few states claim very wide rights of self-defence to protect nationals, anticipate attack, and to respond to terrorist and other past attacks. It seems that the lesson they have learned from the judgment in the *Nicaragua* case is that form is more important than substance. As long as they pay lip-service to the need to act in self-defence, and as long as they report to the Security Council invoking the magical reference to Article 51, somehow their action acquires a veneer of legality and their argument will be treated seriously by commentators. A few of these commentators seem prepared to treat any US action as a precedent creating new legal justification for the use of force.[131] Thus they use the US actions in Tripoli, Panama, the Iran/Iraq conflict, Iraq, Afghanistan, and Sudan as shifting the Charter paradigm and extending the right of self-defence. The lack of effective action against the USA as a sanction confirms them in this view. But the vast majority of other states remain firmly attached to a narrow conception of self-defence. This long-standing disagreement between states on interpretation of the UN Charter seems beyond resolution, and states accordingly seek to avoid doctrinal dispute by appealing to doctrines, such as necessity and proportionality, on which there is universal agreement where at all possible.

---

[131] Arend and Beck, *International Law and the Use of Force* (1993); Weisburd *The Use of Force* (1997); D'Amato, *Prospect and Process* (2nd edn, 1995).

5

Collective self-defence

It is well known that there is comparatively little practice on the use of force in collective self-defence; states have generally avoided direct and open military participation by their armed forces in conflicts between other states. The relatively large number of treaties on collective self-defence is not matched by extensive state practice.[1] Commentators list the following instances where states have actually invoked collective self-defence: USA and Lebanon (1958), UK and Jordan (1958), UK and South Arabian Federation (1964), USA and Vietnam (1961–75), USSR and Hungary (1956),[2] Czechoslovakia (1968), Afghanistan (1979), and France and Chad (1983–4, 1986). But this cannot be taken as a definitive list; different commentators produce different lists.[3] Controversially, some add the UN-authorized actions in Korea and Iraq as further examples of collective self-defence.[4]

The above list includes some episodes where collective self-defence was invoked and foreign troops were introduced into the 'victim' state requesting assistance but force was not used in actual conflict, or was not used beyond the national border of the victim state. States have invoked

---

[1] The main multilateral treaties are the NATO Treaty (1949) 34 UNTS 243; the (now defunct) Warsaw Pact (1955) 219 UNTS 24; the Rio Treaty (1947) 21 UNTS 77; the Security Treaty between Australia/New Zealand/USA (1951) 131 UNTS 83; South East Asia Collective Defense Treaty (1954) 209 UNTS 20; the Baghdad Pact (1955) 233 UNTS 199; Pact of the Arab League (1945) 70 UNTS 237; Arab League Treaty of Joint Defence (1955) 49 AJIL Supplement (1955) 51. There are also hundreds of bilateral treaties which provide for collective self-defence. On the more than sixty Soviet bloc treaties made in the 1970s, see Zipfel, *Die Freundschafts und Kooperationsverträge der Kommunistischen Staaten* (1983). The USA, the UK, and France each have an extensive network of treaties. On French treaties, see Keesings (1996) 41402.

[2] The inclusion of the Soviet intervention in Hungary as an instance of collective self-defence being invoked by a state is very doubtful; apart from a reference to the intervention being in accordance with the Warsaw Treaty, the USSR did not refer to collective self-defence to justify its action (1956 UNYB 67).

[3] Cot and Pellet, *La Charte des Nations Unies* (1991), 787; Alexandrov, *Self-Defence Against the Use of Force in International Law* (1996), 216. It is noteworthy that this list is exclusively collective self-defence of territory. The issue of collective self-defence of ships at sea came up in the Iran/Iraq conflict when the USA, on 29 April 1988, decided to extend the protection offered by its naval forces in the Gulf to friendly neutral vessels. It announced that, following a request from the vessel under attack, assistance would be rendered by a US warship or aircraft. It used this power twice in 1988 to protect a Danish and a Panamanian vessel, but apparently did not expressly rely on collective self-defence; it spoke of assistance to vessels in distress, following a request from the vessel under attack: Gray, 'The British Position with regard to the Gulf Conflict (Iran–Iraq): Part 2', 40 ICLQ (1991) 465 at 468. See de Guttry and Ronzitti, *The Iran–Iraq War (1980–1988) and the Law of Naval Warfare* (1993), 196, 304.

[4] Alexandrov, *Self-Defense Against the Use of Force in International Law* (1996) at 252; he also includes regional action under this heading of collective self-defence.

collective self-defence as a justification for inviting in foreign troops before any armed attack has occurred, in case collective self-defence is needed in the future; that is, as a deterrent or as a precaution. The sending of troops and the provision of other aid has been much more common than the use of those troops in actual fighting against an attacking state. The US use of force against North Vietnam, Cambodia, and Laos in the name of the collective self-defence of South Vietnam and the US use of force against Nicaragua (in the name of collective self-defence of El Salvador, Costa Rica, and Honduras) are exceptional in that the USA used force outside the 'victim' state.

That is, although in theory there is a distinction between collective self-defence and assistance in reply to an invitation by a government to respond to external intervention against that government, in practice the line may not be a clear one.[5] The states sending in their troops make choices as to the justification they offer. They may invoke collective self-defence before it is actually necessary and conversely they do not always expressly invoke collective self-defence even when a case could be made for it on the basis that there has been or might be an armed attack.

Thus, for example, Ethiopia, the USSR, and Cuba all tended to play down the presence of Soviet and Cuban troops in Ethiopia (1977–8) even though there had been an armed attack by Somalia into the Ogaden region of Ethiopia after the overthrow of Emperor Haile Selassie and the armed response by Ethiopia was limited to driving out the invading forces.[6] Also with regard to the collective self-defence of Angola against attacks by South Africa, Cuba at first simply stressed that it had been invited in by the MPLA, which subsequently formed the government on the coming to independence of Angola in 1975. Angola referred to Article 51 in relation to the presence of the Cuban troops only from 1983, after the issue of 'linkage' had become more prominent. On the basis of 'linkage', South Africa argued that its withdrawal from Namibia was linked to that of Cuba from Angola, thus implying an equivalence between the two situations. Angola replied that the Cuban presence had been requested by the legitimate government of Angola for the clear and express objective of repulsing the open and flagrant invasion by South Africa. The first invasion (in 1975) was repulsed by the Angolan people with the assistance of Cuban troops, but South African aggression had continued. There was a continued need for the assistance of Cuban forces in full conformity with

---

[5] Mullerson, 'Intervention by Invitation', in Damrosch and Scheffer (eds), *Law and Force in the New International Order* (1991) 127; Diaz Barrado, *El Consentimento, Causa de Exclusion de la Ilicitud del Uso de la Fuerza en Derecho Internacional* (1989), 78.

[6] Keesings (1978) 28760, 28989. A Friendship Treaty was concluded between the USSR and Ethiopia in November 1978: Keesings (1979) 29435.

Article 51, as every state has the right to individual or collective self-defence.[7]

All the episodes listed above pre-date the judgment in the *Nicaragua* case.[8] After the judgment the USA occasionally again invoked collective self-defence against Nicaragua in Central America.[9] And recently claims to collective self-defence to justify the use of force in defence of Kuwait[10] and Tajikistan[11] again reveal the complexity of such claims. The legality of the third state use of force was controversial in all these cases, both those before and those after the *Nicaragua* case, but the disagreements between states on the legality of these uses of force have generally centred on the facts rather than the law. In almost all these cases the controversy concerned the question whether there had been an armed attack and also whether there had been a genuine request for help by the victim state.

On the whole, however, the states directly involved and those responding to their use of force through international organizations have not disagreed as to the *content* of the applicable law. This may seem surprising, given that the theory of collective self-defence has been controversial since the debate over its express inclusion in the UN Charter. Collective self-defence was included at the instance of the Latin American states to make clear the compatibility of the existing American system and the new UN system. After prolonged debate collective self-defence was included in Chapter VII on the powers of the Security Council rather than in Chapter VIII on regional arrangements.[12] There has subsequently been controversy as to whether collective self-defence was a new concept when it was included in the Charter in 1945.[13] Some of the judges in the *Nicaragua* case

---

[7] For example, SC 2481st meeting, 2565th meeting. On the history of Cuban involvement in Angola, see *Repertoire of the Practice of the Security Council 1975–1980*, 260. The Security Council expressly rejected the doctrine of linkage; see, for example, SC Res 539.

[8] *Case concerning Military and Paramilitary Activities in and against Nicaragua*, 1986 ICJ Reports 14 (hereafter *Nicaragua* case).

[9] For example, 1988 UNYB 170; S/PV 2800, S/PV 2802, A/42/931.

[10] The USA and the UK invoked collective self-defence after the Iraqi invasion of Kuwait in 1990 to justify their naval operations undertaken after the imposition of an economic embargo on Iraq but before the specific authorization of force by the Security Council. They imposed a 'naval interdiction' to stop ships violating the embargo. In this instance controversy over legality centred on the question whether the USA and the UK were entitled to act without Security Council authority. See Warbrick, 'The Invasion of Kuwait by Iraq', 40 ICLQ (1991) 482, 964; Greenwood, 'New World Order or Old?', 55 MLR (1992) 153 at 161, 164–5.

[11] On Tajikistan, see below at 127.

[12] Judge Oda and Judge Schwebel go into the history of the drafting of the UN Charter provisions on collective self-defence in their Dissenting Opinions, 1986 ICJ Reports 212 at para 91–6; 266 at para 194.

[13] Brownlie, *International Law and the Use of Force by States* (1963), 328, 229–30; Higgins, *The Development of International Law through the Political Organs of the United Nations* (1963), 208; Kelsen, *Law of the United Nations* (1950) at 793, Delivanis, *La légitime défense en droit international public moderne* (1971), Part II, Chapter 2; Macdonald, 'The Nicaragua case: New Answers to Old Questions', 1986 Canadian Yearbook of International Law 127 at 143.

took the view that it was an innovation. Thus, for example, Judge Oda said that the term 'collective self-defence' was unknown before 1945 and therefore expressed doubt as to whether it was an inherent right.[14] Judge Jennings agreed that it was a novel concept.[15] Whether or not collective self-defence was a totally new concept, the post-1945 practice has been crucial in the crystallization of the concept.

Early debates on Article 51 of the UN Charter focused on whether collective self-defence was an autonomous right allowing any third state to use force in defence of the victim of an armed attack or whether it was a collection of rights to individual self-defence only to be exercised if the third state was itself a victim or if the interests of the third state were somehow engaged.[16] What were the conditions for its exercise: did it require a preexisting treaty arrangement for collective action? Some argued that there was a need of prior agreement for collective self-defence, otherwise the use of force would be contrary to the spirit of Article 51;[17] other writers like McDougal insisted on a common interest rather than a pre-existing treaty.[18]

THE *NICARAGUA* CASE

The ICJ decision in the *Nicaragua* case on the legality of the US use of force and intervention in Nicaragua renewed the passion of the debate on the scope of collective self-defence. The judgment has been much attacked and much misinterpreted. It plays a crucial role in this area. The Court's decision, its first extended discussion of the law on the use of force, was based on customary international law because of the US reservation to its Optional Clause acceptance. The Court found that the US multilateral treaty reservation prevented it from applying the UN Charter and other multilateral treaties, such as the OAS Charter and the Rio Treaty, which in fact bound the parties. However, the reservation did not stop the Court from deciding the case on the basis of customary international law, which continued to exist alongside treaty law.[19] Moreover, the Court could properly adjudicate because the provisions of multilateral treaties did not

---

[14] Oda, Dissenting Opinion at 253, paras 90–7.

[15] Jennings, Dissenting Opinion at 530–1.

[16] Alexandrov, *Self-Defense Against the Use of Force in International Law* (1996) at 101; Higgins, *The Development of International Law through the Political Organs of the United Nations* (1963) at 208; see also *Nicaragua* case, Jennings, Dissenting Opinion at 544–6.

[17] Delivanis, *La légitime défense en droit international public moderne* (1971), Part II, Chapter 2; Kulski, 'The Soviet System of Collective Security Compared with the Western System', 1950 (44) AJIL 453.

[18] McDougal and Feliciano, *Law and Minimum World Public Order* (1961); Bowett, *Self-Defence in International Law* (1958), 216.   [19] *Nicaragua* case paras 172–6.

diverge from customary international law to such an extent that a judgment of the Court on custom would be a wholly pointless exercise. The Court went on to say that, although it had no jurisdiction to determine whether the conduct of the USA constituted a breach of the Charter of the UN and that of the OAS, it could and must take them into account in ascertaining the content of customary international law.[20]

The Court's exposition of the law on collective self-defence, the justification used by the USA to support its use of force and intervention in and against Nicaragua, was relatively brief. The parties, in view of the circumstances in which the dispute had arisen, had relied only on the right of self-defence in the case of an armed attack which had already occurred; the lawfulness of a response to the imminent threat of armed attack was not raised.[21] Also the parties agreed that any exercise of self-defence must be necessary and proportionate. The Court accordingly went on to define the other specific conditions which had to be met for the exercise of collective self-defence.[22]

First, the Court considered what constituted an armed attack: the sending of armed bands rather than regular army could constitute an armed attack, provided that the scale and effects of the operation were such as to be classified as an armed attack and not a mere frontier incident. Assistance to rebels in the form of the provision of weapons or logistical or other support could amount to a threat or use of force or intervention, but did not constitute an armed attack.[23] Second, 'it is also clear that it is the

[20] Ibid. para 183. Judge Ago expressed 'serious reservations with regard to the seeming facility with which the Court—while expressly denying that all the customary rules are identical in content to the rules in the treaties—has nevertheless concluded in respect of certain key matters that there is a virtual identity of content as between customary international law and the law enshrined in certain major multilateral treaties' (Separate Opinion at 183, para 6). Judge Jennings was similarly sceptical as to whether custom could have developed since the adoption of the UN Charter on the basis of the rules in the Charter (Dissenting Opinion at 531). Other judges in their Separate Opinions argued that the US multilateral treaty reservation should not be given any effect and that the Court could apply the UN Charter and other multilateral treaties (Judge Sette Camara, Separate Opinion 192; Judge Ni, Separate Opinion 201).

[21] *Nicaragua* case para 194. The *Rio Treaty*, by which the parties were in fact bound, requires an armed attack in its express provision for collective self-defence in Article 3 (see *Nicaragua* case para 196–7). There is an important distinction between Article 3, which allows collective self-defence in cases of armed attack, and Article 6, which provides for cooperation in response to other types of outside intervention. Many other collective self-defence treaties make the same distinction. Judge Schwebel, in his Dissenting Opinion, blurred this distinction.

In state practice there are no instances of anticipatory collective self-defence being expressly invoked to justify the actual use of force, except perhaps in the Harib fort incident, 1964 UNYB 181; this use of force by the UK was condemned by the Security Council as a reprisal. Judge Schwebel (Dissenting Opinion para 172–3) apparently argued that there is a right of anticipatory self-defence, but he did not support this by reference to any state practice on collective self-defence. [22] *Nicaragua* case para 194.

[23] Ibid. para 195.

State which is the victim of the armed attack which must form and declare the view that it has been so attacked. There is no rule in customary international law permitting another state to exercise the right of collective self-defence on the basis of its own assessment of the situation. Where collective self-defence is invoked, it is to be expected that the State for whose benefit this right is used will have declared itself to be the victim of an armed attack.'[24] Third, the Court held that 'there is no rule permitting the exercise of collective self-defence in the absence of a request by the State which regards itself as the victim of an armed attack'.[25] The Court also held that the requirement in Article 51 of the UN Charter that the state claiming to use the right of individual or collective self-defence must report to the Security Council was not a customary law requirement, although 'the absence of a report may be one of the factors indicating whether the state in question was itself convinced that it was acting in self-defence'.[26]

The Court was criticized for its treatment of collective self-defence in the separate and dissenting opinions on contrasting grounds. Judge Ruda said that the Court should not have gone into the topic at all, given that it had held that there was no armed attack.[27] Judge Oda said that if it were going to consider collective self-defence, it had been far too brief on this controversial topic.[28]

The judgment on the merits in *Nicaragua* attracted strong criticism, especially from US writers.[29] They were unhappy at the brevity of the Court's reasoning on collective self-defence and at its approach to customary international law. Or it may be more accurate to say that, because some of the writers were unhappy with the substantive conclusions of the Court that the USA had illegally used force and intervened in Nicaragua, they therefore attacked its legal reasoning. How far were the Court's conclusions on collective self-defence justified on the basis of customary international law and compatible with treaty law? To what extent were they based on sound policy considerations?

---

[24] Ibid.   [25] Ibid. paras 196–8.   [26] Ibid. para 200.

[27] Judge Ruda (Separate Opinion, 174 at 176, para 12), was critical of this. He said that there was no need for the Court to go into collective self-defence; it should not have discussed the law on request and declaration by the victim state. It was enough for the Court to determine that there had been no armed attack.

[28] Judge Oda, Dissenting Opinion at 212, paras 90, 97.

[29] For criticism of the Court's doctrine of collective self-defence, see, for example, Franck, 'Some Observations on the ICJ's Procedural and Substantive Innovations', 81 AJIL (1987) 116; D'Amato, 'Trashing Customary International Law', 81 AJIL (1987) 101; Hargrove, 'The *Nicaragua* Judgment and the Future of the Law of Force and Self-defense', 81 AJIL (1987) 135; Norton Moore, 'The *Nicaragua* case and the Deterioration of World Order', 81 AJIL (1987) 151; see also Macdonald, 'The *Nicaragua* case: New Answers to Old Questions', 1986 Canadian Yearbook of International Law 127 at 149.

THE MEANING OF ARMED ATTACK

The actions of armed bands and irregular forces

As was discussed in the previous chapter, the Court asserted that on the central question of what constitutes an armed attack the *Definition of Aggression* gave guidance. An armed attack included the actions of armed bands where these were imputable to a state.[30] This limited use of the *Definition of Aggression* seems justified in the light of state practice.[31]

A central issue in all the episodes where collective self-defence was expressly invoked by states was whether there had been an armed attack such as to justify the third state assistance to the victim state. In state practice it has been accepted since the early days of the UN that the actions of armed bands and irregular forces could constitute an armed attack by a state. This has been accepted in the context of collective self-defence as well as individual self-defence.[32] During the US intervention in Lebanon in the name of collective self-defence in 1958 there was initially some uncertainty on this issue.[33] The USA and Lebanon did not at first mention armed attack, although they both reported to the Security Council that the US intervention was in response to a request by Lebanon under Article 51 of the UN Charter. But subsequently Lebanon expressly argued that there was an armed attack by the United Arab Republic (Egypt and Syria) and that there was no difference between a regular army and irregular forces for the purposes of Article 51.[34] China also took this position and no state challenged it.[35] The reason why the claim to collective self-defence was controversial in Security Council and General Assembly debates was that states were sceptical as to whether there had in fact been any armed attack, whether by regular or irregular troops; they claimed that the USA was simply trying to protect an unpopular leader from internal unrest at a time of growing Arab nationalism and republicanism.

Again, in the case of Vietnam, the USA argued that the infiltration from North Vietnam amounted to an armed attack justifying collective self-defence of South Vietnam. It famously asserted that from 1959 until 1964

---

[30] *Nicaragua* case para 195.

[31] Judge Ago, in his Separate Opinion 181 para 7, expressed reservations about the legal significance of General Assembly resolutions. In contrast, Judge Schwebel was prepared to accept the *Definition of Aggression* as reflecting customary international law (Dissenting Opinion, para 168). See Gray, 'The Principle of Non-use of Force', in Lowe and Warbrick (eds) *The United Nations and the Principles of International Law* (1994), 33.

[32] Judge Schwebel, Dissenting Opinion para 157–8; Brownlie, 'International Law and the Activities of Armed Bands', 7 ICLQ (1958) 712; Gill, 'The Law of Armed Attack in the Context of the *Nicaragua* case', 1 Hague Yearbook of International Law (1988) 30.

[33] 1958 UNYB 36.   [34] SC 833rd meeting, 18 July 1958.

[35] SC 831st meeting, 17 July 1958, para 99.

the North infiltrated over 40,000 men into the South. It said that in these circumstances armed attack was not as easily fixed by date and hour as in the case of traditional warfare, but the infiltration of thousands of men clearly constituted an armed attack under any reasonable definition.[36] States did not deny that the actions of irregular troops could be attributed to a state, but they doubted whether in fact there was an invasion of one state by armed bands from another rather than an uprising throughout Vietnam.[37] Similarly, with regard to its intervention in Afghanistan in 1979 the USSR claimed collective self-defence against at first unspecified 'foreign intervention'; it was not controversial that the actions of armed bands could constitute an armed attack, but there was doubt as to the existence of such an attack.[38]

Most recently, in Tajikistan there was controversy as to the existence of armed attacks from Afghanistan against Tajikistan.[39] After Tajikistan attained independence in 1991 civil war broke out and opposition forces operated against the government from Afghanistan. Russia argued that it was justified in using force in collective self-defence of Tajikistan against these incursions. In 1993–5 Russia and Tajikistan repeatedly accused Afghanistan of involvement in the attacks; Afghanistan denied these claims. This continued even after the conclusion of a border agreement between Afghanistan and Tajikistan, an *Agreement on a Temporary Cease-fire and the Cessation of Other Hostile Acts on the Tajikistan/Afghanistan Border and within the Country* between the warring parties in Tajikistan and the creation of a UN observer force (UNMOT) to monitor the border/cease-fire. The UN Secretary-General made various reports on the situation but did not come to any public conclusions as to the occurrence of armed attacks and the right of Tajikistan and Russia to act in collective self-defence against Afghanistan.

The supply of arms

What proved more controversial than the attribution of the actions of armed bands to a state was the ICJ's assertion in the *Nicaragua* case that the supply of arms, financial and logistic support could not amount to an armed attack. The USA contended that Nicaragua had intervened in El Salvador and other neighbouring states in order to foment and sustain armed attacks upon the governments of those states and that its subversive intervention in the

---

[36] Department of State Bulletin, 28 March 1966; see 60 AJIL (1966) 565.

[37] Wright, 'Legal Aspects of the Vietnam Situation', 60 AJIL (1966) 750; see also Falk (ed.), *The Vietnam War and International Law* (1968).

[38] Cot and Pellet (eds), *La Charte des Nations Unies* (1991), 787; Doswald-Beck, 'The Legal Validity of Military Intervention by Invitation of the Government', 56 BYIL (1985) 189.

[39] 1993 UNYB 383, 514; 1994 UNYB 454, 591; 1995 UNYB 495.

governing circumstances was tantamount to an armed attack. The Court said that such assistance as the supply of arms, financial and logistic support could be regarded as a threat or use of force, or amount to intervention in the internal or external affairs of other states, but that it did not amount to an armed attack.[40] The Court gave no authority for this statement and was criticized for its failure to do so by some commentators. But the Court's choice not to elaborate on the basis for its finding may be explained by the fact that the parties had not disagreed about the meaning of armed attack.[41] Rather, the central disagreement was whether, on the application of the law to the particular facts, the actions of the Nicaraguan government amounted to an armed attack. On the facts of the case the Court found that there had been no significant assistance to the opposition in El Salvador since 1981 and that Nicaragua could not be held responsible for the limited assistance that had been given.[42] Therefore there was actually no need for the Court to go into the question of the definition of armed attack; the decision on the general question of what counted as an armed attack was not decisive.

In state practice the supply of arms, money, and logistic support have not generally been treated as armed attacks in the context of collective self-defence. Occasionally there have been hints of such a position. For example, in Lebanon in 1958 the USA and Lebanon at first simply said that the infiltration of armed men, arms, and supplies from Syria in the UAR threatened the independence of Lebanon and that this gave the right of collective self-defence. They did not expressly mention armed attack at this stage; they invoked Article 51 as a precaution, saying that their forces were not there to engage in hostilities.[43] In the Security Council debates

[40] *Nicaragua* case para 195.

[41] This was accepted by Schwebel (Dissenting Opinion para 160, 172); see also Rostow, 'Nicaragua and the Law of Self-Defense revisited', 11 Yale JIL (1987) 437.

[42] *Nicaragua* case para 230. The Court was criticized by some for its reluctance to attribute these actions to Nicaragua, but its position on this point is consistent with its position on the *contras*. Just as the Court did not make the USA responsible for all the acts of the *contras* and did not accept that the *contras* were mere agents of the USA, so it did not attribute to Nicaragua all action helping the opposition in El Salvador; see Gill, 'The Law of Armed Attack in the Context of the *Nicaragua* case', 1 Hague Yearbook of International Law (1988) 30.

Judge Schwebel disagreed with the conclusion of the Court on these facts (Dissenting Opinion para 166). On the question of fact, Judge Jennings (Dissenting Opinion 544) said:

As to the case before the Court, I remain somewhat doubtful whether the Nicaraguan involvement with Salvadorian rebels had not involved some forms of 'other support' besides the possible provision, whether officially or unofficially, of weapons. There seems to have been perhaps overmuch concentration on the question of the supply, or transit, of arms; as if that were of itself crucial, which it is not. Yet one is bound to observe that here, where questions of fact may be every bit as important as the law, the United States can hardly complain at the inevitable consequences of its failure to plead during the substantive phase of the case.   [43] SC 827th meeting.

some states (the UK, France, Canada, and China) supported the right of Lebanon to request and the USA to send troops, but on the facts this cannot be interpreted as amounting to an endorsement of the actual use of force in the exercise of collective self-defence. It can be seen as simply an endorsement of the right of the USA to send in its troops to help the government of Lebanon. Certain states, such as the UAR, the USSR, and Sweden, denied the existence of an armed attack and said that because of this the USA had no right to use force against the UAR.[44] Lebanon, in later defending its position against the criticisms that had been made by other states in the Security Council, expressly justified its invitation to the USA on the basis that there had been an attack. It affirmed a conception of armed attack that did not include the mere supply of arms, but only armed attack by regular army and irregular troops.[45]

The US justification of its intervention in Vietnam also at first seemed to be based on a wide view of armed attack. In its 1966 Department of State *Memorandum on The Legality of US Participation in the Defense of Vietnam* it said in the first paragraph that it was assisting South Vietnam to defend itself against armed attack from the North and that 'this armed attack took the form of externally supported subversion, the clandestine supply of arms and the infiltration of armed personnel'.[46] But the USA subsequently focused on the movement of troops across the border between North and South Vietnam; in its reports to the Security Council the USA, in claiming to act in collective self-defence, generally spoke only of the use of force by regular and irregular troops.[47] The lesson that emerges from this practice is that the supply of arms alone does not constitute an armed attack. This position was acceptable to Judges Schwebel and Jennings, but some commentators have apparently taken a more extreme position.[48]

FRONTIER INCIDENTS

Also controversial was the distinction made by the International Court of Justice in the *Nicaragua* case between armed attack and frontier incident.

[44] SC 827th–831st meetings, 15–17 July 1958.   [45] SC 833rd meeting, 18 July 1958.
[46] 60 AJIL (1966) 565.

[47] Thus on the extension of the war into Cambodia, see 1972 UNYB 153; Stevenson, 'US Military Actions in Cambodia: Questions of International Law', in Falk (ed.), *The Vietnam War and International Law*, Vol 3 (1972), 23 at 31.

[48] Norton Moore, 'The *Nicaragua* case and the Deterioration of World Order', 81 AJIL (1987) 151 at 154; Norton Moore, 'The Secret War in Central America and the Future of World Order', 80 AJIL (1986) 43; Reisman, 'Allocating Competences to Use Coercion in the Post-Cold War World', in Damrosch and Scheffer (eds), *Law and Force in the New International Order* (1991), 26.

The distinction requires detailed discussion because of the prevalence of frontier incidents in state practice; this is the most common form of force between states and the least discussed. The Court first drew this distinction in the context of its discussion of the applicable law. It said that as regards certain aspects of the principle prohibiting the use of force, it would be necessary to distinguish the most grave forms of the use of force (those involving an armed attack) from less grave forms. Accordingly, in its examination of the exceptions to the prohibition on the use of force, and specifically in its consideration of the right of individual and collective self-defence, the Court discussed the nature of an armed attack and referred expressly to frontier incidents. It said that just as individual self-defence is subject to the state concerned having been the victim of an armed attack, reliance on collective self-defence does not remove the need for this: 'The Court sees no reason to deny that, in customary law, the prohibition of armed attacks may apply to the sending by a state of armed bands to the territory of another state, if such an operation, because of its scale and effects, would have been classified as an armed attack *rather than as a mere frontier incident* had it been carried out by regular armed forces.'[49]

When the Court came to apply customary international law to the facts of the case, it asked whether the US actions using force against Nicaragua were justified as collective self-defence.[50] Did Nicaragua engage in an armed attack against El Salvador, Costa Rica, and Honduras? The Court said that the limited provision of arms from Nicaragua to the opposition in El Salvador did not amount to an armed attack.[51] Therefore the concept of frontier incident did not play a decisive role in this part of the judgment. In contrast, the Court held that there had been certain trans-border incursions from Nicaragua into Costa Rica and Honduras imputable to the government of Nicaragua.[52] Here, it seems that the distinction between frontier incident and armed attack was important to the Court. If these trans-border incursions amounted to armed attacks, then it would be possible that the USA might have a claim to collective self-defence of Costa Rica and El Salvador. However, the Court was rather non-committal (and it did not expressly mention frontier incidents or elaborate on the distinction between armed attack and frontier incident at this point in its judgment). It said only that it had very little information as to the circumstances or possible motivations of the incursions and this rendered it difficult to decide whether they could be treated for legal purposes as amounting either singly or collectively to an armed attack by Nicaragua on either or both of these states.

[49] *Nicaragua* case para 195.   [50] Ibid. paras 226, 229.   [51] Ibid. para 230.
[52] Ibid. para 231.

The distinction between armed attack and frontier incident in the *Nicaragua* case

The Court did not elaborate in any detail on the distinction between frontier incidents and armed attack. The first distinguishing features it mentioned were the 'scale and effects' of the attack;[53] this formula is comparable to the exclusion of 'acts and consequences not of sufficient gravity' from the *Definition of Aggression* and would seem to cover scale in place and time and also the scale of the impact of the attack. It is clear from the context of the Court's pronouncement that the difference envisaged is one of degree rather than of kind; that is, both frontier incidents and armed attacks were attributable to the state. The Court's concept of frontier incident was not limited to acts of non-state organs.

The second set of distinguishing features mentioned by the Court are more obscure; they are the 'circumstances and motivations' of the attack.[54] This phrase is very general; the implication seems to be that the Court would include within 'frontier incident' episodes where there was no intent to carry out an armed attack, including accidental incursions and incidents where officials disobeyed orders. The question of motivation is a controversial one. Can a state's motive be anything more than an inference from the action in question? Is the intent of individual soldiers to be attributed to the state? Factors of motive and intent were much discussed during the drafting of the *Definition of Aggression*; there was fundamental disagreement as to whether an act could constitute an act of aggression simply because the use of force was intentional or whether there should be some further intention on the part of the state to commit aggression (*animus aggressionis*).[55] The Court in *Nicaragua* left these questions of intent and motive with regard to frontier incidents unresolved.

Criticism of the distinction between armed attack and frontier incident

At first sight it might seem that the distinction drawn in a sketchy way in the *Nicaragua* case between armed attacks and lesser incursions such as frontier incidents was illogical and unnecessary. Given that all self-defence, whether individual or collective, must be necessary and proportionate, a minor frontier incursion would justify only a very limited

---

[53] *Nicaragua* case para 195.   [54] Ibid. para 231.
[55] Schwebel, 'Aggression, Intervention and Self-Defense in Modern International Law', 136 RCADI (1972–II) 463; Ferencz, 'Defining Aggression: Where it stands and where it's going', 66 AJ (1972) 491.

response. Thus there would seem to be no need to distinguish between armed attacks allowing self-defence and mere frontier incidents. The necessity and proportionality requirements would provide adequate safeguard against excessive use of force.[56]

Many harsh criticisms were made of the Court for its narrow view of armed attack, and its consequent limitation of the US right to act in collective self-defence. As part of this, writers condemned the Court's distinction between frontier incidents and armed attacks. In the context of the law on self-defence Dinstein is critical of the Court in *Nicaragua*. He says that 'In reality there is no cause to remove small scale armed attacks from the spectrum of armed attacks' and he describes the question of frontier incidents as 'particularly bothersome'.[57] Many others writing on the *Nicaragua* case also throw doubt on the distinction.[58] For example, Hargrove says Article 51 in no way limits itself to especially large, direct or important attacks.[59] Reisman accuses the Court of developing a theory that is tolerant of different forms of protracted and low-intensity conflict; he argues that this will lead to an increase in violence in international politics.[60] This argument echoes that of Fitzmaurice, writing in 1933, who argued that it was important not to treat frontier incidents as a justified resort to force; this would encourage frontier incidents and place innocent states in a difficult position.[61] However, Reisman seems to misinterpret the Court's reasoning on armed attack; the Court did not say that frontier incidents could not cumulatively amount to an armed attack and thus justify self-defence. It actually spelled out that trans-border incursions could be taken singly or collectively to constitute an armed attack.[62]

The writers critical of the reasoning in the *Nicaragua* case follow the same line as earlier commentators on the UN Charter who said that any attack, even small border incidents, allowed self-defence.[63] Thus Brownlie

[56] For example, this is the view of Higgins, *Problems and Process* (1994), 251.

[57] Dinstein, *War, Aggression and Self-Defence* (2nd edn, 1994), 11. But Dinstein accepts the distinction between frontier incidents and other more significant uses of force in the context of determining whether a state of war exists.

[58] For example, Schacter, 'In Defense of International Rules on the Use of Force', 53 University of Chicago Law Review (1986) 113; Macdonald, 'The *Nicaragua* case: New Answers to Old Questions', 1986 Canadian Yearbook of International Law 127 at 151.

[59] Hargrove, 'The *Nicaragua* Judgment and the Future of the Law of Force and Self-defense', 81 AJIL (1987) 135 at 139.

[60] Reisman, 'Allocating Competences to use Coercion in the post Cold-War World, Practices, Conditions, and Prospects', in Damrosch and Scheffer (eds), *Law and Force in the New International Order* (1991), 26 at 39–40.

[61] Fitzmaurice in Ferencz (ed.), *Defining International Aggression: The Search for World Peace* (1975), Vol 2 at 152.   [62] *Nicaragua* case para 231.

[63] For example, Kunz, 'Individual and Collective Self-Defense in Article 51 of the Charter of the United Nations', 41 AJIL (1947) 872 at 878; Badr, 'The Exculpatory Effect of Self-defense in State Responsibility', 10 Georgia Journal of International and Comparative Law (1980) 1.

had expressed doubts about the concept of frontier incidents. He writes of the concept as 'vague', and says that from the point of view of assessing responsibility the distinction between frontier incident and armed attack is only relevant in so far as the minor nature of the attack is *prima facie* evidence of absence of intention to attack, of honest mistake, or simply the limited objectives of an attack. For him, the question as to whether the particular use of force is permissible self-defence is merely one of proportionality.[64]

Arguments for the distinction between armed attack and frontier incident

But it is clear, despite the criticisms of the *Nicaragua* case, that there were nevertheless serious reasons for the Court's distinction between armed attacks and mere frontier incidents. Its concern was with *collective* self-defence; it wanted to limit *third state* involvement. Its insistence on a high threshold for armed attack would serve to limit third party involvement. If there was no armed attack, there could be no collective self-defence. The use of necessity and proportionality alone would not exclude third party involvement, merely limit the scope of their permissible response.[65]

Judge Jennings, in his Dissenting Opinion in the *Nicaragua* case, expressed some limited sympathy with the Court's approach to collective self-defence. He said that 'It is of course a fact that collective self-defence is a concept that lends itself to abuse. One must therefore sympathize with the anxiety of the court to define it in terms of some strictness. There is a question, however, whether the court has perhaps gone too far in this direction.'[66] Jennings did not, however, specifically criticize the concept of frontier incident.

Interestingly, Judge Schwebel, in his otherwise sweeping rejection of the majority judgment in the *Nicaragua* case, did not uncompromisingly reject the Court's position on this question of the scope of armed attack. He said:

While I disagree with its legal *conclusions*—particularly as they turn on the holding that there has been no action by Nicaragua tantamount to an armed attack upon El Salvador to which the United States may respond in collective self-defence—I recognize that there is room for the Court's *construction of the legal meaning of an armed attack*, as well as for some of its other conclusions of law. The

---

[64] Brownlie, *The Use of Force by States* (1963) at 366. He referred to intent, mistake, and limited objective as distinguishing features of frontier incidents.

[65] For some support for this view, see Farer, 'Drawing the Right Line', 81 AJIL (1987) 112; Diaz Barrado, *El Consentimento Causa de Exclusión de la Ilicitud del Uso de la Fuerza en Derecho Internacional* (1989). [66] Jennings, Dissenting Opinion 528 at 543.

Court could have produced a plausible judgment—unsound in its ultimate conclusions, in my view, but not implausible—which would have recognized not
only the facts of United States intervention in Nicaragua but the facts of
Nicaragua's prior and continuing intervention in El Salvador; which would have
treated Nicaragua's intervention as unlawful (as it undeniably is); but which
would also have held that it nevertheless was not tantamount to an armed attack
upon El Salvador or that, even if it were, the response of the United States was
unnecessary, ill-timed or disproportionate.[67]

The distinction and the *Definition of Aggression*

The distinction between mere frontier incidents and other more significant uses of force is not one that was invented by the Court. Although the
concept of frontier incident had not before *Nicaragua* attained the status of
a term of art, it was already familiar from earlier practice and had been
specifically discussed during the protracted attempts of states to define
aggression, particularly during the drafting of the 1975 *Definition of
Aggression*. The proposal to include a *de minimis* clause (to exclude minor
incidents, including frontier incidents, from the category of aggression)
was first made by Finland in 1972 in order to give the Security Council the
opportunity not to condemn when the acts or the consequences are not
grave.[68] Eventually Article 2 of the *Definition of Aggression* was adopted:

The first use of armed force by a state in contravention of the Charter shall constitute prima facie evidence of aggression although the Security Council may, in
conformity with the Charter, conclude that a determination that an act of aggression has been committed would not be justified in the light of other relevant circumstances, *including the fact that the acts concerned or their consequences are not
of sufficient gravity.*

Although this does not expressly refer to frontier incidents, it reflects the
general support for a distinction between frontier incidents and aggression and followed extensive discussion of frontier incidents.[69]

Of course, the flexibility of Article 39 of the UN Charter means that the
distinction between aggression and frontier incident is not likely to be
crucial for the decision-making of the Security Council under Chapter VII;
its powers are the same whether it finds an act of aggression, a breach of
the peace or a threat to the peace. Moreover, the Security Council in practice has been reluctant to identify and denounce acts of aggression.[70] The

---

[67] Schwebel, Dissenting Opinion 272, para 15 (italics added).
[68] See Ferencz, *Defining International Aggression: The Search for World Peace* (2 vols, 1975) at 367.
[69] Ferencz, ibid. at 248; Schwebel, 'Aggression, Intervention and Self-Defense in Modern
International Law', 136 RCADI (1972–II) 463 at 467–8; Fitzmaurice, 'The Definition of
Aggression', 1 ICLQ (1952) 137 at 139.
[70] Cot and Pellet (eds), *La Charte des Nations Unies* (1991), 661.

less dramatic choice, but more important in this context, will be whether the frontier incident amounts to a breach of the peace or a threat to the peace.[71]

Furthermore, there are questions about the interrelationship of aggression, frontier incident, and armed attack. As part of the debate about the role that a definition of aggression might play, and of the usefulness of such a definition, the lack of any express correlation between the terms used in Articles 2(4) ('the use of force'), 51 ('armed attack') and 39 ('act of aggression') of the UN Charter gave rise to considerable controversy.[72] During the early discussions of the *Definition of Aggression* the Netherlands representative suggested that it might be more useful to define armed attack rather than aggression. In this context he said that insignificant incidents did not amount to armed attack allowing self-defence.[73] However, his proposal to define armed attack was not accepted. But, just because the concept of frontier incident was being discussed in the context of work on a definition of aggression, this does not mean that these discussions have no relevance for the scope of the right of self-defence. Some commentators apparently assumed that any act of aggression would necessarily allow self-defence. Thus Broms said that the *de minimis* clause limits the likelihood of a state arguing that a very minor incident amounts to an act of aggression leading to self-defence.[74] If this is a complete identification of aggression and armed attack it goes too far. But in *Nicaragua* the Court itself used the *Definition of Aggression* to help it to determine the scope of an armed attack; it was in this context that it drew the distinction with frontier incident. Some later writers supported this and said that Article 51 required serious acts, and that small border incidents did not count.[75] The legality of the third state use of force was controversial in all the cases where collective self-defence was invoked by

[71] Higgins, *The Development of International Law through the Political Organs of the United Nations* (1963), 181; as Higgins pointed out, it is important to remember that just because an act is too minor to count as aggression does not mean that it is legal; it could still be a breach of the peace, open to condemnation by the UN. In the early days of the UN the Security Council condemned even minor uses of force, but this does not seem to be true today.

[72] Bowett, *Self-Defence in International Law* (1958) at 250–6; Roling, 'The Ban on the Use of Force and the UN Charter', in Cassese (ed.), *The Current Legal Regulation of the Use of Force* (1986); Mullerson, 'The Principle of the Non-Threat and Non-Use of Force in the Modern World', in Butler (ed.), *The Non-Use of Force in International Law* (1989), 29.

[73] Ferencz, *Defining International Aggression: The Search for World Peace* (1975) at 238; see also Fitzmaurice, 'Definition of Aggression', 1 ICLQ (1952) 137 at 142.

[74] Broms, *The Definition of Aggression in the UN* (1968), 151; 'The Definition of Aggression', 154 RCADI (1977–I) 299 at 346; see also Hargrove, 'The Nicaragua Judgment and the Future of the Law of Force and Self-defense', 81 AJIL (1987) 135 at 139.

[75] Mullerson, 'Self-Defense in the Contemporary World', in Damrosch and Scheffer (eds), *Law and Force in the New International Order* (1991), 13; Lamberti Zanardi, 'Indirect Military Aggression', in Cassese (ed.), *The Current Legal Regulation of the Use of Force* (1986), 111; see also Rifaat, *International Aggression* (1979), Chapter 11.

states. But, although the existence of an armed attack was problematical in most of the above episodes, in none of them has the distinction between armed attack and frontier incident been a relevant consideration.[76]

OTHER LIMITS ON THE RIGHT OF COLLECTIVE SELF-DEFENCE

As mentioned above, the Court's findings in the *Nicaragua* case on the nature of the incursions from Nicaragua into Costa Rica and Honduras were somewhat inconclusive as regards the question whether these were frontier incidents not amounting to an armed attack. After the Court had looked at these incursions and at the supply of arms to the opposition in El Salvador it continued, 'There are however *other* considerations which justify the court in finding that neither these incursions nor the alleged supply of arms to the opposition in El Salvador may be relied on as justifying the exercise of the right of collective self-defence.'[77] The Court went on to apply the conditions that it had identified as limiting the right to collective self-defence in its earlier discussion of customary international law. It found that there had been no timely declaration by El Salvador that it was the victim of an attack and no declaration at all by Honduras and Costa Rica. Also none of the three had made any request for help to the USA before its forcible intervention. These factors together all showed that the USA was not acting in self-defence of the three states.[78]

The only authority the Court mentioned for its requirement of a request by the victim state was the *Rio Treaty*, Article 3(2), which says that measures of collective self-defence are decided 'on the request of the state or states directly attacked'. As regards its requirement of a declaration by the victim state that it had been the victim of an armed attack, the Court offered no authority. That is, it offered almost no justification for the conditions it apparently imposed on collective self-defence. One obvious inference is that the Court was influenced by the fact that the parties were actually bound by a treaty commitment that the victim state request assistance.[79] Moreover, the approach adopted by the Court seems correct in principle, as any other approach would allow the third state to pronounce on the existence of an armed attack and to decide that it was going to use force even against the wishes of the victim state.[80]

---

[76] In the case of Tajikistan questions arose as to whether cross-border incursions from Afghanistan constituted armed attacks allowing collective self-defence. However, the central issue was the responsibility of Afghanistan rather than the characterization of the incursions.
[77] *Nicaragua* case para 231.   [78] Ibid. paras 232–4.
[79] *Inter-American Treaty of Reciprocal Assistance* (1947) 21 UNTS 77.
[80] See *contra* Macdonald, 'The *Nicaragua* case: New Answers to Old Questions', 1986 Canadian Yearbook of International Law 127 at 143. He argued that 'if there is an armed

Judges Jennings and Schwebel, however, attacked the Court's reasoning and conclusion on these points. Their arguments seem to be based on policy considerations. Both were critical of the court's 'formalistic' model of collective self-defence. Schwebel's concern was with covert action; he asked, 'Where is it written that a victim state may not informally and quietly seek foreign assistance?'[81] Jennings showed some sympathy with the Court's desire to limit the scope of collective self-defence. He said, 'Obviously the notion of collective self-defence is open to abuse and it is necessary to ensure that it is not employable as a mere cover for aggression disguised as protection, and the Court is therefore right to define it somewhat strictly. Even so, it may be doubted whether it is helpful to suggest that the attacked state must in some more or less formal way have "declared" itself the victim of an attack and then have as an additional "requirement" made a formal request to a particular third state for assistance.' Jennings' argument is apparently based on policy. He goes on, 'It may readily be agreed that the victim state must both be in real need of assistance and must want it and that the fulfilment of both these conditions must be shown. But to ask that these requirements take the form of some sort of formal declaration and request might sometimes be unrealistic.'[82]

Writers similarly have been critical of the Court's reasoning on the grounds of its formalism.[83] Simma, in his commentary on the UN Charter, states categorically, but without any attempt at justification beyond references to secondary sources, that the Court was wrong to require an express request by the victim state.[84] Macdonald agrees that the requirement of a request for help was a 'wholly new and unconsidered limitation on the right to collective self-defence'.[85] These pronouncements by writers are not only misguided as a matter of principle and in the light of state practice; they also rest on a misreading of the Court's judgment.

The Court's judgment may be interpreted in a much less formalistic way than that adopted by the writers critical of the Court. When it came to apply the rule that it had earlier in its discussion of the applicable law stated in apparently rather categorical terms, the Court took a more relaxed approach to the requirement of a declaration and a request. It said

---

attack, what the victim believes to have occurred is otiose because the aid-giving state is also subject to the armed attack'.

[81] Schwebel, Dissenting Opinion paras 191, 221–7. He argued particularly that these requirements were not appropriate in cases of covert action. But this seems to mistake the nature of the right and the role of the Security Council.

[82] Jennings, Dissenting Opinion 544–5.

[83] Norton Moore, 'The Nicaragua case and the Deterioration of World Order', 81 AJIL (1987) 151; Morrison, 'Legal Issues in the Nicaragua Opinion', 81 AJIL (1987) 160.

[84] Simma, *The United Nations Charter: A Commentary* (1994) 675 at para 33.

[85] See Macdonald, 'The *Nicaragua* case: New Answers to Old Questions', 1986 Canadian Yearbook of International Law, 127 at 150.

that it is evident that it is the victim state, being most directly aware of that fact, which is *most likely* to draw general attention to its plight. It is also evident that if a victim state wants help it will *normally* make an express request.[86] This is clearly something less than a strict formal rule: 'Thus in the present instance the Court is entitled to take account, in judging the asserted justification of the exercise of collective self-defence by the United States, of the actual conduct of El Salvador, Honduras and Costa Rica at the relevant time, as indicative of a belief by the State in question that it was the victim of an armed attack by Nicaragua, and of the making of a request by the victim State to the United States for help in the exercise of collective self-defence.'[87] In fact it is clear that the Court did not *require* a declaration and a request.

Nor did it intend the declaration and request to be *decisive* as to legality. After its examination of whether there had been a declaration and a request, the Court concluded that 'the condition *sine qua non* required for the exercise of the right of collective self-defence by the United States is not fulfilled in this case'. The reference to '*the* condition *sine qua non*' apparently refers to an armed attack.[88] The Court thus apparently took the absence of a declaration, request for assistance (and of a report to the Security Council) simply as *confirmation* that there had been no armed attack.[89]

State practice also supports the Court's position that normally a request and a declaration would be made. Some collective self-defence treaties, like the *Rio Treaty*, expressly require a request by the victim state.[90] In every case where a third state has invoked collective self-defence it has based its claim on the request of the victim state even where there was no express treaty provision requiring this.[91] Also the state claiming to be the victim has generally asserted that it has been the victim of an armed attack. But in almost all the cases of collective self-defence listed above there has been controversy over the existence or the genuineness of the

---

[86] *Nicaragua* case para 232.   [87] Ibid. paras 233, 234.   [88] Ibid. para 236–7.

[89] Greig, 'Self-Defence and the Security Council: What does Article 51 require?', 40 ICLQ (1991) 366 at 375, supports this view.

[90] The Arab League *Treaty of Joint Defence*, Article IV(3), 55 AJIL Supplement 51, and the France/Djibouti Protocol (1982), 1430 UNTS 103 also require a request. Other treaties require 'consultation' (UK/Mauritius *Agreement on Mutual Defence and Assistance* (1968) 648 UNTS 3; UK/Malta *Agreement on Mutual Defence* (1964) 588 UNTS 55) or 'agreement' on the response to an armed attack (USA/Liberia *Agreement on Cooperation* (1959) 357 UNTS 94).

[91] USSR/Hungary (1956), 1956 UNYB 67; USA/Lebanon (1958) S/PV 827, 1958 UNYB 36 at 38; UK/Jordan (1958) 1958 UNYB 41; USA/Vietnam (1965) S/6174, 60 AJIL (1966) 565; USSR/Czechoslovakia (1968) S/PV 1441, 1968 UNYB 298; USSR/Afghanistan A/41/55, 1980 UNYB 296; Libya/Chad (1980) 1981 UNYB 222; France/Chad (1983, 1986) 1983 UNYB 180, 1986 UNYB 168, 1987 UNYB 176, S/17837, S/18554; Angola/Cuba (from 1975) S/PV 2440, S/PV 2481, 1983 UNYB 173; USA/Honduras (1988) S/PV 2802, A/42/931, 1988 UNYB 170; Russia/Tajikistan (1993) S/26241, 1993 UNYB 514.

request. With regard to the interventions in Lebanon and Jordan in 1958, the USSR argued that the USA put pressure on Lebanon to issue an invitation,[92] and that the UK intervention was planned before the request from Jordan and that the request was not free. The true motive of the USA and the UK was to repress the rise of Arab nationalism.[93] With regard to Vietnam, those who challenged the legality of the US intervention said that South Vietnam was not a separate state and had no right to seek outside assistance.[94] In the Soviet invasions of Czechoslovakia and Afghanistan the invitations came from governments installed by the invading state.[95] In Chad there was an ongoing civil war and the legitimacy of the government and its right to request outside help was not always clear. But Libya relied on a request in 1980 and said that it had left when so requested.[96] France also said that a request was necessary and it responded to a request.[97]

Third state interest?

After his criticism of the Court's requirement of a declaration and a request by the victim state, Judge Jennings went on to say that the reasoning was also objectionable in that the Court was giving the impression that the third state need not itself have an interest for it to exercise collective self-defence.[98] Many others follow the Jennings approach.[99] Some have even argued that the right to collective self-defence is essentially the right of the party giving aid to the victim, and that the International Court of Justice itself should not be taken to have rejected this position.[100] But this insistence on a third party interest all seems rather far-fetched in the light of state practice since 1945. States themselves have not used this argument; attacks by states on the legality of actions taken in the name of collective self-defence have not mentioned the absence of a third state interest or of a treaty commitment as a ground of illegality. In many of the

---

[92] 1958 UNYB 36.   [93] 1958 UNYB 41.

[94] Wright, 'Legal Aspects of the Viet-Nam Situation', 60 AJIL (1966) 750.

[95] Doswald-Beck, 'The Legal Validity of Military Intervention by Invitation of the Government', 56 BYIL (1985) 189.   [96] 1981 UNYB 223.

[97] France 1983 UNYB 180, 1984 UNYB 185, 1986 UNYB 168, 1987 UNYB 176, S/17837, S/18554, S/PV 2721; *Repertoire of the Practice of the Security Council (1981–84)* 261; see Alibert, 'L'Affaire du Tchad', 90 RGDIP (1986) 368.

[98] Jennings, Dissenting Opinion 545.

[99] Dinstein, *War, Aggression and Self-Defence* (2nd edn, 1994), Chapter 9; Bowett, *Self-Defence in International Law* (1958) at 216; Macdonald, 'The *Nicaragua* case: New Answers to Old Questions', 1986 Canadian Yearbook of International Law at 151; Delivanis, *La légitime défense en droit international public moderne* (1971).

[100] Macdonald (above note 99) argued that 'if there is an armed attack, what the victim believes to have occurred is otiose because the aid-giving state is also subject to the armed attack'.

episodes the intervening state did in fact have a pre-existing treaty relationship with the 'victim' state,[101] but in the other cases where there was
no such treaty this was not mentioned as a ground of illegality even by
those otherwise critical of the use of force.[102]

The duty to report to the Security Council under Article 51

Also the failure of the USA to report on its use of force to the Security
Council under Article 51 was taken by the Court as an indication that the
USA was not exercising the right of collective self-defence.[103] Judge
Schwebel criticized this, but the Court's position is an accurate reflection
of earlier practice on collective self-defence. The USA itself, with regard to
its intervention in Vietnam, pointed out that it was not bound under
Article 51 to report because neither North nor South Vietnam were members of the UN. Nevertheless, it said it would report because Article 51
was an appropriate guide.[104] The other states claiming to use collective
self-defence in other episodes also reported under Article 51. Indeed,
there is a contrast here with individual self-defence, with regard to which
states' reporting was much more erratic and which has improved only
since the *Nicaragua* case. In collective self-defence all the states expressly
invoking collective self-defence reported.[105] And after the decision on the
merits of the *Nicaragua* case the Central American states and the USA
referred their subsequent claims to collective self-defence to the Security
Council.[106] Moreover, several collective self-defence treaties specifically

[101] There were pre-existing treaties between Hungary, Czechoslovakia, Ethiopia,
Afghanistan and the USSR; the UK and the South Arabian Federation; El Salvador, Costa
Rica and Honduras and the USA; Chad and France (France invoked a 1976 Cooperation
Agreement, but had to stretch its terms; see Alibert, 'L'Affaire du Tchad', 90 RGDIP (1986)
343). To justify its collective self-defence of Tajikistan Russia invoked a bilateral Treaty of
Friendship (S/26110), and an agreement between five members of the CIS (S/26892, 1993
UNYB 514). In some of these cases the treaty was concluded not long before the use of force,
so it seems that even though it is not a legal requirement it may be seen as adding legitimacy.

[102] Thus the absence of a treaty in the cases of USA/Lebanon (1958), UK/Jordan (1958),
Cuba/Angola (from 1975), and USA and UK/Kuwait (1990) was not singled out as a ground
for criticism.

[103] *Nicaragua* case para 235; see Greig, 'Self-Defence and the Security Council: What does
Article 51 require?', 40 ICLQ (1991) 366.

[104] As discussed in the previous chapter, the USA did not just report to the Security Council once at the start of the conflict, but made several separate reports of individual actions or
series of actions; 1965 UNYB 185, 1966 UNYB 153, 1970 UNYB 215.

[105] USA/Lebanon, SC 827th meeting, 1958 UNYB 38; Jordan/UK, S/4053, S/4071, 1958
UNYB 40; USA/Vietnam, 1965 UNYB 185, 1966 UNYB 146, 1970 UNYB 215, 1972 UNYB 153,
S/10631; USSR/Czechoslovakia, SC 1441st meeting, 1968 UNYB 298; Libya/Chad, 1981
UNYB 223; France/Chad, S/PV 2721, S/17837, S/18554, S/19136, 1983 UNYB 180, 1984
UNYB 185, 1986 UNYB 168, 1987 UNYB 176; USSR/Afghanistan, 1980 UNYB 296 at 299, 300;
Cuba/Angola, 1983 UNYB SC 2440th, 2481st meetings, 1983 UNYB 173; USA/Honduras,
1988 UNYB 170; Russia/Tajikistan, S/26110, 26241, 1993 UNYB 514.

[106] For example, 1988 UNYB 170; S/PV 2800, 2802, A/42/931.

require parties to report to the Security Council.[107] It may not be mandatory to report in the sense that failure to report will not in itself mean that
the action cannot be self-defence, but failure will be *evidence* that the
action was not in fact self-defence. As with the UK's controversial intervention to protect the South Arabian Federation (before it was a member
of the UN), the USSR and the USA both said that the UK should have
gone to the Security Council earlier if its action had been justified as self-
defence.[108] The UK itself repeated this argument against the USSR and its
failure to turn earlier to the Security Council over Afghanistan.[109]

CONCLUSION

Writers on collective self-defence are clearly split into two camps, and
their reactions to the *Nicaragua* case reflect these different viewpoints.
First, some view collective self-defence as a valuable means to help protect weak victim states from oppression.[110] They therefore attack the
Court's limitations on collective self-defence. For them the Court's view
of armed attack is too narrow, the alleged requirements of a declaration
and request by the victim state are unduly formalistic and restrictive.
They argue that the court's approach will encourage aggression of a low-
key kind.[111] This sort of enthusiasm for collective self-defence was also
apparent in earlier writers on the Charter; they were clearly writing under
the influence of the Second World War and saw the provision for collective self-defence in Article 51 as a useful means to protect small states. For
example, McDougal and Feliciano said that defence must be collective if
it is not to be an exercise in individual suicide.[112]

The opposing camp are those writers who have taken a much more
suspicious approach to collective self-defence. They see it rather as a threat
to world peace. Thus they argue that there is a need for a high threshold
of armed attack and distinction between armed attack and lesser use of
force in order to reduce the involvement of superpowers. Otherwise there
would be a risk of the internationalization of civil conflicts and the

---

[107] Australia/New Zealand/USA 131 UNTS 83; USA/Japan 373 UNTS 179; S E Asia 209
UNTS 28; Arab League 70 UNTS 237. [108] 1964 UNYB 181 at 184.
[109] 1980 UNYB 300.
[110] For example, Macdonald, 'The *Nicaragua* case: New Answers to Old Questions', 1986
Canadian Yearbook of International Law 127 at 151.
[111] Reisman, 'Allocating Competences to use Coercion in the post Cold-War World, Practices, Conditions, and Prospects', in Damrosch and Scheffer (eds), *Law and Force in the New
International Order* (1991), 26.
[112] McDougal and Feliciano, *Law and Minimum World Public Order* (1961) at 246; Delbruck,
'Collective Self-Defence' in Bernhardt (ed.), *Encyclopaedia of Public International Law* (1982),
Vol 13, 114.

expansion of inter-state conflicts.[113] They also said that there is a danger that Article 51 on collective self-defence would help remote, undemocratic states.

In this regard it is interesting that the Court itself in *Nicaragua*, although concerned to limit the right of collective self-defence, expressly ruled out any consideration of the *motives* of states engaged in collective self-defence. Thus it declined to undertake an examination of any additional motive beyond the protection of El Salvador, Costa Rica, and Honduras that the USA might have in using force against Nicaragua.[114] The USA asserted that it had responded to requests for assistance from El Salvador, Honduras, and Costa Rica in their self-defence against aggression by Nicaragua. Nicaragua claimed that the references made by the USA to the justification of self-defence were merely pretexts for its activities. The true motive was to impose its will on Nicaragua and force it to comply with US demands. However, the Court said that if the USA could establish that Nicaragua had supported the opposition in El Salvador and that this support amounted to an armed attack and the other appropriate conditions for collective self-defence were met, then it could legally invoke collective self-defence. The possibility of an additional motive, even one perhaps more decisive for the USA, could not deprive the USA of its right to resort to collective self-defence. The only significance of the alleged additional motive was that special caution was called for in considering the allegations of the USA concerning conduct by Nicaragua which may provide a sufficient basis for self-defence. This provides a marked contrast to the policy-oriented approach of McDougal and Feliciano. In their discussion of collective self-defence they say, 'A first step in the determination of reasonableness (that is lawfulness) is thus an inquiry into the substantiality of the collective "self" alleged for security and defence, and *into whether a purported grouping for common protection is in reality a façade for other unlawfully expansive purposes.*'[115]

Does state practice reflect the ideal picture of collective self-defence as a protection for small states rather than as a pretext for furthering Cold War or neo-colonial interests? The more cynical view appears to be the more accurate as regards the actual use of force. All the state practice on collective self-defence since the Second World War has been controversial. The USSR has subsequently disavowed its invasion of Hungary and Czechoslovakia and acknowledged that the Brezhnev doctrine of limited

---

[113] Farer, 'Drawing the Right Line', 81 AJIL (1987) 112; Higgins, 'The Attitude of Western States towards Legal Aspects of the Use of Force', in Cassese (ed.), *Current Legal Regulation of the Use of Force* (1986); also Delivanis, *La légitime défense en droit international public moderne* (1971), Part II, Chapter 2.   [114] *Nicaragua* case para 127.
[115] McDougal and Feliciano, *Law and Minimum World Public Order* (1961) at 248, 252.

sovereignty was not compatible with international law.[116] Some of the other episodes may be seen as showing a fundamental clash of perceptions; the situation could be seen either as one of a civil war with outside interference to further the political aims of the third state or as collective self-defence against an outside attack. The US intervention in Vietnam is just the most dramatic instance of this. The episodes where the USA or the UK intervened in Arab states may also be seen in this way: were they propping up unpopular rulers against regional pressure for change or were they saving the victims of outside aggression? And the same question arose of the French intervention in Chad. In Tajikistan the key question is how far Afghanistan is responsible for the operations across its border into Tajikistan.

On the positive side, it is possible to argue that during the Cold War the simple existence of collective self-defence treaties—not only NATO and the now defunct Warsaw Pact, but also the treaties between the USA, the USSR and former colonial powers and smaller states—may have acted as a deterrent to attack and thus protected small states. But this conclusion is necessarily speculative. The same state practice would be equally open to an alternative construction that these treaties in fact served to legitimate intervention by other states parties.

The USA walked out of the Court hearings in the *Nicaragua* case after it lost its attempt to challenge the admissibility and jurisdiction.[117] In view of its conformity with state practice and the failure of the dissenting judges and critical commentators to demonstrate that the decision was wrong in law rather than on the facts, the ICJ's judgment on the merits of the *Nicaragua* case remains an authoritative statement of the law in this area.

---

[116] McWhinney, 'New Thinking in Soviet International Law', 1990 Canadian Yearbook of International Law 309 at 332; Gray, 'Self-determination and the Break-up of the Soviet Union', 12 Yearbook of European Law (1992) 465.   [117] 24 ILM (1985) 246.

6

The UN and the use of force

The Security Council has been more active in its use and authorization of the use of force in recent years than at any time in the history of the UN, but its activities bear little relation to the original scheme of the Charter. Since 1988 it has initiated more peacekeeping operations than in the previous forty years, ranging from minor operations such as UNMOT on the border of Tajikistan and Afghanistan to major operations such as those in Cambodia and Angola, Kosovo and East Timor; all these operations were conducted without any express provision for peacekeeping in the Charter. The Security Council has also authorized member states to use force against Iraq and in Yugoslavia, Somalia, Rwanda, Haiti, Albania, and East Timor. These operations too are rather different from the original plan of those who established the UN.

The aim of the drafters of the UN Charter was not only to prohibit the unilateral use of force by states in Article 2(4) but also to centralize control of the use of force in the Security Council under Chapter VII.[1] The initial plan was that the Security Council would have its own standing army to use in response to threats to the peace, breaches of the peace, and acts of aggression. But the standing army never materialized; states did not make the agreements to provide troops to the UN as set out in Article 43. It is notorious that during the Cold War the Security Council was not able to carry out its 'primary responsibility for the maintenance of international peace and security' under Article 24 and its power to take decisions binding on member states under Article 25 was little used because of the veto power of the five permanent members of the Security Council under Article 27 of the UN Charter. The formal scheme of Chapter VII under which the Security Council could take provisional measures (Article 40) or determine that there was a threat to the peace or breach of the peace or act of aggression (under Article 39) and take economic measures (Article 41) or (should the Security Council consider that measures under Article 41 would be inadequate or had proved inadequate) action by air, sea or land forces (Article 42) did not stand up to the pressure of the Cold War. I will give only a brief account of the Security Council's actions during the Cold War in order to determine how far the early actions set the pattern

---

[1] On Chapter VII of the UN Charter see Simma (ed.), *The Charter of the United Nations: A Commentary* (1994), 605; Cot and Pellet (eds), *La Charte des Nations Unies* (1991). Article 2(7) of the UN Charter provides that the application of enforcement measures under Chapter VII shall not be prejudiced by the principle that the UN should not intervene in matters which are essentially within the domestic jurisdiction of states.

for more recent action. This chapter will show how the Charter scheme has been transformed in practice, how the UN Security Council has used its powers to respond to threats to the peace, breaches of the peace, and acts of aggression. The focus will be on the practice of the UN, and certain operations will be considered in detail in order to illuminate the application in practice of Chapter VII of the Charter and the development through practice of the institution of peacekeeping.

THE UN IN THE COLD WAR

Chapter VII action

The veto of the five permanent members of the Security Council under Article 27(3) was used 279 times between 1945 and 1985; from 1946 until 1970 it was almost exclusively the USSR, facing a Western majority in the General Assembly, that prevented the adoption of resolutions by the Security Council. In 1970 the USA made its first veto, and from then on came to replace the USSR as overwhelmingly the main user of the veto.[2] But of course it was not only the actual use of the veto that prevented action by the Security Council; threats to use the veto also prevented the adoption of resolutions or secured their revision to something more acceptable to the permanent member concerned.

During the Cold War the Security Council occasionally threatened to use Chapter VII; often it called for action without taking any binding decisions. Very rarely did it succeed in taking binding decisions under Chapter VII in response to threats to the peace, breach of the peace, and acts of aggression.[3] When it did act under Chapter VII its approach was generally flexible rather than formalistic; it did not usually specify the exact article of the Charter under which it was acting.[4] Security Council Resolution 598, demanding a mandatory cease-fire in the 1980–8 Iran/Iraq conflict, was unusual in that it expressly stated that the Security Council was acting under Articles 39 and 40. This reluctance by the Security Council to identify the precise legal basis, if any, for its resolutions has led to protracted and not always fruitful speculation by some commentators as to the legal basis of Security Council operations. It is clear from the

[2] Article 27(3) of the UN Charter provides that decisions of the Security Council on non-procedural matters shall be made by an affirmative vote of nine members, including the concurring votes of the permanent members. See Patil, *The UN Veto in World Affairs* (1992); Sonnenfeld, *Resolutions of the United Nations Security Council* (1988), 43–52; Bailey and Daws, *The Procedure of the UN Security Council* (3rd edn, 1998) at 226.
[3] For a list of resolutions passed under Chapter VII, see Bailey and Daws, *The Procedure of the UN Security Council* (3rd edn, 1998) at 272–3.
[4] See Sarooshi, *The United Nations and the Development of Collective Security* (1999) for a detailed discussion of the possible bases of Security Council action in the UN Charter.

practice of the Council that no formal pronouncement with an express reference to Article 39 is required for action under Chapter VII; the use of the language of Article 39 is apparently sufficient.[5]

The Security Council has been extremely reluctant to find that there has been an act of aggression; it has done so only with regard to Israel, South Africa, and Rhodesia.[6] It is also generally reluctant to condemn states by name. It has been readier to find a breach of the peace; it has done so with regard to Korea, Iraq/Kuwait, Argentina's invasion of the Falklands, and the 1980–8 Iran/Iraq conflict. Similarly it has passed many resolutions determining the existence of a threat to the peace.[7]

The first time the Security Council took economic measures under Article 41 was against Rhodesia (now Zimbabwe) after the Smith regime illegally declared independence of the UK in 1965 in order to establish white minority rule. In 1966 the Security Council imposed an embargo on raw materials, oil, and arms in Resolution 232; this expressly stated that it was acting under Articles 39 and 41. In 1968 it expanded this to a more comprehensive embargo in Resolution 253, which stated that the Security Council was acting under Chapter VII. It made no reference to Article 41 until paragraph 9, which requested 'all member states to take all possible action under Article 41 to deal with the situation in Southern Rhodesia, not excluding any of the measures provided in that article'. The later resolutions, designed to strengthen sanctions against Southern Rhodesia, also made express reference to Article 41. In contrast, when the Security Council subsequently took economic measures with regard to other states it did so without express reference to Article 41. In other ways these first sanctions set the pattern for subsequent measures.

First, the Security Council has consistently taken a wide view of the 'threat to international peace and security' under Article 39. In these first resolutions on Southern Rhodesia it said that the situation resulting from the proclamation of independence by the illegal authorities in Southern Rhodesia was extremely grave and its continuance constituted a threat to international peace and security. This readiness to look at the wider consequences of a civil conflict or illegal overthrow of a government and to treat it as a threat to international peace and security has been apparent in much of the later practice of the Security Council. Second, the resolutions imposing sanctions were directed against a non-state entity and

---

[5] See Freudenschuss, 'Article 39 of the UN Charter Revisited: Threats to the Peace and Recent Practice of the UN Security Council', 46 Austrian Journal of Public and International Law (1993) 1; Bailey and Daws, *The Procedure of the UN Security Council* (3rd edn, 1998) at 271.

[6] SC Res 573, 611, 387, 567, 568, 571, 574, 577, 455. The General Assembly has been ready to denounce acts of aggression; such resolutions were usually discounted by permanent members as not authoritative findings under Chapter VII.

[7] On practice under Article 39, see Kirgis, 'The Security Council's First Fifty Years', 89 AJIL (1995) 506.

addressed to non-member states as well as members. Resolutions 232 and 253 specifically urged non-member states to act in accordance with the provisions of the present resolution. Resolution 314 was addressed to 'all states'. The legal basis for this was spelled out in Resolutions 314 and 409 as residing in Article 2(6) of the UN Charter.[8] Subsequent resolutions followed this pattern of reference to 'all states'.

Third, in Resolution 221, passed to secure the effectiveness of the voluntary embargo called for in Resolution 217, the Security Council authorized the UK to use force to intercept ships on the high seas. This resolution did not include any reference to Chapter VII or to any specific article, although it did determine that the possibility of a breach of the oil embargo by tankers discharging oil intended for Southern Rhodesia in Mozambique amounted to a threat to the peace. It called upon the UK to prevent, by the use of force if necessary, the arrival in Mozambique of oil destined for Southern Rhodesia. Clearly such authorization does not fit within Article 41, which expressly excludes 'measures involving the use of armed force'. But Resolution 221 has been the model for many subsequent resolutions; it is sometimes said to be based on Article 42 and sometimes Chapter VII in general. This lack of concern with the specification of a precise legal basis for its actions has proved typical of the Security Council. Many commentators are content to base such resolutions authorizing force to secure the implementation of economic measures on 'Article 41 and a half'.[9]

Again in Resolution 418 (1977) imposing an arms embargo on South Africa, the first mandatory sanctions against a member state, the Security Council did not refer to Article 41 specifically; it made only a general reference to Chapter VII. This approach has been followed in almost all subsequent resolutions authorizing economic measures or the use of force. The resolution held that the military build-up by South Africa and its persistent acts of aggression against neighbouring states seriously disturbed the security of those states; South Africa was at the threshold of producing nuclear weapons. Therefore, having regard to the policies and acts of the South African government, the acquisition of arms by South Africa constituted a threat to the maintenance of international peace and security. The Security Council decided that all states should observe a mandatory arms embargo.

The action against Korea in 1950 was the only use of force authorized by the Security Council during the Cold War in response to a breach of the

---

[8] Article 2(6) of the UN Charter says, 'The Organization shall ensure that states which are not Members of the United Nations act in accordance with these Principles so far as may be necessary for the maintenance of international peace and security.'

[9] See Sarooshi, *The United Nations and the Development of Collective Security* (1999), 194.

peace by a state.[10] It was not quite what was envisaged in Chapter VII of the Charter and there is still controversy about its legality. The Security Council said in Resolution 82 that North Korea had made an armed attack against South Korea and this constituted a breach of the peace. Neither was a member state and some states saw this conflict as a struggle within one divided state for decolonization rather than an invasion of one pro-Western state by a socialist state. The absence of the USSR (in protest at the representation of China in the United Nations by the Taiwan government) enabled the Security Council to act.[11] It passed Resolution 83 recommending member states to 'furnish such assistance to South Korea as may be necessary to repel the armed attack and to restore international peace and security in the area'. But this action was far from what was provided in the Charter. The Council (in the absence of any standing army under Article 43 agreements) recommended action by states; it did not take any binding decision. And it did not itself establish a UN force. In Resolution 84 it recommended all member states providing military force and other assistance to make such forces available to a unified command under the USA; it requested the USA to designate a commander, but authorized the force to use the UN flag. Sixteen states contributed forces, but the USA played the dominant role. It was requested to provide the Security Council with reports as appropriate on the course of the action taken.[12]

The exact legal basis for the action against North Korea was not specified in the resolution recommending states to send troops and this has led to speculation ever since. Some argue that the action could not have been under Article 42 because that provision is not autonomous but depends on member states having made agreements under Article 43. Others reject this because Article 42 makes no reference to Article 43 and there is no indication elsewhere in the Charter that Article 42 must remain inoperative in the absence of Article 43 agreements. Moreover, given that Article 42 allows Security Council decisions to use force, this must be taken to include the lesser power to make recommendations to member states. Other writers argue that the Korean action was taken under Article 39 or under Chapter VII generally, or that it was collective self-defence.[13] There is little in the resolutions or in the Security Council

---

[10] 1950 UNYB 220; Sarooshi at 169.

[11] On the controversy about the interpretation of Article 27(3) on voting in the Security Council, see Simma (ed.), *The Charter of the United Nations: A Commentary* (1994) at 454; Bailey and Daws, *The Procedure of the UN Security Council* (3rd edn, 1998) at 257.

[12] On the return of the USSR, the Security Council was again unable to act; the General Assembly stepped in: 1950 UNYB 220; Franck, *Nation against Nation* (1985), 33–5.

[13] See Simma (ed.), *The Charter of the United Nations: A Commentary* (1994) at 633. The *Certain Expenses* case, ICJ Reports (1962) 151 at 167, rejected the argument that Article 42 is inoperative in the absence of agreements under Article 43. The Court said that 'It cannot be said that the Charter has left the Security Council impotent in the face of an emergency situation when agreements under Article 43 have not been concluded.'

debates to resolve this controversy and it is not clear that it had any practical significance.

The division of powers between the Security Council and the General Assembly

The inaction of the Security Council during the Cold War led the General Assembly to assume a role greater than originally envisaged. The Charter provides for a division of functions between the two organs. Article 11(2) says that the General Assembly may discuss questions relating to the maintenance of international peace and security and make recommendations (except as provided in Article 12); but any such question on which action is necessary shall be referred to the Security Council. Article 12 is designed to prevent clashes between the two bodies; it provides that, while the Security Council is exercising its functions with regard to a particular dispute or situation, the General Assembly shall not make any recommendation unless the Security Council so requests. But these two provisions have been flexibly interpreted in such a way that there is no strict division of functions.

The General Assembly, concerned at the inaction of the Security Council and its failure to play the role provided in the Charter, passed the *Uniting for Peace Resolution* in 1950. This allowed it to call emergency meetings in the event of Security Council failure because of lack of unanimity of the permanent members to exercise its primary responsibility for the maintenance of peace and security in any case where there appears to be a threat to the peace, breach of the peace or act of aggression. The General Assembly may then recommend collective measures, including the use of armed force if necessary.[14] Using this procedure it recommended the establishment of peacekeeping forces in the Middle East. The legality of this was upheld by the International Court of Justice in the *Certain Expenses* case; it explained away the provision of Article 11(2) that questions on which action was necessary should be referred to the Security Council on the basis that the Security Council has a primary but not an exclusive responsibility for the maintenance of international peace and security. The Court also relied on the less convincing argument that it is only enforcement action and not peacekeeping action that must be referred to the Security Council.[15]

Article 12 has also been gradually eroded. The General Assembly has made recommendations even when the Security Council was dealing

[14] GA Res 377(V).
[15] *Certain Expenses* case, ICJ Reports (1962) 151. Since UNEF it has been the Security Council rather than the General Assembly which has established peacekeeping forces.

actively with an issue. If the Security Council was not actually exercising its functions at that moment, or if a resolution was blocked by a veto, the General Assembly has assumed it is free to make recommendations, provided that these did not directly contradict a Security Council resolution.[16] The General Assembly has accordingly passed a series of resolutions condemning certain behaviour when the Security Council could not agree on a resolution or could not take measures against a wrongdoing state. Some Western states were unhappy at this; they said that the repetition of resolutions condemning states was a pointless rhetorical exercise. This was the response when the General Assembly called for the imposition of sanctions on South Africa after the USA and the UK had blocked this in the Security Council. Recently the General Assembly regarded itself as free to call on the Security Council to lift the arms embargo on Bosnia-Herzegovina when the Security Council had been divided as to whether to do so. Technically it may be possible to make out a case on the basis of the practice of the two bodies that this did not contravene Article 12, but it seems to be precisely the type of situation that Article 12 was designed to prevent.[17]

Another blurring of the divide between the General Assembly and the Security Council during the Cold War occurred because many states not members of the Security Council chose to address the Security Council to set out their positions.[18] States such as France, Australia, and the UK repeatedly complained that this was inappropriate; they accused these states of turning the Security Council into a mini-General Assembly. Thus France said that there was a growing tendency to transform the debates of the Security Council, which should be action oriented, into a substitute for General Assembly debate and a forum for confrontation. The UK said that it would prefer speeches to be given only by member states and those specially affected.[19] In recent years this use of the Security Council by non-members has become much less common.

Peacekeeping during the Cold War

In response to the inability of the Security Council to take enforcement action under Chapter VII, the institution of peacekeeping evolved during the Cold War.[20] There was no express basis for this in the Charter, but the

[16] Simma (ed.), *The Charter of the United Nations: A Commentary* (1994) at 254; Blum, *Eroding the United Nations Charter* (1993), 103; Gray, 'Bosnia and Herzegovina: Civil War or Inter-State Conflict: Characterisation and Consequences', 67 BYIL (1996) 155.   [17] Gray, ibid.
[18] On participation of non-member states, see UN Charter, Articles 32, 34, 35; Bailey and Daws, *The Procedure of the UN Security Council* (3rd edn, 1998), 154.
[19] For example, Australia S/PV 2619; France S/PV 2608; UK S/PV 2713.
[20] UN Publications, *The Blue Helmets: A Review of United Nations Peacekeeping* (3rd edn, 1996); Higgins, *United Nations Peacekeeping 1946–1967* (4 vols); Morphet, 'UN Peacekeeping

institution has evolved through the practice of the United Nations and its legality is no longer challenged by any state. Commentators have speculated that a legal basis may be found in the power of the General Assembly to establish subsidiary organs, or under Chapter VI on peaceful settlement, or under Article 40 on provisional measures.[21] All of these may be theoretical possibilities, but in practice, there has been no express reference to any of these in the resolutions establishing peacekeeping forces and the debate seems to be without practical significance. The UN Blue Books on Peacekeeping and the UN Home Page on Peacekeeping do not concern themselves with this problem.

Between 1948 and 1988 fifteen peacekeeping forces were established. It is common to divide the practice of peacekeeping in the Cold War into four periods: the nascent (1948–56), the assertive (1956–67), the dormant (1967–73), and the resurgent (1974–87).[22] Different writers have drawn up different lists of these forces over the years, but the UN's own list can probably be treated as authoritative.[23] There was a wide variety of types of operation which came to share the name of peacekeeping. Most of the Cold War peacekeeping operations were interposed between states; very few were established to play a role in ending civil conflict.

The earliest were limited observation forces; the first major forces were UNEF established by the General Assembly in the Middle East from 1956 to 1967, and ONUC, established by the Secretary-General with Security Council authorization in the Congo[24] from 1960 to 1964. The former operation led to agreement on the basic principles underlying what later came to be known as peacekeeping operations; the latter revealed the difficulties that arise when these principles are compromised.

After UNEF was terminated the UN Secretary-General produced a report examining the 'new and unique experiment' and setting out guidance for future operations.[25] The mandate of UNEF under General Assembly Resolutions 998 and 1000 had been 'to secure and supervise' the cease-fire and withdrawal of foreign forces from Egypt, and later to maintain peaceful conditions in the area by its deployment along the armistice line between Egypt and Israel. It had been agreed that the force should not include troops from the permanent members of the Security

and Election-Monitoring', in Roberts and Kingsbury (eds), *United Nations, Divided World* (2nd edn, 1993), 183; Hill and Malik, *Peacekeeping and the United Nations* (1996); White, *Keeping the Peace* (1993).

[21] Simma (ed.), *The Charter of the United Nations: A Commentary* (1994) at 590.
[22] Hill and Malik, *Peacekeeping and the United Nations* (1996), Chapter 2.
[23] UNDPKO website, http://www.un.org/Depts/dpko; UN Publications, *The Blue Helmets: A Review of United Nations Peacekeeping* (3rd edn, 1996).
[24] Subsequently Zaire, and now the Democratic Republic of the Congo.
[25] Report of the Secretary-General, *Summary study of the experience derived from the establishment and operation of the Force*, A/3943.

Council or of any other country which for geographical or other reasons might have a special interest in the conflict. It operated with the consent of the host state and was withdrawn when Egypt terminated its consent in 1967. In determining the composition of the force serious consideration was to be given to the views of the host state. UNEF had been interposed between regular, national military forces which were subject to a cease-fire. It had a clear-cut mandate and was neutral in relation to international political issues. It operated under a *Status of Forces Agreement* (SOFA), with the host state establishing the rights and privileges of the UN forces.

Interestingly, the Secretary-General said that the nature of peacekeep-ing precluded the employment of UN forces in situations of an essentially internal nature. Nor should such a force enforce any specific political solu-tion; it would require specific authority for offensive action. It should use force only in self-defence. A wide interpretation of this right was not acceptable because it would blur the distinction between these operations and those under Chapter VII.

Most of the UN operations which later became known as peacekeeping operations followed these principles. But ONUC departed from them and showed the dangers of so doing. It was originally created to assist the government of the Congo in the chaotic aftermath of independence in 1960. Its mandate was to give the government military and technical assistance after the collapse of essential services until national security forces were able fully to meet their tasks, but it became embroiled in the conflict when its original mandate was expanded. Resolution 161, although not formally passed under Chapter VII, used the language of Article 39 in its concern that the danger of civil war constituted a threat to international peace and security. It authorized ONUC to use force going beyond self-defence in order to prevent civil war; the resolution urged ONUC 'to take all appropriate measures to prevent the occurrence of civil war in the Congo ... including the use of force, if necessary, in the last resort.' Later Resolution 169 went further and not only affirmed the terri-torial integrity of the Congo but authorized the Secretary-General to use force to end the attempted secession of the province of Katanga and to expel foreign mercenaries. This led ONUC to assume responsibilities that went beyond normal peacekeeping. Its numbers were increased to 20,000 to respond to the expansion of its mandate and it was involved in fight-ing against those seeking secession.[26] The type of controversy that arose over the extension of peacekeeping in the Congo has recurred with regard to the operations in Yugoslavia and Somalia.

---

[26] See Higgins, *United Nations Peacekeeping 1946–1967*, Vol III, 5; Abi-Saab, *The United Nations Operations in the Congo 1960–1964* (1978); Virally, 'Les Nations Unies et L'affaire du Congo', 1960 AFDI 557.

Of the fifteen forces established in the Cold War five still exist: three in the Middle East, UNMOGIP in Kashmir, and UNFICYP in Cyprus. This highlights a problematic characteristic of peacekeeping: that it may help to freeze the situation, or even protect an aggressor's territorial gains.[27]

A NEW LEGAL ORDER? CHAPTER VII AFTER THE COLD WAR

The end of the Cold War brought with it a steep decline in the use of the veto. In 1990 the only vetos were two by the USA, one on a resolution about its 1989 intervention in Panama and one on a resolution to establish a Commission on Israel's activities in the occupied territories. There were then no vetos until 1993; the first was by Russia on the funding of the peacekeeping force in Cyprus. The USA did not use its veto for five years from 1990; when it did revert to this, it was again to protect Israel from condemnation of its breaches of international humanitarian law in the occupied territories. This was its thirtieth veto in protection of Israel since 1972.

The UN response to the Iraqi invasion of Kuwait gave rise to hopes of a new era for the UN and of a New World Order.[28] This was only the second time that the Security Council had authorized armed action against an aggressor state. The Security Council met the day after the invasion and passed Resolution 660, declaring that there had been a breach of international peace and security; expressly acting under Articles 39 and 40 it condemned the invasion and demanded the withdrawal of Iraqi forces from Kuwait. It called on Iraq to withdraw and imposed economic sanctions in Resolution 661. When this proved ineffective to secure Iraq's withdrawal from Kuwait, Resolution 678 authorized member states cooperating with the government of Kuwait to use 'all necessary means' to uphold and implement Resolution 660, calling on Iraq to withdraw from Kuwait and to restore international peace and security in the area.[29] It is clear from the Security Council debates that this formula was understood to mean the use of force. The same (or similar) euphemistic formula has been used in almost all the subsequent resolutions authorizing the use of force by states. In the case of Iraq no further resolution was passed until

---

[27] This has led to argument about payment with regard to UNIFIL in Lebanon and UNFICYP in Cyprus; some states have argued that payment should be by Israel and Turkey respectively. See Martinez, 'Le financement des opérations de maintien de la paix de L'Organisation des Nations Unies', 81 RGDIP (1987) 102.

[28] UN Blue Book Series, Vol IX, *The UN and the Iraq/Kuwait Conflict 1990–1996.*

[29] The resolution was passed by 12–2 (Cuba, Yemen) – 1 (China), 1990 UNYB 189 at 204. On abstentions in the Security Council, see Bailey and Daws, *The Procedure of the UN Security Council* (3rd edn, 1998) at 250.

the cease-fire three months later and there was considerable controversy over lack of UN control over the operation conducted by the coalition forces. No time limit was set to the member state action; Security Council involvement was secured only by the duty on the member states to keep it informed.[30]

As with the Korean action, there was debate as to the legal foundation of the coalition action in *Operation Desert Storm* against Iraq. Unlike the resolutions on Korea, Resolution 678 does refer to Chapter VII, but it does not refer to any specific article. Also in contrast to the Korean action, the coalition forces in Iraq did not operate under UN flag or UN command; they were simply authorized to act against Iraq by the Security Council. Some claim this as an Article 42 action; others regard it as justified by Chapter VII generally; yet others say that it is collective self-defence authorized by the Security Council.[31] The Secretary-General, in his *Agenda for Peace*, did not treat it as Article 42 action, but said simply that the Security Council had authorized member states to use force.[32] The question is only of practical significance if the legal basis affects the scope of the permissible action that could be taken by states. Because the coalition forces did not in fact continue to use force to secure the overthrow of the government of Saddam Hussein the disagreement as to the legal basis of the operation does not seem to have had practical consequences. It is doubtful whether this would have counted as necessary and proportionate action if the force had been based on collective self-defence, but it could conceivably have been justified under Chapter VII as action necessary to restore international peace and security. Despite the uncertainty as to its legal basis, this operation marked the start of a new era for the UN and Resolution 678 provided a model for later authorization of the use of force by member states. However, the optimism prevalent at the time of Resolution 678 has since dissipated.

ARTICLE 41: TRANSFORMATION?

The Security Council has made vastly increased use of Article 41 in recent years. It is only if such measures would be inadequate or have already proved to be inadequate that the Security Council may turn to measures involving armed force under Article 42. As in the case of the measures against South Africa, it has done so without express mention of the arti-

---

[30] The Security Council met in private during the operation: 1991 UNYB 168. On the concern over lack of Security Council control, see, for example, Sarooshi, *The United Nations and the Development of Collective Security* (1999) at 174 and works cited there.
[31] Sarooshi, ibid.; Greenwood, 'New World Order or Old? The Invasion of Kuwait and the Rule of Law', 55 MLR (1992) 153.   [32] 31 ILM (1992) 953.

cle; the Security Council simply refers to Chapter VII in general. Starting with the comprehensive sanctions against Iraq after its invasion of Kuwait, the Security Council has taken measures with regard to Yugoslavia, Somalia, Libya, Liberia, Cambodia, Haiti, Angola, Rwanda, Sudan, Sierra Leone, Kosovo, Afghanistan, and Ethiopia and Eritrea. It has authorized force to secure the effective implementation of measures in many of these cases (those of Iraq, Yugoslavia, Somalia, Haiti, and Sierra Leone).[33] For example, Resolution 787 on sanctions against Yugoslavia (Serbia and Montenegro) 'calls upon states acting nationally or through regional agencies or arrangements to use such measures commensurate with the specific circumstances as may be necessary under the authority of the Security Council to halt all inward and outward maritime shipping in order to inspect and verify their cargoes and destinations and to ensure strict implementation of the provisions of resolutions 713 and 757'. As in the earlier authorization of the UK to use force to enforce the embargo on Rhodesia, the precise legal basis for this was not specified and remains unclear.

The above list of Article 41 measures includes several cases of sanctions against non-state actors, as in the first measures against Rhodesia; Article 41 does not specify any limitation on those against whom sanctions may be taken. Thus the Security Council condemned the failure of the Khmer Rouge in Cambodia to carry out their obligations under the 1991 *Paris Peace Agreements* and imposed an embargo on the supply of petroleum products to areas occupied by any party not complying with the agreements.[34] Second, more extensive measures were taken against UNITA in Angola when it refused to comply with the peace agreement and with Security Council resolutions.[35] Third, in September 1994 sanctions were imposed against the Bosnian Serbs for their refusal to accept the peace settlement for the former Yugoslavia.[36] Also sanctions were imposed on the unrecognized Taliban regime in Afghanistan after their failure to surrender a terrorist leader, Usama Bin Laden, to a country where he would be brought to justice.[37] More recently arms embargoes that were initially imposed as blanket prohibitions on the export of arms to a state have been modified to allow the provision of arms to the legitimate government or international forces but to prohibit their supply to illegitimate forces. This was done with regard to Rwanda and Sierra Leone.[38]

The Secretary-General's view is that Article 41 measures are designed not to punish but to secure compliance with international obligations.

---

[33] Iraq: SC Res 665, 670; Yugoslavia: SC Res 757, 787; Somalia: SC Res 794; Haiti: SC Res 875; Sierra Leone: SC Res 1132. [34] SC Res 792.
[35] SC Res 864, 1127, 1173, 1176, 1295.   [36] SC Res 942.   [37] SC Res 1267.
[38] In SC Res 1011 and SC Res 1132, 1171, 1299.

Some of the measures are clearly not directed against any wrongdoer.[39] Thus certain of the arms embargoes were imposed not because a state had broken international law, but to try to secure that a conflict did not escalate. The arms embargoes on Yugoslavia, Somalia, Liberia, Rwanda, Ethiopia, and Eritrea were of this type, and those on Yugoslavia and Somalia were imposed with the consent of the governments. Some of these measures have been described as a symbolic substitute for any real action by the international community, faced with the need to be seen to take some action in response to serious conflict. Other arms embargoes were imposed in response to a breach of international law, such as those against the illegal regimes in Rhodesia and South Africa, and subsequently those against Libya for its sponsorship of terrorism and in 1998 against FRY for its behaviour in Kosovo.[40] Arms embargoes were also imposed against those who seized power illegally in Haiti and Sierra Leone. In some of these cases the state affected by the arms embargo challenged its legality or sought its removal on the ground that the embargo violated its right to self-defence. This was argued unsuccessfully by Bosnia-Herzegovina in an attempt to secure exemption from the arms embargo imposed on the whole of Yugoslavia, and with more success by Rwanda.[41] The embargo was lifted as far as arms destined for the government were concerned, but otherwise remained in place.[42]

Where measures were taken under Article 41 in response to a breach of international law, and so may accurately be described as sanctions, generally the resolutions specify the breach of international law and the action needed to secure the lifting of the measures. For example, Resolution 757 imposing sanctions on Yugoslavia (Serbia and Montenegro) specified that this was in response to non-compliance with Resolution 752 demanding an end to intervention in Bosnia; it said that all states should adopt the comprehensive measures listed until the Security Council decided that Yugoslavia (Serbia and Montenegro) had complied with Resolution 752. But sometimes it is unclear or controversial exactly what action would be required by the wrongdoing state. The question of terminating the sanctions against Iraq, in place since Resolution 661 in 1991, has led to divisions between members of the Security Council. The cease-fire Resolution 687 requires the destruction of Iraq's chemical, biological, and nuclear weapons and long-range ballistic missiles and an undertaking by Iraq not to develop any such weapons in the future; when this is achieved, the Security Council will lift the sanctions imposed in Resolution 661. There

[39] The contrary assertion of Frowein in Simma (ed.), *The Charter of the United Nations: A Commentary* (1994) at 632 does not seem to be supported by practice.
[40] Even in this case Russia insisted that the aim of the arms embargo was not to punish Yugoslavia: SC 3868th meeting, March 1998.   [41] See Chapter 4 below.
[42] SC Res 1011.

have been many conflicts over the implementation of this provision. Iraq has repeatedly claimed to have complied with its disarmament obliga-tions and has repeatedly been found by the UN inspection team to have been concealing its weapons. The USA has been accused of wanting to impose wider conditions on Iraq, going beyond disarmament, in order to perpetuate the sanctions.[43] Nevertheless, there are reports that certain members of the Security Council are ready to consider lifting the sanc-tions. As the Secretary-General said, the humanitarian situation in Iraq poses a serious moral dilemma for the UN. The UN has always been on the side of the weak and the vulnerable, yet here it is accused of causing suffering to an entire population. The UN is in danger of losing the prop-aganda war about who is responsible for the situation in Iraq, President Saddam Hussein or the UN.[44]

There was also some concern over the sanctions against Libya, imposed in Resolution 748, adopted by 10–0–5; this said that the sanctions were imposed because of Libya's refusal to provide a full and effective response to US, UK, and French requests for the surrender of Libyan nationals, allegedly responsible for terrorist attacks. The sanctions would be lifted after Libya demonstrated by concrete actions its renunciation of terrorism. Libya challenged the validity of this resolution in the *Lockerbie* case before the ICJ. It argued either that the resolution does not in fact require the surrender of the alleged terrorists or, if it does, it is *ultra vires* and invalid.[45] Support for the sanctions from African and Arab states showed signs of crumbling from 1997 onwards. After the two alleged ter-rorists were surrendered for trial in a Scottish court in the Netherlands the sanctions were suspended in 1999.[46] Similar resolutions more explicitly seeking the surrender of alleged terrorists from Sudan and Afghanistan were also passed and followed by the imposition of sanctions.[47]

The increased use of sanctions in recent years has intensified concern over effectiveness, humanitarian considerations of the impact of the measures on the population of the target state and the economic impact on the neighbouring states.[48] The Secretary-General, in his *Supplement to the Agenda for Peace*, writes of the difficulties of determining the objectives of Article 41 measures, of monitoring and of avoiding unintended effects. He describes sanctions as a blunt instrument that may harm vulnerable

[43] Gray, 'After the Ceasefire: Iraq, the Security Council and the Use of Force', 65 BYIL (1994) 135.   [44] UN Press Release SC/6834.

[45] *Cases Concerning Questions of Interpretation and Application of the 1971 Montreal Convention arising from the Aerial Incident at Lockerbie (Jurisdiction and Admissibility)*, ICJ Reports (1998); 37 ILM (1998) 587.   [46] SC Res 1192; S/PRST/1999/10; 38 ILM (1999) 926.

[47] SC Res 1044, 1054, 1070 on Sudan; SC Res 1267 on Afghanistan.

[48] Leigh, 'The Political Consequences of Economic Embargoes', 89 AJIL (1999) 74; see also, for example, the SC debate on sanctions against Iraq, SC 4120th meeting.

groups, interfere with the work of humanitarian agencies, and conflict with the development objectives of a state. Also they may be counter-productive in that they may provoke a patriotic response as opposed to a rejection of those whose behaviour led to the imposition of sanctions.[49] These considerations have led to attempts to create 'smart sanctions' that directly affect those responsible for the transgression without unduly harming the general population. Thus in Haiti and Angola the measures were designed to restrict the freedom to travel of those who had illegally violated peace agreements or Security Council resolutions and also to freeze foreign bank accounts of those responsible for the unlawful action; in the case of Angola measures were also taken to prohibit trade in diamonds from the areas controlled by UNITA.[50] The Security Council is currently still working on the improvement of the sanctions system.

PEACEKEEPING AFTER THE COLD WAR: EXPANSION AND RETREAT

The Security Council vastly increased its peacekeeping activities after the Cold War. The numbers give a clear picture of the scope of the change. In the forty years from 1945 to 1988 there were fifteen operations; in the ten years from 1988 to 1998 over twenty-five new forces were established.[51] The majority of these new forces were deployed within states involved in civil wars rather than between states. In his 1995 *Supplement to An Agenda for Peace* the Secretary-General noted this transformation in the nature of peacekeeping. He wrote of peacekeeping as being in a time of transition and discussed the difficulties that had arisen. Because most peacekeeping after the Cold War had been within states challenges had arisen that had not been encountered since the Congo operation in the 1960s. UN forces were faced by irregular forces rather than regular armies, civilians were the main victims of the conflicts, civil conflict brought humanitarian emergencies and refugees, state institutions collapsed. All these factors meant that international intervention had to go beyond military and humanitarian operations to bringing about national reconciliation and re-establishing effective government. Peacekeeping in such contexts was more complex and more expensive than more limited operations such as

[49] *Supplement to Agenda for Peace* S/1995/1. The Security Council in SC Res 1196 on the situation in Africa also confirmed the importance of ensuring that embargoes should have clear objectives.

[50] This was done in the case of UNITA, where the measures implemented by SC Res 1173 and 1176 (1998) were directed against the leaders of UNITA and the areas of Angola controlled by it. The prohibition on the sale of diamonds from these areas was reinforced by the creation of a panel of experts in SC Res 1237 (1999) to make the sanctions effective. Targeted measures were also taken against those responsible for the coup in Haiti in SC Res 917.

[51] See list of peacekeeping forces on UN website, http://www.un.org/Depts/dpko.

monitoring a cease-fire or controlling a buffer zone. This was to be a second generation of peacekeeping.[52] According to the Secretary-General, the concept of peacekeeping is not static; there are as many types of peacekeeping operations as there are types of conflict.[53]

The forces established in 1999 in Kosovo and East Timor marked a further development:

they are qualitatively different from almost any other the Organisation has ever undertaken. In each place the United Nations is the administration, responsible for fulfilling all the functions of a State—from fiscal management and judicial affairs to everyday municipal services, such as cleaning the streets and conducting customs formalities at the borders. This is a new order of magnitude for an organization that more customarily provides States with technical assistance in such areas, rather than assuming complete responsibility for them. And it is a new order of magnitude for peacekeeping operations as well, making them extraordinarily complex and almost as dependent on civilian experts as on military personnel.[54]

Accordingly UNMIK and UNTAET could be seen as the third generation of peacekeeping.

The end of Cold War conflicts

UN peacekeeping forces played a major role in the settlement of long-standing conflicts that had been fuelled by the Cold War. In 1988 the USSR announced its intention of withdrawing its troops from Afghanistan; this was followed by the 1988 *Geneva Accords*, a set of four agreements involving Afghanistan, Pakistan, the USA, and the USSR. As part of this settlement the Security Council established UNGOMAP with the relatively limited mandate to investigate and report on possible violations of the Geneva Accords. Although it was set up as part of the UN Secretary-General's Good Offices Mission, its use of military personnel meant that it was classified as a peacekeeping operation. It monitored the withdrawal of Soviet forces and also operated on the border between Afghanistan and Pakistan, investigating reports of violations of the non-interference and non-intervention obligations in the peace accords. It was terminated in 1990.[55]

The interconnected peace settlements in Namibia, Angola, and Mozambique also involved the creation of new UN peacekeeping operations. The United Nations had been concerned with Namibia since 1948, when South Africa first purported to incorporate the mandated territory. In 1966

---

[52] S/1995/1; 1995 UNYB 175.   [53] 1993 UNYB 3.
[54] Address of Deputy-Secretary-General, Press Release DSG/SM/91.
[55] UN Publications, *The Blue Helmets: A Review of United Nations Peacekeeping* (3rd edn, 1996) at 661.

the UN General Assembly terminated the South African mandate over Namibia and placed it under the responsibility of the UN, but South Africa continued illegally to occupy Namibia. In 1978 the Security Council agreed on a plan for Namibian independence in Resolution 435; Western states sought a negotiated solution and the USA and the UK opposed further Chapter VII action against South Africa other than the arms embargo in Resolution 918. South Africa subsequently linked the question of the independence of Namibia and its compliance with Resolution 435 with the withdrawal of Cuban forces from Angola. The General Assembly and the Security Council rejected this linkage, but it nevertheless formed the basis of the agreement eventually reached in 1988 between Angola, Cuba, and South Africa. In 1989 the Security Council finally began to implement the Resolution 435 Settlement and, as part of this, agreed on the establishment of UNTAG. This was in many ways an unusual operation, with functions going beyond traditional peacekeeping; it was the first of the 'second generation of peacekeeping'. At its maximum it comprised 8,000 personnel. Its mandate was to ensure free and fair elections and to create the conditions that would make such elections possible. UNTAG included military, civilian, and police components. The military section was responsible for monitoring the cease-fire, the withdrawal of South African troops, and some border monitoring. In March 1990 Namibia finally reached independence and UNTAG was terminated.[56]

The fate of Angola was tied to that of Namibia; it had been subjected to civil war ever since its independence from Portugal in 1975, with Cuba and the USSR supporting the government and South Africa and the USA supporting the opposing UNITA forces.[57] Also SWAPO operated from Angola in its operations to liberate Namibia from South African occupation. As part of the wider regional settlement in 1988, Angola, South Africa, and Cuba agreed on the withdrawal of Cuban troops from Angola; Angola and Cuba asked for the establishment of a UN military observer force to verify compliance with their bilateral agreement on troop withdrawal. A small force, UNAVEM, was created and successfully completed this limited mission. Negotiations on the settlement of the internal conflict in Angola between the government and UNITA led to the 1991 *Peace Accords* for Angola and the creation of UNAVEM II. This was now given a much more extensive mandate; it was to verify implementation of the *Peace Accords*. This involved monitoring the cease-fire, the collection of the armed forces of the two parties into assembly areas and the demobilization of those forces, the formation of joint armed forces, the police, and supervising the elections. But serious problems arose; after the elections

---

[56] UN Publications, *The Blue Helmets: A Review of United Nations Peacekeeping* (3rd edn, 1996) at 201.	[57] Ibid. 231.

in October 1992 UNITA resorted to fighting and the situation deteriorated in early 1993. UNAVEM II operated as a channel for communications between the parties, but its mandate came to seem unrealistic in
the absence of an effective cease-fire. The Security Council reacted to
UNITA's non-cooperation with the peace process by imposing an arms
and oil embargo on it. Negotiations eventually led to the *Lusaka Protocol*
in October 1994 and a new attempt at securing a cease-fire. In 1995
UNAVEM III took over from UNAVEM II; it was assigned political, military, police, humanitarian, and electoral functions. But the authorized
number of troops were not provided and, like its predecessor, it ran into
difficulties because of delays and non-cooperation, mainly by UNITA. Its
mandate was terminated in July 1997 and it was replaced by an observer
mission. But the security situation worsened and MONUA was not able
to carry out its mandate; it was terminated in February 1999. Angola was
once again in a state of war. The United Nations held UNITA and its
leader, Jonas Savimbi, responsible for this crisis.[58]

The UN experience in Mozambique was happier. Like Angola, Mozambique had been involved in civil war almost since the date of its independence from Portugal in 1975; again South Africa and Western states
denied the legitimacy of its government and supported forces aiming
to overthrow it. The SWAPO liberation movement operated from
Mozambique against South African occupation of Namibia. In 1992 a
General Peace Agreement was signed between the parties and the UN was
asked to oversee the implementation of this Agreement. The Security
Council created UNOMOZ and over two years it verified the cease-fire
and secured the assembly and demobilization of the opposing armed
forces; it assisted in the creation of a new joint army; its police component
monitored the national police; it coordinated humanitarian activities;
assisted the massive repatriation programme; and secured the implementation of free and fair elections in October 1994.[59]

In Cambodia the 1991 *Paris Agreements* were intended to end many
years of conflict. After the 1978 intervention in Cambodia by Vietnam to
overthrow the Khmer Rouge regime of Pol Pot, states' support for the
competing parties divided partly on Cold War lines. The Vietnamese
announced the withdrawal of their troops in 1989 and the permanent
members of the Security Council worked together to achieve a negotiated
solution. Under the Peace Agreement the UN was to organize free elections, coordinate the repatriation of refugees, coordinate economic rehabilitation and reconstruction, supervise and verify the withdrawal of

[58] S/PRST/1999/3; S/1999/49.
[59] UN Publications, *The Blue Helmets: A Review of United Nations Peacekeeping* (3rd edn,
1996) at 319; UN Blue Book Series, Vol V, *The United Nations and Mozambique 1992–1995*.

foreign forces, the cease-fire and demobilization; coordinate the release of prisoners of war and foster an environment of peace and stability. The UN sent in an advance mission, UNAMIC; then UNTAC, one of the largest and most ambitious peacekeeping forces in the history of the UN, was deployed in 1992. UNTAC was made up of seven distinct components: human rights, electoral, military, civil administration, police, repatriation, and rehabilitation. At its largest it comprised 20,000 personnel. It was terminated in 1993.[60]

Finally, in Central America the long-lasting conflicts involving significant outside intervention by Eastern and Western blocs were terminated by the 1986 *Esquipulas II Agreement* between the five states of the region. As part of this agreement Costa Rica, El Salvador, Guatemala, Honduras, and Nicaragua agreed on the deployment of the first substantial UN peacekeeping operation in Latin America. Initially ONUCA was established to verify the commitments by the states parties to stop aid to opposition forces in other states and not to allow the use of their territory for attacks on other states. Mobile teams of military observers were created. The mandate was subsequently expanded to include verification of the cessation of hostilities and demobilization of irregular forces; and subsequently to monitor the separation of forces and the cease-fire in Nicaragua. ONUCA completed its mandate in 1992.[61]

In El Salvador it was replaced by ONUSAL in 1991; negotiations between the government and the opposition FMLN led to a series of agreements, culminating in the 1992 *Chapultepec Agreement*. Under these preliminary agreements ONUSAL was to monitor agreements between the government and FMLN; its initial mandate was to verify compliance with the *Human Rights Agreement*. The *Chapultepec Agreement* further expanded the role of ONUSAL to cover verification of the cease-fire and the separation of forces, prevention of the movement of forces, and the supervision of the destruction of its weapons by FMLN. ONUSAL was to have three, later four, divisions—Human Rights, Military, Police, and Electoral—to supervise the different aspects of the Peace Agreement. It completed its functions in 1995.[62]

This brief survey of UN peacekeeping operations in those conflicts where the end of the Cold War facilitated settlement shows that the forces played an extensive role involving a very wide range of activities. Only UNGOMAP in Afghanistan was a limited force of a traditional kind; the others were large and complex operations with functions including disarmament, election monitoring, human rights, and the re-establishment of

[60] *The Blue Helmets* at 447; UN Blue Book Series, Vol II, *The United Nations and Cambodia 1991–1995.*   [61] Ibid. 413.
[62] Ibid. 423; UN Blue Book Series, Vol IV, *The United Nations and El Salvador 1990–1995.*

civil society. They involved significant civilian participation as well as more traditional military functions such as monitoring cease-fires. In the terms of the *Agenda for Peace*, these were peace-building as well as peace-keeping operations.

The start of new conflicts

But the end of the Cold War also contributed to the outbreak of new conflicts. The break-up of Yugoslavia and the competing claims of Croats, Bosnians, and Serbs led to conflict; the UN undertook several operations in the former Yugoslavia. The break-up of the USSR into its fifteen constituent republics also brought with it pressures for further subdivision on ethnic lines and the first UN peacekeeping force in the former USSR was established in Georgia in 1993. Conflict had broken out because of the determination of the Abkhazians to pursue independence, although at the time that Georgia became independent the Abkhazians were only a 20 per cent minority within Abkhazia. After a cease-fire was agreed between Georgian government and Abkhazian secessionist forces in July 1993 the Security Council created UNOMIG, an observer force of up to 88 members with a traditional mandate to verify compliance with the cease-fire and investigate reports of violations. However, as soon as deployment began the cease-fire broke down; Abkhazian forces occupied the whole of the territory and displaced the Georgian inhabitants. Resolution 881 in November 1993 authorized the continued presence of UNOMIG, with an interim mandate to suit the changed circumstances. It was simply to maintain contacts with both sides and monitor the situation. After another cease-fire was agreed CIS peacekeeping forces were deployed; accordingly the mandate of UNOMIG was amended. Its strength was increased to 136 observers and it was given new tasks: the verification of the new cease-fire, the observation of the CIS peacekeeping forces, verification that the parties and their heavy military equipment were withdrawn from certain security zones, and monitoring the withdrawal of volunteer forces from outside Abkhazia. Political stalemate continued because of the fundamental disagreements between the government and the Abkhazian separatists on the recognition of the territorial integrity of Georgia and the repatriation of refugees.[63]

After the former USSR republic Tajikistan became an independent state previous political and economic structures broke down and civil war broke out; initially many of the opposition forces retreated to Afghanistan and conducted cross-border attacks. The UN became involved in seeking a peaceful settlement and the *Tehran Agreement* was reached between the

---

[63] *The Blue Helmets* at 569.

opposing Tajik forces in September 1994. In this the parties agreed to halt hostile acts on the Tajik/Afghan border and within Tajikistan and to establish a Joint Commission to oversee the implementation of the Agreement. The Security Council created UNMOT, a small operation initially of fifty-five mixed military and civilian personnel, to investigate cease-fire allegations on its own initiative or at the request of the Joint Commission. The situation worsened in 1996, but talks continued. In November 1997 the situation was calmer and UNMOT's mandate was expanded to include monitoring disarmament and demobilization. Its civilian component was to take on new functions in monitoring human rights, police, and elections. After the successful holding of the first multi-party elections UNMOT was terminated in May 2000.[64]

Also, when the USSR and the USA and other powers withdrew support from governments which they had helped to keep in power during the Cold War, those governments were weakened and in many cases civil war resulted. UN peacekeeping operations played a role in some of these conflicts. Thus, for example, the UN became involved in peacekeeping operations in Somalia when civil war broke out after the overthrow of the Siad Barre regime, which had long been supported by Western states. In Liberia, when the government of the Western-backed President Doe was overthrown, the UN sent a peacekeeping force to supplement the work of a regional force.[65] In the Central African Republic the reluctance of France to continue to prop up the government contributed to instability; a UN force was successfully deployed.

In other African states it was internal as much as Cold War factors which contributed to the outbreak of conflict.[66] The DRC plunged into conflict after the overthrow of President Mobutu, supported in power by France during the Cold War; conflicts in neighbouring Rwanda, Uganda, and Angola spilled over into the DRC. Here and in Sierra Leone the parties struggled for power and control of the rich resources of the state. In Sierra Leone a UN peacekeeping force was established in 1999 but ran into difficulty at the end of the year; in the DRC the Security Council provided for the establishment of a UN force but its deployment was delayed.

---

[64] *The Blue Helmets* at 589.   [65] See Chapter 7 below.
[66] See Report of the Secretary-General, *The causes of conflict and the promotion of durable peace and sustainable development in Africa*, S/1998/318, 37 ILM (1998) 913.

The extension of peacekeeping

Optimism about the role that peacekeeping forces would be able to play after the end of the Cold War was one of the factors that led to an expansion of their mandates. They not only took on wider roles in the re-creation of civil society as described above, there was also a blurring of the differences between peacekeeping and enforcement action. The Secretary-General, in his 1992 *Agenda for Peace,* had envisaged a more ambitious role for peacekeeping forces. He wrote of a new concept of peacemaking; this would involve UN forces operating under Article 40, of the UN Charter to enforce rather than merely monitor cease-fires.[67] The expansion of the traditional model of peacekeeping and blurring of the distinction between peacekeeping and enforcement was most marked in Yugoslavia and Somalia; UN experience in these conflicts led to a rethinking of the relationship and a much more cautious attitude, by both the Secretary-General in his 1995 *Supplement to An Agenda for Peace* and the Security Council. Thus in Yugoslavia and Somalia the traditional distinctions between the two types of operation seemed to break down. As described above, the generally agreed principles that had evolved through state practice required that peacekeeping forces should be impartial, not take sides, lightly armed, not use force except in self-defence, operate with the consent of the host state, and should not usually include forces from permanent members of the Security Council or states with a political interest in the host state. They had no express basis in the UN Charter and did not operate under Chapter VII of the Charter.

Yugoslavia

In Yugoslavia and Somalia peacekeeping and enforcement action blurred together when peacekeeping forces were given functions that went beyond traditional peacekeeping. In Yugoslavia UNPROFOR was set up in 1991 as a traditional peacekeeping force, The first sixteen resolutions on UNPROFOR were all passed without any reference to Chapter VII. But it was sent in to Croatia and then Bosnia in the absence of a firm cease-fire and without the cooperation of the parties. Divisions in the Security Council and lack of agreement as to strategy led to a long series of over thirty resolutions on UNPROFOR and the gradual expansion of its mandate. Its initial mandate under Resolution 743 in February 1992 was 'to create the conditions of peace and security required for the negotiation of

---

[67] *Agenda for Peace* para 44, 31 ILM (1992) 953.

an overall settlement of the Yugoslav crisis'. This was expanded to authorize the protection and operation of Sarajevo airport in Bosnia, the monitoring of UN-protected areas in Croatia, and the delivery of humanitarian
aid.

The first major expansion of its mandate was in Resolution 776 (12–0–3,
September 1992), which authorized UNPROFOR to use force to secure the
delivery of humanitarian aid. China abstained on this vote because the
resolution impliedly referred to Chapter VII through its reference back to
Resolution 770, which had been passed under Chapter VII. China said
that this changed the nature of the peacekeeping force; UNPROFOR
should, as a UN peacekeeping operation, follow the generally recognized
guidelines established in past UN peacekeeping operations in implementing its mandate. This resolution contained disturbing elements
which departed from these guidelines. On the one hand, it recognized
that UNPROFOR should observe the normal rules of engagement of UN
peacekeeping forces in implementing its new mandate, namely to use
force in self-defence. On the other hand, it approved the use of force in
self-defence when troops are blocked by armed forces. China was concerned that UNPROFOR would run the risk of plunging into armed
conflict.[68] This fear was borne out by events; it proved difficult for
UNPROFOR to secure the delivery of aid by force and each party saw the
delivery of aid to the other parties as a threat to it and so they were not
willing to cooperate.

From February 1993 the Security Council began to use Chapter VII in
its resolutions on UNPROFOR. The first time it did this was apparently on
the initiative of France which said that, given the problems encountered
by UNPROFOR, it was unthinkable to continue the present mandate in
its current form. France said that the reference to Chapter VII was not
intended to change the nature of the force from peacekeeping to peacemaking; they were motivated by the need to guarantee the safety of
UNPROFOR. China challenged this, saying that the resolution establishing UNPROFOR had not invoked Chapter VII and that the safety of
UNPROFOR personnel could be dealt with by their right of self-defence
without invoking Chapter VII. Resolution 807 expressed concern at the
lack of cooperation of the parties and at the cease-fire violations; it
determined that the situation constituted a threat to peace and security in
the region and then went on: 'determined to ensure the security of
UNPROFOR, and to this end acting under Chapter VII', they demanded
that the parties comply fully with the UN peacekeeping plan in Croatia,
observe Security Council resolutions, and respect fully UNPROFOR's
unimpeded freedom of movement.[69] Almost all the subsequent resolutions

[68] SC 3114th meeting (1992) at 11–12.   [69] SC 3174th meeting (1993).

on UNPROFOR also invoked Chapter VII; as France acknowledged, not to have resorted to Chapter VII in later resolutions would have been the worst of signals for the parties. France said that the reference to Chapter VII did not imply any automatic authority to resort to force other than in self-defence, but gave UNPROFOR the authority it needed to surmount the obstacles in the way of the execution of its mandate.[70]

UNPROFOR was later also authorized to use force in protection of the safe havens. The Security Council, faced with calls to act in response to ethnic cleansing, especially that by the Bosnian Serbs, proclaimed several 'safe areas' in 1993; it followed this by extending the mandate of UNPRO-FOR in Resolution 836 to enable it not only to monitor the cease-fire and to participate in the delivery of humanitarian relief in the safe areas, but also 'acting in self-defence to take the necessary measures including the use of force' in reply to bombardments and armed incursions into the safe areas. But member states were not willing to provide the 30,000 troops estimated by the UN Secretary-General to be necessary for the performance of this mandate. The 7,000 troops actually provided were militarily incapable of protecting the safe areas against attack by the Bosnian Serbs and the protection for one ethnic group was seen as undermining the impartiality of UNPROFOR.[71]

Despite the invocation of Chapter VII in these resolutions, UNPROFOR was still obstructed in the performance of its mandate by all the parties; the Security Council responded with the creation of the Rapid Reaction Force (RRF) in June 1995. This was a mobile, well-armed force, to operate under the existing mandate of UNPROFOR. But states were divided as to whether this was really a continuation of UNPROFOR or a new enforcement force. China argued that the RRF would constitute a *de facto* change in the peacekeeping status of UNPROFOR; it was being established for enforcement action and would thus become a party to the conflict. Russia agreed that the resolution gave the impression that the RRF was intended to operate against one party to the conflict, the Bosnian Serbs. But the UK and France insisted that no change in the nature of UNPROFOR was intended. Both Croatia and Bosnia put obstacles in the way of the operation of the RRF on the ground.[72]

When in 1995 Croatia demanded the withdrawal of UNPROFOR from its territory, it was replaced by UNCRO. The Security Council affirmed its determination to ensure the security and freedom of movement of

---

[70] SC 3344th meeting (1994); 3527th meeting (1995).

[71] Akashi, 'The Use of Force in a UN Peacekeeping Operation: Lessons Learnt from the Safe Areas Mandate', 19 Fordham ILJ (1995) 312; 1994 UNYB 522; Report of the Secretary-General pursuant to GA Resolution 53/35 (1998), *Srebrenica report*.

[72] Gray, 'Host-State Consent and UN Peacekeeping in Yugoslavia', 7 Duke Journal of Comparative and International Law (1996) 241.

personnel of the new peacekeeping operation and to that end acted under
Chapter VII in Resolution 981 establishing UNCRO. The force was nevertheless still regarded as a peacekeeping force, dependent on Croatia's consent for its deployment in its territory. It was given a mandate more
acceptable to Croatia because the name of the force (UN Confidence
Restoration Operation in Croatia) was designed to acknowledge Croatia's
sovereignty over the whole of its territory. Its mandate was essentially to
create the conditions that would facilitate a negotiated settlement consistent with the territorial integrity of Croatia and which guarantees the
security and rights of all communities living in a particular area of
Croatia. Despite Croatia's success in renegotiating the mandate of the
force, it did not cooperate with UNCRO. It overran the areas where
UNCRO operated in 1995 and its mandate became unworkable.[73]

After the 1995 Peace Agreement the UN created new peacekeeping
operations. In Bosnia UNMIBH replaced UNPROFOR; in Croatia UNCRO
was replaced by UNTAES and UNMOP. The last was to monitor the
demilitarization of the Prevlaka peninsula and was established without
any reference to Chapter VII. But the Security Council again blurred the
distinction between peacekeeping and enforcement operations in its creation of UNTAES; this alone of the three operations was created under
Chapter VII, even though with the consent of Croatia. The Security
Council in Resolution 1037 determined that the situation in Croatia continued to constitute a threat to international peace and security. 'Acting
under Chapter VII', it decided to establish a UN peacekeeping operation
for an initial period of twelve months. The reference to Chapter VII seems
to have been inspired by concern over the need to ensure the security and
freedom of movement of the personnel of the UN peacekeeping operation in Croatia. The mandate of the military component of UNTAES
was to supervise the demilitarization agreed in the Basic Agreement on
the Region of Eastern Slavonia, Baranja and Western Sirmium between
the government of Croatia and the local Serbian community, to monitor
the safe return of refugees, to contribute by its presence to the maintenance of peace and security in the region, and otherwise to assist in
implementation of the Basic Agreement. The UN Secretary-General had
expressed some concern over the creation of this force; he argued that it
should have proper enforcement powers if it was to be able to carry out its
functions. There was a danger that it would run into the same sort of problems as UNPROFOR had earlier. But despite the reference to Chapter
VII, the new force was not given enforcement powers. It was member
states who were authorized to take all necessary measures in defence of

---

[73] UN Publications, *The Blue Helmets: A Review of United Nations Peacekeeping* (3rd edn, 1996) at 543.

UNTAES.[74] The force was terminated in January 1998 although a major part of its mandate, the repatriation of displaced Serbs, was left undone.

Thus the use of Chapter VII in the resolutions on UNPROFOR, UNCRO, and UNTAES increased expectations as to what they might achieve, but did not in itself give these forces enforcement powers in the absence of further express provision. The lack of realistic mandates and of adequate resources meant that the forces were not able to fulfil the expectations raised.

Somalia

The UN commitments in the former Yugoslavia led to reluctance to get involved in Somalia even though the scale of the loss of life there was much greater than that in the former Yugoslavia.[75] This led to accusations of double standards; the Security Council was said to care less about conflict in Africa than in Europe.[76] The Security Council first responded to the civil war in Somalia by issuing a statement in January 1991, but it was not until a year later in January 1992 that the Security Council passed Resolution 733, expressing grave alarm at the rapid deterioration of the situation and the heavy loss of life and widespread material damage. It determined that the situation was a threat to peace and security and imposed an arms embargo. In April 1992 it established a peacekeeping force; Resolution 751 said that the Security Council was deeply disturbed by the magnitude of the human suffering caused by the conflict and concerned that the continuation of the situation constituted a threat to international peace and security.

As in Bosnia, there was no real cease-fire in place and the peacekeeping force was sent in even though there was no peace to keep. Its mandate led it into conflict with the warring parties. Its initial mandate was not only to monitor the cease-fire in the capital, Mogadishu, but also to provide security for those delivering humanitarian aid. This was the first time in the history of the UN that a force was established with the primary purpose of making possible the delivery of emergency assistance to a civilian population. Its purpose was to deter attacks on humanitarian relief operations and it was to use force only in self-defence. But UNOSOM I proved unable to operate beyond Mogadishu or to carry out its mandate in the absence of cooperation of the warring parties.

[74] SC Res 1037, 1120.

[75] UN Publications, *The Blue Helmets: A Review of United Nations Peacekeeping* (3rd edn, 1996) at 285; UN Department of Peacekeeping, Lessons Learned Unit, *The Comprehensive Report on Lessons Learned from UN Operations in Somalia, April 1992–March 1995*; Clarke and Herbst (eds), *Learning from Somalia: The Lessons of Armed Humanitarian Intervention* (1997); UN Blue Book Series, Vol VIII, *The United Nations and Somalia 1992–1996.*

[76] See below at 187.

The Security Council responded to this by sending a different type of force. In December 1992 it authorized the deployment of member states in a multinational non-UN force, UNITAF, to 'use all necessary means to establish a secure environment' for humanitarian relief operations. Operational command was assumed by the USA and it contributed more than two-thirds of the troops. The authorization of this operation was another new departure for the UN.[77] It was the first time that Chapter VII was used, not to authorize force against a wrongdoing state such as Iraq, but for humanitarian aims in a civil war. More than twenty states contributed forces and at the maximum UNITAF reached 37,000 troops, of which the vast majority were US citizens. It was created as a temporary operation, and when the USA decided to terminate its participation the force could not go on. It achieved limited success in securing the delivery of humanitarian relief, but it was not able to operate throughout Somalia and it did not secure the disarmament of the warring factions. It handed over to another UN force in March 1993 without having established a secure environment for humanitarian operations.

The Security Council in Resolution 814 (adopted unanimously) replaced both UNOSOM I and UNITAF by UNOSOM II, the first peace-enforcement operation under the command of the UN, created under Chapter VII, with functions that went beyond traditional peacekeeping.[78] UNOSOM II was mandated in Resolution 814 to operate throughout Somalia: to monitor the cessation of hostilities and compliance with the cease-fire agreements; to prevent any resumption of violence and, if necessary, to take appropriate action against any faction violating the cease-fire; to secure disarmament of the organized factions; to maintain security at ports, airports and lines of communication needed for deliveries of humanitarian assistance; to protect the UN civilian staff; to clear mines; and to assist refugees to return home. This innovative combination of peacekeeping and Chapter VII proved only partially successful. UNOSOM II was drawn into conflict with one of the warring factions and was not able to carry out its mandate in the absence of an effective cease-fire.

---

[77] On authorization to member states to use force, see below at 187.

[78] For the first time the USA contributed troops to serve under UN command; this led to serious problems in securing unity of command. The USA tended to operate outside the UN command structure. The Secretary-General, in the *Supplement to an Agenda for Peace* (S/1995/1 at para 41), said that the experience in Somalia underlined again the necessity for a peacekeeping force to act as an integrated whole. That necessity is all the more imperative when the mission is operating in dangerous conditions. There must be no attempt by troop-contributing governments to provide guidance, let alone give orders, to their contingents on operational matters. To do so creates divisions within the force. It can also create the impression that the operation is serving the policy objectives of the contributing governments rather than the collective will of the UN as formulated by the Security Council. Such impressions inevitably undermine an operation's legitimacy and effectiveness.

Resolution 837 was passed in response to the murder of UN peacekeepers by one of the factions led by General Aidid; it extended UNOSOM II's mandate and drew it into conflict with the faction. This resolution authorized the UN forces to arrest and try those responsible for the killings. Under this mandate US troops suffered losses when their operation in pursuit of General Aidid went wrong. After this the USA was no longer willing to continue the operation and announced a complete withdrawal of its forces by March 1994.

Accordingly UNOSOM II's mandate was redefined in a more limited way in February 1994 in Resolution 897; this determined that there was still a threat to international peace and security and was again passed under Chapter VII, but nevertheless marked a return to traditional peace-keeping. UNOSOM II was no longer to use force to secure disarmament or in response to cease-fire violations. It would use force only in self-defence. In the continued absence of cooperation from the warring parties and the reluctance of contributing states to maintain their troops in Somalia the operation was terminated in March 1995. According to the Secretary-General, this was the first UN operation to be withdrawn by the Security Council before completing its mission.[79] Somalia still has no properly functioning central government.

Contemporaneous peacekeeping and enforcement operations

The second way in which the Security Council blurred the traditional distinctions between peacekeeping and enforcement action in Yugoslavia and Somalia was through the establishment of both peacekeeping and enforcement forces to operate at the same time. In these conflicts the Security Council first established a peacekeeping force and later authorized states to take enforcement action. This happened first in Yugoslavia, where UNPROFOR was operating on the ground as a peacekeeping force; the Security Council subsequently authorized NATO member states to use force under Chapter VII. The first resolution to do this was Resolution 770 in August 1992; it called upon states acting nationally or through regional arrangements or agencies to take all measures necessary to facilitate, in coordination with the UN, the delivery by relevant UN humanitarian organizations and others of humanitarian assistance to Sarajevo and other parts of Bosnia. That is, it authorized the use of force to ensure the safety of humanitarian convoys, if necessary by clearing a path through hostile forces. It was followed by Resolution 816, authorizing states 'under the authority of the Security Council and subject to close

---

[79] Report of the Secretary-General, *The causes of conflict and the promotion of durable peace and sustainable development in Africa*, S/1998/318, 37 ILM (1998) 913 at para 31.

coordination with the Secretary-General and UNPROFOR' to take all necessary measures in the air-space of Bosnia to ensure compliance with the ban on flights over Bosnia that the Security Council had imposed earlier in an attempt to secure the safety of humanitarian operations. Under this resolution NATO set up *Operation Deny Flight*. The scope of the right to use force was limited to responding to violations of the no-fly ban; it did not allow pre-emptive action against surface-to-air weapons systems on the ground. Resolution 836 on the protection of safe havens proved more important. The Security Council had declared that six towns were safe havens, but had failed either to demilitarize them (except Srebrenica and Zepa) or to provide adequate numbers of peacekeeping forces to protect them. Therefore it turned to NATO to protect the safe havens. Resolution 836 (June 1993) decided that member states could take all necessary measures, through the use of air power, in and around the safe areas in Bosnia to support UNPROFOR in the performance of its mandate to deter attacks and reply to bombardments and armed incursions on the safe areas.[80]

The first use of force by NATO under these resolutions was in February 1994 against aircraft violating the no-fly zone. It followed this by at first minor and then more serious uses of force to protect the safe areas in 1994 and 1995. It became clear that NATO air attacks could not deter action on the ground by the Bosnian Serbs against the safe areas; also UN peacekeeping forces on the ground were vulnerable to attack and were endangered by member state operations against Bosnian Serbs. This was made very clear when the Bosnian Serbs responded to a NATO air attack in April 1995 by taking UNPROFOR troops hostage. UNPROFOR forces were unable to defend the safe areas of Srebrenica and Zepa; the Security Council then withdrew its forces from areas it could not defend and thus made it possible for the NATO air forces to act. Finally, NATO used force in *Operation Deliberate Force*, a major operation to defend Sarajevo under Resolution 836. This brought an end to the conflict in Bosnia and led to the conclusion of the December 1995 Peace Agreement.[81]

All these resolutions authorizing states to use force, to secure the delivery of humanitarian aid, to enforce the no-fly zone, and to protect safe havens asserted the obligation on member states to act in close coordination with the Secretary-General. In practice this was interpreted to require not merely that NATO inform the Secretary-General of its use of force, but that the Secretary-General's consent was needed before NATO could act. This was to secure coordination with UNPROFOR operations and to

[80] SC Res 908 and 958 later supplemented this provision to deal with actions against safe areas originating in Croatia.

[81] See UN Publications, *The Blue Helmets: A Review of United Nations Peacekeeping* (3rd edn, 1996), 485; 1994 UNYB 522 at 523, 525; *Srebrenica report* para 117–23, 452; *General Framework Agreement* 38 ILM (1999) 75.

avoid actions that would endanger UNPROFOR forces on the ground. This restriction on NATO's freedom to use force led to divisions in the Security Council; the USA, without troops on the ground, was more enthusiastic about air-strikes against Bosnian Serbs than troop-contributing states France and the UK, and called for greater freedom for NATO to act. Again this shows the difficulties of combining the two types of operations.

After the end of the conflict the combination of the two types of force was more successful. Following the Peace Agreement the Security Council combined in Bosnia a UN Mission (UNMIBH) including a civilian police force (IPTF) and IFOR. The latter was a multinational force of NATO and non-NATO member states under unified command established under Chapter VII. In Resolution 1031 the Security Council determined that the situation in Bosnia was still a threat to international peace and security. It authorized member states to establish IFOR; this 50,000-strong force was to 'use all necessary means to effect the implementation of and to ensure compliance' with the Peace Agreement. At the end of 1996 IFOR was replaced by a smaller multinational stabilization force, SFOR; its mandate in Resolution 1088 was essentially the same as that of IFOR.

Again in Somalia the Security Council's attempts to combine peace-keeping and enforcement forces proved not wholly successful. As described above, it first established a peacekeeping force, UNOSOM I, then in Resolution 794 authorized states to conduct a joint operation (UNITAF) to 'use all necessary means to establish as soon as possible a secure environment for humanitarian relief operation'. There was meant to be a clear division of functions between the two forces, but UNITAF failed to deliver the secure environment for humanitarian assistance that it was mandated to provide. It was unwilling to undertake the disarmament functions that the UN had expected it to carry out and which would have given the peacekeeping force the security to carry out its mandate.[82]

Thus the combination of two different types of operations at the same time during on-going armed conflict led to serious problems in Yugoslavia and in Somalia. It emerged that peacekeeping and enforcement actions were not necessarily compatible during armed conflict. Peacekeeping operations were endangered by forcible intervention and the states authorized to use force were hampered by the presence on the ground of vulnerable peacekeeping forces. There were fundamental problems as to who could authorize operations and of coordination between

---

[82] See UN Department of Peacekeeping, Lessons Learned Unit, *The Comprehensive Report on Lessons Learned from UN Operations in Somalia, April 1992–March 1995*. Subsequently, when UNITAF and UNOSOM I were replaced by UNOSOM II, the USA at the same time maintained its own forces in support of UNOSOM II but outside the UN command; UN Publications, *The Blue Helmets: A Review of United Nations Peacekeeping* (3rd edn, 1996) at 301.

the two forces. The combination of the two types of operation has proved more successful after the conclusion of conflict.[83]

LESSONS FROM YUGOSLAVIA AND SOMALIA: A RETURN TO TRADITIONAL PEACEKEEPING?

The lessons of Yugoslavia and Somalia are now widely accepted. Peacekeeping and enforcement forces may not be compatible. The two types of action are not simply activities on a continuum; it is not possible gradually to increase the functions of peacekeeping forces to include elements of enforcement without endangering the impartiality of the force. If a peacekeeping force is to be given Chapter VII enforcement functions it must be given commensurate forces, equipment, and logistical support. The Secretary-General, in his 1995 *Supplement to An Agenda for Peace*, abandoned the expansive optimism of the earlier *Agenda for Peace* and retreated to the more traditional concept of peacekeeping. He stressed the basic principles of consent of the parties, impartiality, and the non-use of force except in self-defence. Three aspects of recent mandates had led peacekeeping operations to undermine these basic principles: the tasks of protecting humanitarian operations during continuing warfare, protecting civilian populations in safe areas, and pressing the parties to achieve national reconciliation at a pace faster than they were ready to accept. It has repeatedly been asserted that peacekeeping forces must never again be deployed into an environment in which there is no cease-fire or peace agreement.

The Security Council in a Statement welcomed the Secretary-General's analysis in the *Supplement to An Agenda for Peace* and also reiterated the practical requirements of successful peacekeeping: the need for a clear mandate, a fixed time frame, an effective command structure, and secure financing.[84] Other bodies have also affirmed the traditional approach to peacekeeping in recent years. The USA, in President's Decision Directive on Reforming Multilateral Peace Operations, stressed the need for the traditional model of peacekeeping to be followed.[85] The CIS and OSCE provisions on peacekeeping similarly follow the traditional pattern.[86] The UN Special Committee on Peacekeeping report on the undertaking of a comprehensive review of the whole question of peacekeeping also stressed the importance of respect for the principles of consent, impartiality, and

---

[83] This may also be seen in Kosovo and East Timor; see below at 189.
[84] S/PRST/1995/9; see also Special Peacekeeping Committee Press Release GA/PK/163.
[85] 33 ILM (1994) 795.
[86] CSCE 31 ILM (1992) 1385; CIS 35 ILM (1996) 783. See Chapter 7 below.

non-use of force, except in self-defence; the need for clear mandates, objectives, and command structures.[87]

Subsequent operations show that these lessons from Yugoslavia and Somalia have had a deep impact on states. They generally have not deployed peace-keeping forces until a cease-fire was in place, and in Security Council resolutions they stress that the presence of a force depends on the continuation of a cease-fire and cooperation of parties. The Security Council's role in Rwanda reflected a marked caution.[88] Member states were not willing to commit resources to Rwanda at the same time that they were heavily involved in the former Yugoslavia and Somalia. The Security Council's first involvement was in response to incursions by Tutsi rebels (the RPF) against the government of Rwanda from Uganda. In July 1993 the Security Council established a border monitoring force, UNOMUR, on the Uganda side of the border with Rwanda.[89] When a comprehensive peace agreement was made between government and opposition forces in Rwanda, the UN agreed to assist in the implementation of the agreement. In October 1993 the Security Council established UNAMIR at the joint request of the government and the RPF opposition with the mandate of 'contributing to the establishment and maintenance of a climate conducive to the secure installation and subsequent operation of the transitional government'. It was to monitor the cease-fire and oversee demilitarization and demobilization and assist with mine clearance. It comprised 2,500 lightly armed and equipped military personnel.

However, the parties were not all committed to the implementation of the peace agreement and in April 1994, after the Presidents of Rwanda and Burundi died together in a plane crash, the country sank into conflict. There were terrible massacres of Tutsis and moderate Hutus by supporters of the Rwandan government; between 500,000 and a million people were killed in three months. UNAMIR's mandate to implement the peace agreement became irrelevant; nor did it have the resources to prevent this genocide. The Belgian contingent was unilaterally withdrawn from UNAMIR and its strength was reduced to 1,500.[90] Senior military officials

---

[87] Report of the Special Committee on Peacekeeping, A/54/839; see also UN Press Release GA/SPD/179 (May 2000).

[88] UN Publications, *The Blue Helmets,: A Review of United Nations Peacekeeping* (3rd edn, 1996) at 339; UN Department of Peacekeeping, *Comprehensive Report on Lessons Learned from UNAMIR*; UN Blue Book Series, Vol X, *The United Nations and Rwanda 1993–1996*.

[89] UNOMUR ended in 1994 when RPF became the new government of Rwanda.

[90] The participation of Belgian forces was an example of a departure from the convention that states with historic interests in an area should not participate in peacekeeping forces there, see below at 184.

said that 'the force level was too small for military action to protect the victims of the slaughter and the force's capabilities had not been put together with a conflict situation in mind. With an extremely weak logistics base, UNAMIR was also rapidly running out of food and medical supplies . . . It had no ambulances and mainly soft-skin vehicles for the transportation of troops.'[91]

During the massacres in April 1994 the Secretary-General accordingly gave the Security Council a choice between three options: a large Chapter VII force with the power to avert massacres, a small group of around 270 military personnel to act as intermediary between the two parties, or complete withdrawal. The Security Council chose the second option. Resolution 912 altered UNAMIR's mandate; it was to act as an intermediary in an attempt to secure a cease-fire, assist in humanitarian operations, and monitor developments. The situation deteriorated and there were mass movements out of the state. It was not until May 1994 that the Security Council attempted to authorize more effective action. In Resolution 918 it imposed an arms embargo on Rwanda and expanded UNAMIR's mandate to authorize it to contribute to the security of refugees and civilians through the establishment of secure humanitarian areas and the provision of security for humanitarian operations; it was to take action in self-defence against person or groups who threaten protected sites and populations. But the Secretary-General ran into serious difficulty in trying to obtain more troops; states did not want to become involved in another civil war. After the massacres UNAMIR had only 500 troops on the ground.

The RPF forces gained control over almost the whole of the country and declared a cease-fire in July 1994. After the civil war ended UNAMIR eventually reached its full strength of 5,500 troops in October 1994; states were still reluctant to contribute civilian police to assist in the rebuilding of society. In early 1995 former government forces were re-arming and the situation was tense. The new government of Rwanda informed the UN that UNAMIR no longer had a role to play; it had been established at a time of genocide and civil war in order to contribute to the security of displaced persons. This was now the responsibility of the new government, as was national security and the protection of humanitarian convoys. Accordingly UNAMIR's mandate was redefined in a more limited way in June 1995 and its size was reduced until it was eventually withdrawn by March 1996.

It is clear that states' reluctance to play a major role in Rwanda was strongly influenced by the experience of Yugoslavia and Somalia. The

---

[91] UN Department of Peacekeeping, *Comprehensive Report on Lessons Learned from UNAMIR*, Part 2, para 10.

failure to prevent the genocide in Rwanda has, according to the Secretary-General, 'had especially profound consequences in Africa. Throughout the continent, the perception of near indifference on the part of the international community has left a poisonous legacy that continues to undermine confidence in the Organization.'[92]

THE RELATION OF PEACEKEEPING AND CHAPTER VII

It also seems to have been accepted after the experience of Yugoslavia and Somalia that peacekeeping should be kept separate from Chapter VII actions; after these operations the Security Council did not set up peace-enforcement operations during armed conflict; it did not base its establishment of new peacekeeping operations on Chapter VII. Thus the forces in Georgia, Liberia, Tajikistan, Central African Republic, and Sierra Leone were not established under Chapter VII.

In contrast, in 1999 both UNMIK in Kosovo and UNTAET in East Timor were created under Chapter VII. After the end of the 1999 NATO operation against Yugoslavia to bring an end to the humanitarian catastrophe in Kosovo Yugoslavia accepted a political solution to the Kosovo crisis. This included the withdrawal of its military, police, and paramilitary forces from Kosovo. The Security Council re-engaged in the search for peace in Kosovo. Under Resolution 1244 it both authorized member states to use force and also authorized the Secretary-General to establish an international civilian administration, UNMIK. This was to promote the establishment of substantial autonomy and self-government in Kosovo, perform basic civilian administration functions, organize the development of provisional institutions for democratic and autonomous self-government, facilitate a political process designed to determine Kosovo's future status, support the reconstruction of key infrastructure, support humanitarian aid, and maintain civil law and order, including establishing local police forces. Never before had the United Nations assumed such broad, far-reaching, and important executive tasks. The invocation of Chapter VII was thus necessary not to give UNMIK any wide right to use force, but, first, to authorize force by member states, and, second, to legitimize the very wide powers of UNMIK to restore a semblance of normal life to the province and to make clear that its operations do not depend on the consent of Yugoslavia.

In East Timor UNTAET, referred to in Resolution 1264 as a peacekeeping force, was also established under Chapter VII. In 1999 Indonesia had

---

[92] Report of the Secretary-General, *The causes of conflict and the promotion of durable peace and sustainable development in Africa*, S/1998/318, 37 ILM (1998) 913 para 11.

finally agreed to the holding of a consultation process, organized by the UN through UNAMET, to determine the wishes of the inhabitants of East Timor, the Portuguese territory it had invaded and occupied in 1975. After the inhabitants had indicated in the consultation process that they sought independence widespread and serious disorder broke out as pro-Indonesia militias spread terror by their attacks on the people of East Timor; nearly half of the population fled their homes. The UN Security Council in Resolution 1264 first authorized a multinational force to restore peace and security; it also agreed that this force would be replaced as soon as possible by a peacekeeping force. Accordingly in Resolution 1272 it acted under Chapter VII in establishing UNTAET, to be endowed with overall responsibility for the administration of East Timor and empowered to exercise all legislative and executive authority. It was to have a military component of up to 8,950 troops and was also authorized 'to take all necessary measures' to fulfil its mandate. The resolution (in contrast to Resolution 1264) did not refer to any consent by Indonesia to the establishment of UNTAET, beyond a reference to the importance of cooperation between Indonesia, Portugal, and UNTAET in the implementation of the resolution. Here the reference to Chapter VII was necessary because UNTAET was to take over the enforcement powers of the multinational force as soon as possible; also UNTAET itself was 'given a robust mandate' and empowered to use force by the reference to all necessary measures.[93] In February 2000 the multinational force transferred military command of the territory to UNTAET.

The use of force by peacekeeping operations

Traditionally peacekeeping forces were limited to the use of force in self-defence. This was not expressly spelled out in the resolutions establishing their mandates, but was affirmed in the reports of the Secretary-General that usually set out the details of the operations. Thus in the case of UNEF the Secretary-General affirmed the right of self-defence and warned that this should be used only under strictly defined conditions, because if there was a wide interpretation of self-defence this might blur the distinction between peacekeeping and Chapter VII action.[94] Nevertheless, it was understood that this right to self-defence included the right to resist attempts by forceful means to prevent the force from discharging its duties under its mandate. This was also generally set out in the UN Secretary-General's reports rather than made express in Security Council

---

[93] Report of the Secretary-General on the Situation in East Timor, S/1999/1024 (4 October 1999).   [94] Report of the Secretary-General on UNEF, A/3943 para 179.

resolutions.[95] UNIFIL was exceptional in that Resolution 467 (1980) expressly quoted the Secretary-General's report on the operation and provided that 'The Force shall not use force except in self-defence.' Also 'Self-defence would include resistance to attempts by forceful means to prevent it from discharging its duties under the mandate of the Security Council.'

When UNPROFOR ran into problems in Bosnia and Croatia the Security Council made express its right to self-defence in Resolutions 776, 836, and 871. In the first of these UNPROFOR was authorized, in accordance with the Secretary-General's report, to use force to protect humanitarian convoys; this authorized it to act in self-defence, including situations in which armed persons attempted by force to prevent them from carrying out their mandate. Resolution 836 on the protection of safe areas was unusual in that it expressly authorized UNPROFOR to use force in self-defence. This approach was followed in Resolution 871, which authorized UNPROFOR in carrying out its mandate in Croatia, acting in self-defence, to take the necessary measures, including the use of force, to ensure its security and freedom of movement. Some concern arose that express provision in some resolutions for self-defence might give rise to the false inference that if a resolution did not expressly authorize the right of self-defence a peacekeeping force could not legally use force in self-defence.

Perhaps in response to this concern, in later resolutions on Rwanda and Angola a different approach was adopted. Instead of *authorizing* the use of force the resolutions *recognized* the right of peacekeeping operations to use force in self-defence. Resolution 918 on UNAMIR thus 'recognizes that UNAMIR may be required to take action in self-defence against persons or groups who threaten protected sites and populations, United Nations and other humanitarian personnel or the means of delivery and distribution of humanitarian relief'. Subsequently even this more cautious approach has been abandoned and a different formulation was adopted with regard to MINURCA, the first new peacekeeping force created in Africa since 1993. This was established in response to a crisis in the Central African Republic beginning in 1996; it was to replace a member state force, MISAB, set up after the *Bangui Peace Agreements* of January 1997. Resolution 1159 'affirms that MINURCA may take action to ensure its security and freedom of movement'. This mission was successfully completed in February 2000; the Secretary-General said that MINURCA had done much to restore peace and security in the CAR and to create conditions conducive to the successful conduct of national elections, the restructuring of the security forces, the training of the national police, and the launching of major economic and social

---

[95] For example, UN Publications, *The Blue Helmets: A Review of United Nations Peacekeeping* (3rd edn, 1996) at 60, 84.

reforms. The Secretary-General said that it showed how much could be achieved by peacekeeping operations in Africa with the cooperation and political will of the parties, their commitment to peace and national reconciliation, a clear mandate, appropriate resources, and the strong and consistent support of the international community. It had also broken new ground through its close cooperation with international financial institutions to promote political and financial stability.[96]

Sierra Leone and the DRC

In marked contrast, the peacekeeping forces created for Sierra Leone and the DRC were established in much less promising circumstances and ran into serious difficulties. They were expressly given wider responsibilities under Chapter VII. This seems to mark a reversion to the practice in the former Yugoslavia and Somalia. In Sierra Leone a military coup in May 1997 led to disorder; a small UN force, UNOMSIL, was sent in to supplement an existing ECOMOG regional force.[97] The democratically elected President Kabbah was restored in May 1998, but the opposition RUF, led by Sankoh, did not fully accept the election result and disorder continued. After the *Lomé Peace Agreement* of July 1999 UNOMSIL was replaced by UNAMSIL, a larger force of up to 6,000 military personnel, to cooperate with the government in the implementation of the agreement and to assist in the implementation of the disarmament, demobilization and reintegration plan. The Secretary-General had recommended that the new force should be large and capable and should operate on the basis of robust rules of engagement.[98] In Resolution 1270, adopted unanimously, the Security Council decided under Chapter VII that in the discharge of its mandate UNAMSIL may take the necessary action to ensure the security and freedom of movement of its personnel. But it went further, apparently in response to the Rwanda experience; it also authorized UNAMSIL, 'within its capabilities and areas of deployment, to afford protection to civilians under imminent threat of physical violence'. In the debate on this resolution Argentina commented on the use of Chapter VII; it said that it was appropriate that the draft resolution strengthened UNAMSIL's rules of engagement with the additional authority of Chapter VII of the Charter. The protection of civilians under Chapter VII was a pertinent development. It introduced a new legal and moral dimension. It indicated

[96] UN Press Release GA/SPD/164, October 1999.
[97] See Chapter 7 below. Http://www.un.org/Depts/DPKO/Missions/unosil.
[98] Seventh and Eighth Reports of the Secretary-General on UNOMSIL, S/1999/836, S/1999/1003; First Report of the Secretary-General on UNAMSIL, S/1999/1223; UN Press Release SC/6742.

that the Council had learned from its own experiences and would not be unresponsive when innocent civilians were attacked.[99]

Later the Security Council expanded the role and size of UNAMSIL in order to enable it to take over ECOMOG's role. Resolution 1289 again invoked Chapter VII in the body of the resolution in order to revise UNAMSIL's mandate to authorize it to provide security at key locations, important intersections, and major airports; facilitate the free flow of people, goods, and humanitarian assistance; and provide security in the disarmament process. The government of Sierra Leone welcomed the fact that the revised mandate and additional responsibilities of UNAMSIL were fully backed by Chapter VII of the Charter. His government regarded as one of the most significant provisions of the resolution the Council's decision to authorize UNAMSIL to afford protection to civilians under imminent threat of physical violence.[100] The UK stressed that UNAMSIL was not a Chapter VII peace enforcement operation, but said that it was necessary to adopt a robust and serious stance against possible threats.[101] The Secretary-General said that the force would function with the cooperation of the parties, but, through its military presence, capabilities, and posture, would be able to deter attempts to derail the peace process. However, in practice UNAMSIL was not able to fulfil this wide mandate when the opposition forces resorted to violence again in 2000.[102] Hundreds of UN forces were taken hostage by the rebel RUF. The Secretary-General said that UNAMSIL had been designed as a peacekeeping force and was not equipped for an enforcement operation. It was attacked by one of the parties that had pledged cooperation before it was properly deployed.[103] The emergency Security Council debate revealed a division between states. Some, including several West African states, called for the revision of the mandate of UNAMSIL to make it into a Chapter VII force with greater powers; others argued that the existing mandate with its already wide powers under Chapter VII was adequate, and that the immediate problem was to ensure that the mission had the capacity to carry out the tasks this mandate imposed.[104]

Similar references to Chapter VII were made in the Security Council resolutions providing for a peacekeeping force in the DRC. Chapter 3 of this book described the outbreak of conflict in the DRC, the overthrow of

---

[99] SC 4054th meeting; UN Press Release SC/6742.
[100] SC 4099th meeting; UN Press Release SC/6801.   [101] Ibid.
[102] SC 4139th meeting; UN Press Release SC/6857.   [103] Ibid.
[104] UN Press Release SC/6857. In 2000 the UN force was supplemented by UK troops, present at the invitation of the government of Sierra Leone to allow for the safe evacuation of British nationals. The UK made it clear that UK forces would not be deployed in a combat role as part of UNAMSIL, but their presence on the ground helped to stabilize the situation; they also provided 'technical military advice' to the UN and to the government (Statement by the Secretary of State for Defence in the House of Commons, 15 May 2000).

President Mobutu, and the intervention of Uganda, Rwanda, Namibia, Angola, and Zimbabwe in the fighting in 1998. The Security Council expressed concern, but took no further action until the conclusion of the *Lusaka Peace Agreement* in July 1999. This agreement proposed the establishment of an appropriate force to be constituted, facilitated, and deployed by the UN in collaboration with the OAU.[105] The Secretary-General pointed out that in order to be effective any UN peacekeeping mission in the DRC would have to be large and expensive. It would require the deployment of thousands of international troops. It would face tremendous difficulties and be beset by risks. Deployment would be slow. The huge size of the country, the degradation of its infrastructure, the intensity of its climate, the intractable nature of some aspects of its conflict, the number of parties, the high levels of mutual suspicion, the large population displacements, the ready availability of small arms, the general climate of impunity, and the substitute of armed force for the rule of law in much of the territory combine to make the DRC a highly complex environment for peacekeeping.[106]

The preliminary deployment of a small number of UN liaison officers deepened the Secretary-General's appreciation of the difficulties. The Security Council went on to establish an observer mission, MONUC, but the peace agreement remained fragile and the situation deteriorated.[107] Six months after the peace agreement the Security Council passed Resolution 1291 in February 2000, providing for the expansion of the mandate of MONUC and of the size of the force up to 5,537 military personnel. It was to monitor the implementation of the cease-fire agreement and to investigate violations of the cease-fire; and to develop an action plan for the overall implementation of the cease-fire agreement with particular emphasis on disengagement, disarmament, demobilization and resettlement. Under Chapter VII MONUC was to take the necessary action in the areas of deployment of its infantry battalions and, as it deems within its capabilities, to protect UN personnel, facilities, installations, and equipment; ensure the security and freedom of movement of its personnel; and protect civilians under imminent threat of physical violence.

Many states expressed concern about this resolution; it had been adopted as a compromise. It fell far short of matching the mission's mandate with the resources needed for it to succeed. The deployment of a MONUC peacekeeping operation might create inflated and unrealistic expectations.[108] By May 2000 there had still not been any deployment.

---

[105] *Lusaka Peace Agreement*, S/1999/790.
[106] Report of the Secretary-General on the UN Preliminary Deployment in the DRC, S/1999/790.   [107] http://www.un.org/Depts/dpko/monuc/monucM.
[108] SC 4104th meeting; UN Press Release SC/6809.

The response of states to the situations in Sierra Leone and the DRC indicate that the lessons of the former Yugoslavia, Somalia, and Rwanda may be fading. It has proved easier to stipulate conditions for successful peacekeeping than to live up to them in practice. The relation of peacekeeping and Chapter VII is still problematic. The use of Chapter VII in resolutions on peacekeeping has raised expectations, but the repeated failure by member states to establish realistic mandates and to provide the necessary resources has led peacekeeping forces into difficulty. Criticism has been directed at the UN and its forces, criticism that should often more appropriately be directed at member states.

CONSENT TO PEACEKEEPING

Traditionally peacekeeping forces have operated with the consent of the host state.[109] This ostensibly simple principle masks considerable complexity. The difficulties that can arise in practice, and the complexity of the notion of consent, were particularly apparent in the case of Yugoslavia, where UNPROFOR was originally established at the request of the government of Yugoslavia.[110]

The traditional requirement that UN peacekeeping operations have the consent of the host state was established in the case of the first major UN peacekeeping operation, UNEF. When Egypt withdrew its consent to the stationing of UNEF on its territory the UN Secretary-General regarded this as final and the UN forces were precipitately withdrawn.[111] In Yugoslavia Croatia's withdrawal of consent to the continuation of UNPROFOR on its territory led to the withdrawal of this force and its replacement by UNCRO. Rwanda's notification of the end of its consent to UNAMIR terminated that operation, to the regret of the UN Secretary-General; at roughly the same time Burundi refused to consent to the establishment of a peacekeeping force on its territory.[112]

---

[109] *Certain Expenses* case, ICJ Reports (1962) 151; White, *Keeping the Peace* (1993), 202; Higgins, *United Nations Peacekeeping* (4 vols, 1972).

[110] On host-state consent, see Gray,'Host-State Consent and UN Peacekeeping in Yugoslavia', 7 Duke Journal of Comparative and International Law (1996) 241; Wippman, 'Treaty-Based Intervention: Who Can Say No?', 62 University of Chicago Law Review (1995) 607, and 'Military Intervention, Regional Organization and Host-State Consent', 7 Duke Journal of International and Comparative Law (1996) 209.

[111] Report of the Secretary-General on UNEF, A/3943.

[112] On the withdrawal of consent by Croatia, see Gray, 'Host-State Consent and UN Peacekeeping in Yugoslavia', 7 Duke Journal of Comparative and International Law (1996) 241 at 265; on Burundi, see UN Publications, *The Blue Helmets: A Review of United Nations Peacekeeping* (3rd edn, 1996) at 366; on Rwanda, S/1995/1018, UN Blue Book Series, Vol X, *The United Nations and Rwanda 1993–1996* at 600.

In cases where UN peacekeeping forces have been established in states involved in civil conflict the UN has increasingly sought the consent not only of the government but also of the warring parties. It seems that this has been done not out of legal obligation, but as a matter of securing the effectiveness of the operation. Thus in Yugoslavia the UN Secretary-General sought the consent of all the concerned parties to the initial deployment of UNPROFOR in Croatia and its subsequent deployment in Bosnia. This followed the earlier practice in Angola, Namibia, Cambodia, and Mozambique, but was formalized in that the early Security Council resolutions on UNPROFOR expressly referred to the consent of the concerned parties.[113]

There was also consultation on the initial mandate and composition of the force. The latter had in the early days of peacekeeping been the subject of some debate between host states and the UN as to who should have the final say in determining the nationality of the troops in the peacekeeping force. Through practice it became established that the final word was with the UN, but in fact behind-the-scenes discussions took place between the host state, the members of the Security Council, and troop contributing states. In the first peacekeeping operations troops were not accepted from permanent members of the Security Council or from states with interests in the host state. But this practice was abandoned in Cyprus and Lebanon (where the UK and France respectively contributed troops) and was not followed in Yugoslavia. Faced with the difficulty of obtaining troops and the need for well-trained and equipped forces to meet the more ambitious mandates, the former restrictions on troop contribution were abandoned.

The end of the Cold War means that the reasons behind the limitations have partly disappeared in that the fear that contribution of troops by the USA or the USSR would threaten the impartiality of the force and draw the UN into the Cold War is no longer applicable. However, the experience with US participation in UNOSOM II shows that there are dangers in the participation of the one remaining superpower. The Secretary-General, in speaking of the dangers of a divided command in Somalia, showed that US unwillingness to submit to UN command led to the perception that the operation was serving the policy objectives of the contributing governments rather than the collective will of the UN as formulated by the Security Council.[114] Such impressions inevitably undermined an operation's legitimacy and effectiveness. This problem is clear also in the 1994 US Presidential Decision Directive, which makes express the US reluctance to accept UN command: 'The greater the US military

---

[113] See Gray, 'Host-State Consent and UN Peacekeeping in Yugoslavia', 7 Duke Journal of Comparative and International Law (1996) 241. [114] Above note 78.

role, the less likely it will be that the US will agree to have a UN commander exercise operational control over US forces. Any large scale participation of US forces in a major peace enforcement mission that is likely to involve combat should ordinarily be conducted under US command and operational control or through competent regional organisations such as NATO or *ad hoc* coalitions.'[115]

In Yugoslavia the lack of cooperation by the governments of Croatia and Bosnia with UNPROFOR and their reluctance to respect its freedom of movement were further manifested in the difficulties experienced by the UN in securing the conclusion of *Status of Forces Agreements* (SOFAs) on the rights, duties, privileges, and immunities of the UN forces. Such agreements had been concluded between host states and the UN since UNEF.[116] In 1990 the UN produced a model SOFA.[117] But in Yugoslavia no SOFA was concluded with Bosnia until May 1993 and no agreement with Croatia was made on UNPROFOR though Croatia did conclude an agreement on the successor to UNPROFOR, UNCRO. Similar difficulties in other conflicts have also reflected the problems that UN peacekeeping forces face in the absence of cooperation. The Security Council has repeatedly stressed the importance of the conclusion of these agreements.[118]

The difficulty over the conclusion of SOFAs in the former Yugoslavia was only one aspect of the parties' reluctance to go beyond formal consent to the establishment and deployment of UNPROFOR to real cooperation with those forces. In the former Yugoslavia lack of cooperation was the main factor that made it impossible for UNPROFOR to fulfil its mandate. The parties sought a military solution and saw UNPROFOR as an obstruction to this; they interfered with its freedom of movement, undertook offensives across its positions, and even attacked its forces and took them hostage. It was partly in response to these problems that the Security Council turned to Chapter VII in its resolutions on UNPROFOR.

Similarly the caution of the Security Council with regard to securing the consent of the parties was apparent in its resolutions on Angola; the 1991 *Peace Accords* led to the creation of UNAVEM II, but the Security Council said that there would be no deployment until the parties showed their commitment to peace. Even so, UNAVEM II ran into difficulties because of delay and non-cooperation by UNITA. When the cease-fire broke down in early 1993 the peacekeeping force was given a reduced mandate and restricted to the capital. In December 1993 the Security

[115] 33 ILM (1994) 795.

[116] Morphet, 'UN Peacekeeping and Election Monitoring', in Roberts and Kingsbury (eds), *United Nations, Divided World* (2nd edn, 1993) at 187–8; Higgins, *United Nations Peacekeeping 1946–1967*, Vol 1 at 372.   [117] A/45/594.

[118] The Security Council also stressed the need for SOFAs in SC Res 854, 858, 937 on Georgia, SC Res 872 and 1029 on Rwanda, SC Res 976 on Angola.

Council in Resolution 890 reaffirmed its willingness as necessary to review the existing mandate of UNAVEM II to determine whether it was able to carry out its mission effectively; and again in February 1995 the Security Council stressed its intention to review the role of the UN in Angola should the Secretary-General report that the cooperation required from the parties is substantially delayed or not forthcoming. In 1996 it declared in two resolutions that it would place special emphasis during its future discussion of the mandate of UNAVEM III on the progress demonstrated by the parties. From March 1994 it repeatedly noted that Angolans bore ultimate responsibility for the successful implementation of the Peace Agreement and from May 1994 it stressed that its future decisions concerning Angola would take into account the extent to which the parties demonstrated their political will to achieve a lasting peace. These statements clearly reflect the lessons of Yugoslavia and Somalia. The non-compliance of UNITA with the Peace Agreement and the eventual decision of the government to return to force made UN peacekeeping impossible and UNAVEM III was replaced by a more limited force which was in its turn withdrawn.

Again in the case of Tajikistan the Security Council repeatedly emphasized that the primary responsibility rested with the Tajik parties to resolve their difficulties and that the international assistance provided must be linked to the process of national reconciliation and the promotion of democracy. In Resolution 1030 (1995) and later resolutions extending UNMOT's mandate it imposed the proviso that the 1994 *Tehran Agreement* remain in force and the parties continue to be committed to an effective cease-fire, to national reconciliation, and to the promotion of democracy and decided that the mandate would remain in effect unless the Secretary-General reports that these conditions have not been met. In its next resolution (1061) on Tajikistan the Security Council expressed its intention to review the future of the UN commitment in Tajikistan should the prospects for the peace process not have improved during the mandate period. As it turned out, UNMOT successfully completed its mandate.

The caution learned from the experience in Yugoslavia and Somalia may, however, conflict with the determination by many states, especially African states, to avoid a repetition of the terrible events in Rwanda. The need for urgent action to stop massacres or serious fighting may conflict with the requirement of a cease-fire and commitment to cooperation with a UN force. Most recently this tension can be seen in regard to Sierra Leone and the DRC. In the DRC states delayed the deployment of the peacekeeping force authorized by the Security Council. The resolution establishing the peacekeeping force had stipulated that the deployment of MONUC personnel would be carried out only after the Secretary-General had received credible assurances from the parties to the *Lusaka Cease-fire*

Agreement regarding adequate security to allow UN personnel to carry out their functions. Certain states expressed unhappiness at this situation and have complained of double standards despite the efforts of the Security Council to address the special problems of peacekeeping in Africa.[119] Uganda, Tanzania, and Zimbabwe all called for swift action; China called on the Security Council to act in Africa as readily as it had in Kosovo and East Timor.[120]

Authorization of member states to use force

Because the use of peacekeeping forces for enforcement purposes proved unworkable and because the UN itself is not capable of extensive enforcement action the Security Council has continued to authorize states to use force under Chapter VII, following the models of the operation against Iraq and the use of NATO member states in Yugoslavia and UNITAF in Somalia. Thus in Rwanda (1994), Haiti (1994), Albania (1997), and the Central African Republic (1997) the Security Council acted under Chapter VII in authorizing member states to use force.[121] It also authorized states to undertake operations in Kosovo and East Timor. It is clear that these are not the type of operations originally envisaged by Chapter VII.[122]

Only the operation in Haiti can be seen as an action against a state, or rather against a military junta that had illegally seized power; in

[119] The Secretary-General produced at the request of the Security Council a report on *The causes of conflict and the promotion of durable peace and sustainable development in Africa*, S/1998/318, 37 ILM (1998) 913; this said that the UN had deployed more of its peacekeeping operations in Africa than in any other single region. The deployment in 1989 of operations in Angola and Namibia began a new era of complex, post-Cold-War peacekeeping. Of the thirty-two operations launched by the UN during the succeeding nine years, thirteen were deployed in Africa. However, he acknowledged that the setback suffered in Somalia and the bitter experience in the former Yugoslavia had made the international community reluctant to assume the political and financial exposure associated with deploying peacekeeping operations. This reluctance appeared to go well beyond the lessons that Somalia offered and has had a particularly harsh impact upon Africa (para 29). See also the Report of the Secretary-General on *Enhancement of African Peacekeeping Capacity* (A/54/63); January 2000 was made 'the month of Africa' in the Security Council (Press Release SC/6796).

[120] See, for example, Fifth Committee Debate (Press Release GA/AB/3363) and Fourth Committee Debate on peacekeeping (Press Release GA/SPD/165).

[121] In 1997 it also authorized states in SC Res 1078, SC Res 1080 to go into Zaire on a fixed-term, humanitarian mission because of its concern with the situation in the Great Lakes region of Africa (though with the consent of Zaire, S/1996/920), but the operation turned out to be unnecessary.

[122] For a full discussion of the legal basis of these actions, see Sarooshi, *The United Nations and the Development of Collective Security* (1999); Quigley, 'The Privatization of Security Council Enforcement Actions: A Threat to Multilateralism', 17 Michigan JIL (1995–6) 249.

Resolution 940 the Security Council determined that the junta had failed to comply with the *Governors Island Agreement* and was in breach of its obligations under the relevant Security Council resolutions.[123]

In contrast, in Rwanda and Albania the Security Council used Chapter VII to authorize force to further humanitarian ends. Thus in Rwanda the Security Council responded to the request from France for authorization under Chapter VII to establish a safe humanitarian zone; in Resolution 929, passed by 10–0–5, the Security Council stressed the strictly humanitarian character of the operation which was to be conducted in an impartial and neutral fashion; determined that the magnitude of the humanitarian crisis in Rwanda constituted a threat to peace and security in the region; and acting under Chapter VII authorized member states to conduct a temporary operation under national command aimed at contributing in an impartial way to the security and protection of displaced persons at risk in Rwanda and to use 'all necessary means' to achieve its humanitarian objectives.[124] In Albania the Security Council expressly affirmed the sovereignty, independence, and territorial integrity of Albania, and determined that the breakdown of law and order in Albania and the collapse of effective government constituted a threat to peace and security in the region. It therefore welcomed the offer by certain member states to establish a temporary and limited multinational protection force to facilitate the safe and prompt delivery of humanitarian assistance, and to help create a secure environment for the missions of international organizations in Albania. It authorized member states participating in the multinational protection force to conduct the operation in a neutral and impartial way. In contrast to the other operations, it did not use the phrase 'use all necessary means'; rather, it used Chapter VII only to authorize member states to ensure the security and freedom of movement of the personnel of the multinational force.[125] The Security Council also used this formula in the case of the Central African Republic; in Resolution 1125 it welcomed the establishment of MISAB, the Inter-African Mission to Monitor the Implementation of the Bangui Agreements, set up in January 1997 at the request of the Central African Republic, and acting under Chapter VII authorized those states to ensure the security and freedom of movement of their personnel.

---

[123] See below at 196.

[124] Here again there was some concern about the combination of peacekeeping and Chapter VII action at the same time. New Zealand expressed concern that the combination of two separate operations with different command arrangements did not work; there was clear evidence that the initiative was having a negative impact on UNAMIR (1994 UNYB 291).

[125] Kritsiotis, 'Security Council Resolution 1101 (1997) and the Multinational Protection Force of Operation Alba in Albania', 12 Leiden Journal of International Law (1999) 511.

The Secretary-General recognized that this delegation of UN functions to member states was necessary, given the limited resources at the disposal of the UN and its inability to mount an enforcement action. In the *Supplement to the Agenda for Peace* he acknowledged that the Security Council did not then have the capacity to deploy, command, and control an enforcement action. Although it was desirable that in the long term the UN should be able to conduct such operations, it would be folly to undertake them at a time when the UN was hard pressed even to carry out its peacekeeping commitments. However, he spoke of the dangers to the UN if it seemed to be sidelined; its stature and credibility might be adversely affected. The issue of Security Council control is important and it did impose reporting obligations; in all these operations it requested the states concerned to report to the Council on a regular basis on the implementation of the resolution.

There is also a danger that interested states operating under UN authorization would gain legitimacy to further their own interests. The early tradition of not using the forces of permanent members of the Security Council or of those states with geographical or historical interests in the state concerned has been further circumvented through this type of operation. Thus it was the USA that led the operation in Haiti, France in Rwanda and the Central African Republic, and Italy in Albania. There was some suspicion of the motives of these states. In Rwanda *Operation Turquoise* was criticized for providing a safe haven for the perpetrators of genocide. These were, however, all temporary,[126] limited forces operating with the consent of the host states even where this was not expressly indicated in the relevant resolutions.

The UN-authorized operations in East Timor and Kosovo were more ambitious. In the latter the NATO operation against Yugoslavia in 1999 led to agreement on the principles of a political settlement. Yugoslavia agreed to end the violence in Kosovo and to complete a rapid withdrawal of all military, police, and paramilitary forces. These were to be replaced by international civil and security presences. The Security Council reasserted its involvement in Kosovo after the NATO operation; in Resolution 1244 (14–0–1) it acted under Chapter VII in authorizing member states and relevant international organizations to establish the international security presence (KFOR) in Kosovo. This was to include substantial NATO participation, to be deployed under unified command and control and authorized to establish a safe environment for all people in Kosovo and to facilitate the safe return to their homes of all displaced persons and refugees.

---

[126] This contrasts with the open-ended authorizations to member states in Iraq, Yugoslavia, and Somalia.

The resolution spelled out in detail the responsibilities of KFOR; it did not expressly authorize force and it did not say that member states could use or take all necessary means to carry out its mandate. The formula adopted in Paragraph 7 of Resolution 1244 was that the Security Council authorized member states and relevant international organizations to establish the international security presence in Kosovo as set out in Annex 2 *with all necessary means to fulfil its responsibilities under the resolution*. This was apparently a compromise formula, seen by the West as wide enough to cover enforcement action, but by China and Russia as not an express authorization to use force. Russia said that the presence in Kosovo of the international civil and military contingents would be carried out under the Council's thorough control; the resolution's reference to Chapter VII contained no hint of the possibility of any type of force except that set out in the peace agreement. China abstained, to show its unhappiness with the failure to condemn the NATO bombing; it was also unhappy that the resolution failed to impose necessary restrictions on invoking Chapter VII. However, in view of the fact (among other considerations) that Yugoslavia had already accepted the peace plan, China would abstain.[127] The *Military Technical Agreement* between KFOR and the federal and state governments of Yugoslavia was more specific.[128] This recorded the agreement of the government that KFOR would deploy with the authority to take all necessary action to establish and maintain a secure environment for all citizens of Kosovo and otherwise to carry out its mission. No time limit was set. Although there was agreement by Yugoslavia to the deployment and mandate of KFOR, the language and tone of the resolution were less conciliatory than other resolutions authorizing member states to use force, apart from that regarding Haiti. It *demanded* that Yugoslavia put an immediate end to violence and repression in Kosovo and begin complete and verifiable withdrawal of all forces according to a rapid timetable. It also demanded the full cooperation of Yugoslavia in the implementation of the political settlement.

In East Timor the breakdown of law and order and widespread killing after the consultation process led the Security Council to authorize a multinational force (INTERFET) led by Australia to intervene. Under Resolution 1264, passed under Chapter VII, the Security Council authorized the establishment of a multinational force under a unified command structure, pursuant to the request of the government of Indonesia, to restore peace and security in East Timor, to protect and support UNAMET in carrying out its tasks and, within force capabilities, to facilitate humanitarian assistance operations, and authorized the states participating in the multinational force to take all necessary measures to fulfil this man-

---

[127] UN Press Release SC/6686.   [128] 38 ILM (1999) 1217.

date. This multinational force was to be deployed until replaced as soon as possible by a UN peacekeeping operation.

IMPLIED AUTHORIZATION TO USE FORCE

Iraq

Where they were not able to secure express authority to use force, certain states have recently sought to justify their use of force as impliedly authorized by the Security Council. The first indications of this controversial argument emerged with regard to US and UK action against Iraq.[129] After Iraq was driven out of Kuwait by the coalition forces the government of Iraq turned on the Kurds and Shiites who had been incited to rise against the government during the conflict. The Security Council displayed some initial reluctance to involve themselves in what they at first saw as an internal matter for Iraq, but then passed Resolution 688 (10–3–2) condemning the repression of the Kurds and Shiites, demanding that Iraq stop the repression and calling on Iraq to allow access to international humanitarian organizations. This resolution was not passed under Chapter VII and did not authorize force to protect the Kurds and Shiites. Nevertheless, the USA, the UK, and France referred to this resolution in explanation of their action in intervening in Iraq to establish safe havens. They did not offer a full legal argument in justification of this action and the later establishment of no-fly zones over Iraq, first in the north, then in the south.

In the course of a series of clashes between the USA and the UK and Iraq over the no-fly zones the doctrine of implied authorization did not take any clearer form; the UK and the USA spoke of Resolution 688 allowing a response to Iraqi action and said that action to ensure the safety of aircraft in the no-fly zone was in support of the resolution. The UK also belatedly invoked a justification of humanitarian intervention. Russia and China objected strongly to the US and UK interventions. US and UK action in the no-fly zones escalated dramatically from December 1998. They widened the rules of engagement of their air forces, allowing preemptive attacks on ground defences and command centres.[130] All this was done without extensive legal justification. In the face of continued criticism from Russia and China and a call from the Arab League to halt all

---

[129] See Kritsiotis, 'The Legality of the 1993 US Missile Strike on Iraq and the Right of Self-defence in International Law', 45 ICLQ (1996) 162; Wedgwood, 'The Enforcement of SC Resolution 687, 92 AJIL (1998) 724; Lobel and Ratner, 'Bypassing the Security Council: ambiguous authorisations to use force, ceasefires and the Iraqi inspection regime', 93 AJIL (1999) 124.   [130] Keesings (1999) 42754, 42811, 42866.

acts not authorized by the Security Council, the UK simply said that its operations were purely reactive and not aggressive. The no-fly zones were necessary both to limit Iraq's capacity to oppress its own people and to monitor its compliance with obligations. The USA repeated that it was acting in support of Resolution 688.[131]

The doctrine of implied authorization was also used to justify the use of force against Iraq to secure its cooperation with the cease-fire regime established by Resolution 687 after Iraq had been driven out of Kuwait. This regime obliged Iraq to destroy its weapons of mass destruction and created UNSCOM and IAEA teams to monitor and verify Iraq's compliance; despite Iraq's formal acceptance of Resolution 687, there was great trouble over the implementation of this regime. Iraq's obstruction of the weapons inspectors led to military intervention by the USA and the UK. The difficulties escalated from 1996 and in response the Security Council passed two resolutions under Chapter VII. The first, Resolution 1154, stressed that compliance by Iraq with its obligations to accord immediate and unrestricted access to UNSCOM and IAEA was necessary for the implementation of Resolution 687 and that any violation would have severest consequences for Iraq. When Iraq again limited its cooperation with the weapons inspectors the Security Council passed Resolution 1205, expressing alarm and condemning the decision of Iraq to cease cooperation with UNSCOM and demanding that Iraq rescind its decision. When the UN weapons inspectors reported that Iraq was still obstructing their work the USA and the UK began *Operation Desert Fox* in December 1998, a series of air strikes that continued for four days and nights; it used more Cruise missiles than had been used in the whole 1991 campaign to drive Iraq out of Kuwait. The aim was to degrade Iraq's capability to build and use weapons of mass destruction and to diminish the military threat Iraq poses to its neighbours.

At the Security Council debate the USA and the UK put forward an argument of implied authorization. The UK said that there was a clear legal basis for military action in the resolutions adopted by the Security Council. By Resolution 1205 the Security Council had implicitly revived the authority to use force given in Resolution 678. The USA similarly said that its forces were acting under the authority provided by Security Council resolutions. Iraq had flagrantly committed material breaches of the cease-fire regime in Resolution 687. Several member states supported the action without any discussion of its legality, but a majority of the states speaking in the debate did not accept the legality of the action. According to Russia, the action violated international law; the

---

[131] UN Press Release SC/6683, 21 May 1999.

USA and the UK had no right to act independently on behalf of the UN or to assume the function of world policeman. The cease-fire regime in Resolution 687 did not allow unilateral use of force without further Security Council resolutions.[132]

Kosovo

The USA, the UK and other NATO states relied on implied authorization as part of the justification for the NATO operation against Yugoslavia in 1999. This aroused even more controversy than the actions against Iraq; strong arguments were made that such action was incompatible with the Charter and undermined the role of the Security Council.

The Security Council passed three resolutions in 1998 in response to events in Kosovo. It is clear that these did not *expressly* authorize the use of force. Nor did the words of Resolutions 1160, 1199, and 1203 amount to an *implied* authorization of force. This interpretation is confirmed by the fierce opposition of China and Russia in 1998 to any UN authorization of the use of force against Yugoslavia. Thus Russia, in the debate leading up to the adoption of Resolution 1199, warned that 'the use of unilateral measures of force in order to settle this conflict is fraught with the risk of destabilizing the Balkan region and all of Europe and would have long-term adverse consequences for the international system which relies on the central role of the United Nations.'[133] In the debate leading to Resolution 1203 it said that 'Enforcement elements have been excluded from the draft resolution, and there are no provisions in it that would directly or indirectly sanction the automatic use of force, which would be to the detriment of the prerogatives of the Security Council under the Charter.'[134] Costa Rica also warned against any attempt to claim implied authorization under Resolution 1203; it said that any action which implies the use of force requires clear authorization by the Security Council for each specific case.

The resolutions were all passed under Chapter VII of the UN Charter; they all condemned the use of excessive force by Serbian forces against civilians and also acts of terrorism by the Kosovo Liberation Army. In March 1998 Resolution 1160, passed by 14–0–1 (China), imposed an arms embargo on Yugoslavia and called for a political solution to the issue of Kosovo. It concluded by emphasizing that failure to make constructive progress towards the peaceful resolution of the situation in Kosovo

---

[132] UN Press Release SC/6611, 16 December 1998; 'Contemporary Practice of the United States relation to International Law', 93 AJIL (1999) 470; Lobel and Ratner, 'Bypassing the Security Council: ambiguous authorisations to use force, ceasefires and the Iraqi inspection regime', 93 AJIL (1999) 124.   [133] SC 3930th meeting, 23 September 1998.
[134] SC 3937th meeting, 24 October 1998.

would lead to the consideration of additional measures.[135] Resolution 1199, passed by 14–0–1 (China) in September 1998, expressed grave concern at the excessive and indiscriminate use of force by Serbian security forces and the Yugoslav army which had resulted in numerous civilian casualties and the displacement of over 230,000 persons from their homes. It now determined that the deterioration of the situation in Kosovo constituted a threat to peace and security in the region and demanded an end to hostilities. It demanded that the authorities of Yugoslavia and the Kosovo Albanian leadership should take immediate steps to improve the humanitarian situation and to avert the impending humanitarian catastrophe. In particular it spelled out certain concrete measures to be taken by Yugoslavia, including the cessation of all action by the security forces and the withdrawal of security units used for civilian repression. It also called for the full implementation of the commitments made by President Milosevic of Yugoslavia in June 1998 to resolve problems by peaceful means and not to use repression against the peaceful population. It concluded by deciding that, should the concrete measures demanded in this resolution and Resolution 1160 not be taken, it would consider further action and additional measures to maintain or restore peace and stability in the region. Resolution 1203 was passed by 13–0–2 (China, Russia) in October 1998 to welcome the agreements between Yugoslavia and the OSCE and NATO concerning the verification of compliance by Yugoslavia with the requirements of Resolution 1199. It affirmed that the unresolved situation in Kosovo constituted a continuing threat to peace and security in the region; this characterization of the situation was not acceptable to China and Russia. The Security Council demanded full implementation of the agreements. These three resolutions may justify a claim that NATO was acting in pursuance of the aims of the international community, but they cannot support any claim of implied authorization of force against Yugoslavia by NATO.[136]

In the Security Council debates after the NATO campaign started some states stressed the earlier Security Council resolutions passed under Chapter VII calling on Yugoslavia to stop its actions.[137] Although these

---

[135] This resolution was adopted without express reference to a determination by the Security Council that there exists a threat to international peace and security as required by Article 39, because of Russian and Chinese opposition to such a statement.

[136] On implied authorization, see Lobel and Ratner, 'Bypassing the Security Council: ambiguous authorisations to use force, ceasefires and the Iraqi inspection regime', 93 AJIL (1999) 124. For a rejection of the legality of the NATO claim, see Simma, 'NATO, The UN and the use of force: Legal Aspects', 10 EJIL (1999) 1. Rosalyn Higgins, in response to the claim that Resolution 1199 was enough to justify military action, said, 'One must necessarily ask whether this is not to stretch too far legal flexibility in the cause of good': Higgins, 'International Law in a Changing International System', 58 Cambridge Law Journal (1999) 78.

[137] SC 3989th meeting, 26 March 1999.

resolutions did not expressly authorize the use of force by NATO, several states seemed to argue that they nevertheless justified the NATO action. Thus France, the Netherlands, and Slovenia all emphasized that the Security Council had adopted resolutions under Chapter VII, affirming that the situation posed a threat to regional peace and security, and had imposed certain requirements on Yugoslavia; because Yugoslavia flagrantly violated these requirements, NATO had been entitled to act.

Yugoslavia challenged the legality of the NATO action by bringing cases against ten NATO member states before the ICJ. At the provisional measures stage of the case most of the defendant states did not set out their justification for the use of force. But Belgium did go into the law on the use of force; it argued that the armed intervention was in fact 'based on' Security Council resolutions; this is another instance of the argument of implied Security Council authorization. However, Belgium said that it was necessary to go further and to set out also the doctrine of humanitarian intervention.[138]

Thus there was some uncertainty as to the legal basis for the NATO air campaign; some states focused on implied authorization by the Security Council, others on humanitarian intervention. It was clear, despite the failure by the Security Council to condemn the NATO bombing, that a majority of states were not willing to accept a doctrine of implied authorization. Ever since the end of the NATO action many states have gone out of their way to register their rejection of the unilateral action by NATO and to stress the primary role of the Security Council and the need for express authorization. The Non-Aligned Movement, at a ministerial meeting in September 1999, rejected the legality of the NATO operation.[139] Russia and China remain adamant in their opposition. The UN Secretary-General, in his 1999 *Report on the Work of the Organization*, said that 'the moral rights and wrongs of this complex and contentious issue will be the subject of debate for years to come, but what is clear is that enforcement actions without Security Council authorization threaten the very core of the international security system founded on the Charter of the United Nations. Only the Charter provides a universally accepted legal basis for the use of force.'[140] The doctrine of implied authorization is a dangerous one; there is a serious risk that the Security Council will become reluctant to pass resolutions under Chapter VII condemning state action if there is a possibility that such resolutions might be claimed as implied justification for regional or unilateral use of force.

---

[138] *The Legality of Use of Force*, Yugoslavia v. Belgium, Canada, France, Germany, Italy, Netherlands, Portugal, Spain, United Kingdom, United States of America: Provisional Measures, Belgium oral pleadings.　　　　　　[139] UN Press Release GA/SPD/164.

[140] A/54/1 para 66.

UN-AUTHORIZED FORCE TO RESTORE DEMOCRACY

Another new development in UN action has been the authorization to use force to restore a democratically elected government. In response to a military coup in 1991 overthrowing the first democratically elected government in the history of Haiti, the Security Council condemned the coup and demanded the replacement of the constitutionally elected President. After the Security Council agreed on the imposition of an oil and arms embargo in 1993 the junta and the ousted President concluded the *Governors Island Agreement*, requiring the return of the lawful President and the restoration of democracy. The agreement included provision for a peacekeeping force, UNMIH. However, when an advance party of UNMIH tried to land in Haiti they were rebuffed.

The Security Council decided that, in the absence of the implementation of the *Governors Island Agreement*, UNMIH could not be deployed. Accordingly in Resolution 940 (12–0–2, China, Brazil), acting under Chapter VII, it authorized member states to create a multinational force to 'use all necessary means' to facilitate the departure from Haiti of the military leadership and the prompt return of the legitimately elected President, the restoration of the legitimate authorities of the government of Haiti, and to establish and maintain a secure and stable environment that will permit implementation of the *Governors Island Agreement* on the restoration of democratic government. It also authorized the revision and expansion of the mandate of UNMIH, which was to take over from the multinational force when it had established a secure and stable environment. As it turned out, the US-led multinational force was able to land and carry out its mandate peacefully; it was duly replaced by UNMIH in March 1995 when it had established the secure environment necessary to restore and maintain democracy in Haiti. The situation in Haiti remains precarious and the re-established democracy is still not secure.[141]

From its first resolutions on Haiti the Security Council stressed that this was a unique and exceptional case. Certainly the willingness of the Security Council to find that the situation in Haiti created by the failure of the military authorities to fulfil their obligations under the *Governors Island Agreement* and to comply with relevant Security Council resolutions calling for the restoration of the democratically elected government constituted a threat to peace and security in the region goes further in its discretion under Article 39 than any other such finding. The Security Council has not subsequently repeated the type of operation that it proposed in

---

[141] UN Publications, *The Blue Helmets: A Review of United Nations Peacekeeping* (3rd edn, 1996) at 613; UN Blue Book Series, Vol XI, *Les Nations Unies et Haiti 1990–1996*; 1993 UNYB 334, 1994 UNYB 412, 1995 UNYB 440.

Haiti. It has condemned the overthrow of democratic governments in some cases, such as those of Burundi and Sierra Leone, and in the latter case it went on to impose sanctions. But it has been selective in its condemnations, and other recent coups against democratic governments (such as those in Guinea-Bissau, Comoros, and Niger) have passed without formal condemnation.

PREVENTIVE PEACEKEEPING FORCES

The Secretary-General, in his *Agenda for Peace*, stressed the desirability of acting to prevent conflicts. He has since repeatedly argued that the international community needs to move from a culture of reaction to a culture of prevention.[142] This has recently become a more prominent concern for the Security Council.[143]

The first preventive peacekeeping force, UNPREDEP, was established in Macedonia in 1995 to stop the conflict in Bosnia spreading. It was subsequently retained in response to the danger that the conflict in Kosovo in 1998 might spill over into neighbouring states with significant Albanian population. But it remains a sole instance and was terminated in February 1999 when a veto by China, the first veto since March 1997, prevented the renewal of the force.

The Secretary-General, in the *Supplement to the Agenda for Peace*, again stressed the difficulties with preventive action. The greatest obstacle to success is not lack of information or of analytical capacity, but rather the reluctance of one or other of the parties to accept United Nations help. Collectively member states encourage the Secretary-General to play an active role in this field, but individually they are often reluctant to accept this when they are a party to the conflict. Moreover, states may be reluctant to accept intervention in internal conflicts.

STANDBY FORCES

As the Security Council became more active in peacekeeping and involved in more complex, dangerous, and expensive operations, it became difficult for it to find enough troops and personnel. A Security Council resolution mandating an operation was no longer a guarantee that the operation would be carried out as authorized. This was notoriously the experience in Yugoslavia and Rwanda. It also became clear that better provision was

---

[142] UN Press Release SG/2059; A/54/1.
[143] See, for example, UN Press Release SC/6761, SC/6759 (November 1999).

needed to enable a faster deployment of forces when these were urgently required. The original plan for a standing UN army able to take enforcement action under Article 43 agreements has not been revived, but the Secretary-General has been working to create standby peacekeeping forces and has reported to the Security Council on this annually since 1994. Significant progress has been made and so far over eighty states have made standby arrangements.[144] On paper over 140,000 troops are at the disposal of the UN, but this is not the reality. There are serious practical problems with the quality and training of troops, their equipment, and with speed of deployment. The Special Committee on Peacekeeping was revived in 1988 and has been working with the Secretary-General to improve the efficiency of peacekeeping operations. It is currently involved in a comprehensive review of the whole question of peacekeeping operations.[145]

COOPERATION WITH REGIONAL FORCES

Since the end of the Cold War the UN has for the first time sent peacekeeping forces into conflicts where a regional force is already operating. It first did this in Liberia, where a UN force, UNOMIL, was established to cooperate with an existing regional force, ECOMOG. The Security Council has also for the first time authorized regional organizations to use force under Chapter VII in Yugoslavia, Haiti, and Liberia. UN forces have also cooperated with regional forces in the former USSR, in Georgia and Tajikistan, and recently in Sierra Leone, where the UN established an Observer Mission to work with ECOMOG and subsequently a peacekeeping force to replace it.[146]

CONCLUSION

The period since the end of the Cold War has seen a vast expansion in Security Council activity. An overview of the Security Council's activity in this area makes it clear that it has departed radically from what was originally planned by the founders. The Security Council has shown itself to be flexible and non-formalistic in its exercise of its powers; it has not been concerned with establishing the formal basis for its actions; and it has not

---

[144] 1997 (1) UN Chronicle 13; GA/PK/164; S/2000/194.
[145] UN Press Release GA/SPD/179.
[146] SC Res 1181, August 1998; UN Department of Peacekeeping, Lessons Learned *Cooperation between the United Nations and Regional Organizations/Arrangements in a Peacekeeping Environment* (March 1999).

generally referred to the particular articles of the Charter, if any, under which it is acting.

The UN has authorized force under Chapter VII in ways very different from those originally planned. The absence of a UN standing army under Article 43 has not inhibited it. It has authorized force to implement economic measures; it has authorized member states to use force under UN command (Korea); it has authorized member states to act together against wrongdoing states (Iraq), for humanitarian purposes in Rwanda and Albania, and to restore democracy in Haiti. It has also used Chapter VII to authorize peacekeeping forces to use force going beyond self-defence (as in Yugoslavia and Somalia) and as the basis for the establishment of peacekeeping or peace enforcement forces. Thus the distinction between peacekeeping and enforcement action has been blurred in some operations.

Peacekeeping, an institution that emerged without clear, formal legal basis in the Charter, in response to the inability of the Security Council to implement Chapter VII of the UN Charter in the Cold War, and which has developed through practice to enable the Security Council to carry out its primary responsibility for the maintenance of international peace and security under the Charter, has evolved over the years. The majority of peacekeeping operations since the end of the Cold War have been established within rather than between states and they have ranged from simple, small operations to complex rebuilding of societies torn apart by civil war. The term 'peacekeeping' covers a very wide range of operations and it is clear that peacekeeping is a flexible institution which adapts to meet new needs. But the blurring of peacekeeping and enforcement as in Yugoslavia and Somalia, the use of Chapter VII in peacekeeping operations, has led to problems; it seems that abandoning the defining principles of peacekeeping, the principles of consent and impartiality, endangers the success of operations.

7

Regional peacekeeping and enforcement action

INTRODUCTION

The end of the Cold War brought a transformation in regional action to match that in UN action. Regional action is governed by three articles in the UN Charter. Article 52 provides that regional arrangements or agencies may deal with such matters relating to the maintenance of international peace and security as are appropriate for regional action, provided that such arrangements or agencies and their activities are consistent with the purposes and principles of the UN. Article 53 allows the Security Council to utilize regional arrangements or agencies for enforcement action; they are not permitted to take enforcement action without the authorization of the Security Council. Article 54 requires regional arrangements and agencies to keep the Security Council fully informed of their activities for the maintenance of international peace and security.[1]

The increase in UN activity after the end of the Cold War overstretched the UN financially; it also ran into difficulty in securing an adequate number of troops from member states to carry out the peacekeeping operations the Security Council mandated. It was therefore proposed by many that the UN should turn to regional organizations to share the burden. At first the UN Secretary-General, in his 1991 *Agenda for Peace*, was optimistic as to the role to be played by regional organizations now that the Cold War was over. He wrote that the Cold War had impaired the proper use of Chapter VIII and indeed that regional arrangements had on occasion worked against resolving disputes in the manner foreseen in the Charter. This verdict seems justified in so far as it was based on action by the OAS with regard to Cuba (1962) and the Dominican Republic (1965), Arab League action in Lebanon (1976–83), OAU action in Chad (1981), and Organisation of Eastern Caribbean States (OECS) in Grenada (1983). There was controversy as to the legality of all these operations.[2] They have been discussed in

---

[1] On Chapter VIII of the UN Charter, see Simma (ed.), *The Charter of the United Nations: A Commentary* (1994), 605; Cot and Pellet (eds), *La Charte des Nations Unies* (1991).

[2] See Pellet (ed.), *Les forces régionales du maintien de la paix* (1982); Akehurst, 'Enforcement Action by Regional Agencies, with special reference to the Organization of American States', 42 BYIL (1967) 175; Alibert, 'L'Affaire du Tchad', 90 RGDIP (1986) 368; Miller, 'Regional Organization and the Regulation of Internal Conflict', 19 World Politics (1967) 582; Naldi, 'Peacekeeping Attempts by the OAU', 34 ICLQ (1985) 593; Pogany, 'The Arab League and Regional Peacekeeping', 34 Netherlands ILR (1987) 54; Cot, 'The Role of the

detail by many writers, so in its discussion of this early practice this chapter will focus on the general lessons to be learned from an overview; it will examine the common themes that emerged, the limitations on what may be expected from regional peacekeeping, and the uncertainties about the applicable law that remained at the end of the Cold War. During the Cold War there was not much regional peacekeeping activity, and what there was was controversial. Partly because of the divisions between states little in the way of clear rules emerged from Security Council debates and resolutions. Recent practice shows a significant increase in regional activity and a new awareness of the possibilities offered by regional organizations, but some legal uncertainties remain and the problems with regional operations have become even more apparent outside the Cold War context.

The Secretary-General, in his *Agenda for Peace*, did not set forth any formal pattern of relations between the UN and regional organizations or call for any specific division of labour. But he argued that regional organizations possessed a potential that should be utilized for preventive diplomacy, peacekeeping, peacemaking, and post-conflict peace building. The Security Council would keep its primary role in the maintenance of international peace and security, but 'regional action, as a matter of decentralisation, delegation and cooperation with UN efforts could not only lighten the burden of the Council, but also contribute to a deeper sense of participation, consensus and democratisation in international affairs'. The Secretary-General explained how this might be achieved. First, consultations between the UN and regional arrangements or agencies could help to build international consensus on the nature of the problem and the measures required to address it. Second, complementary efforts by regional organizations and the UN in joint undertakings would encourage states outside the region to act supportively. Third, if the Security Council were to choose to authorize a regional arrangement or organization to take the lead in addressing a crisis within its region it could lend the weight of the UN to the validity of the regional effort.[3]

The years since the *Agenda for Peace* have partly fulfilled the Secretary-General's hopes. There has been a significant increase in cooperation between the Security Council and regional organizations.[4] The resolutions

---

Inter-African Peacekeeping Force in Chad', in Cassese (ed.), *The Current Legal Regulation of the Use of Force* (1986), 167; Issele, 'The Arab Deterrent Force in Lebanon 1976–83', ibid., 179; Pirrone, 'The Use of Force in the Framework of the OAS', ibid., 223; Weiler, 'Armed Intervention in a Dichotomized World: the case of Grenada', ibid., 241.

[3] 31 ILM (1992) 953.

[4] On cooperation between UN and regional organizations from the first meeting between the UN Secretary-General and heads of regional organizations, see 1994 UNYB 88; 1995 UNYB 1439; 1996 UNYB 1352; UN Department of Peacekeeping, Lessons Learned, *Cooperation between the United Nations and Regional Organizations/Arrangements in a Peacekeeping Environment: Suggested Principles and Mechanisms* (March 1999).

of the Security Council reflect the transformation of the Cold War situation as regards regional action. These resolutions show an increased awareness of regional organizations and of their growing role in international peace and security. A 1988 study of Security Council resolutions found that references to regional organizations were rare; it cited only two such references in the entire history of the UN.[5] In 1989 there were no references and in 1990 only one, but since 1991 this picture has been transformed. Many resolutions referred to regional organizations in the context of the former Yugoslavia, Western Sahara, Rwanda, Mozambique, Angola, Somalia, Haiti, and the former USSR. Such resolutions sometimes expressly recalled Chapter VIII of the UN Charter, or expressed appreciation of regional efforts aimed at settlement of a conflict, or supported cooperation between the UN and regional organizations, or endorsed regional efforts. Most of these references concerned attempts at the peaceful settlement of a dispute. Some showed the Security Council urging the regional organization to take the leading role; others authorized joint operations; yet others authorized the use of force by a regional organization.[6]

As these resolutions indicate, the aspirations of the Secretary-General as set out in the *Agenda for Peace* have been met in some respects. First, regional organizations have taken the leading role in some conflicts. The Security Council has left it to the CSCE (now the OSCE) to take the leading role in the conflict between Armenia and Azerbaijan over the Armenian-populated enclave of Nagorno-Karabakh in Azerbaijan. After the escalation of the conflict in 1993 the Security Council saw its role as essentially one of support for the efforts of the CSCE. The CSCE agreed in principle on the establishment of peacekeeping forces, but these were never deployed.[7] The Security Council has also relied on the CSCE to deal with ethnic conflict in other former USSR republics, in Moldova, in South Ossetia in Georgia, and in Chechenya in Russia. In the Federal Republic of Yugoslavia in 1998 the OSCE agreed on the deployment of 2,000 unarmed observers in Kosovo in response to the conflict between the federal government and the ethnic Albanian population of Kosovo.[8]

The UN has also sought to induce the OAU to take a more active role in the resolution of conflicts in Africa. The Security Council turned to the OAU to take the leading role in Burundi.[9] After the abortive coup of October 1993 the OAU announced that it was sending a team of military observers. Burundi had originally asked the UN for 1,000 troops, but the

    [5] Sonnenfeld, *Resolutions of the UN Security Council* (1988), 103.
    [6] Gray, 'Regional Arrangements and the United Nations', in Fox (ed.), *The Changing Constitution of the United Nations* (1998), 91.   [7] 1994 *Annual Register* 433.
    [8] 38 ILM (1999) 24. The force was withdrawn in March 1999 when the federal government refused to agree to a peaceful settlement of the conflict, involving the stationing of NATO troops on its territory.   [9] 1994 UNYB 276.

UN, apparently made cautious by its experience in Somalia, refused this request. The Security Council limited its involvement to welcoming the OAU military observers.[10] After the coup in July 1996 the Security Council again limited itself to a resolution welcoming OAU efforts and mentioning the possibility of sanctions.[11]

In general the Security Council has encouraged the OAU to take a more active role. Following a cooperation agreement in 1990 between the OAU and the UN, the OAU established a *Mechanism for Conflict Prevention, Management and Resolution* in 1993. These provisions were adopted despite the traditional opposition of the OAU to intervention.[12] In 1997 the Security Council in a statement welcomed the important contributions of the OAU through its Mechanism to preventing and resolving conflicts in Africa and looked forward to a stronger partnership in conformity with Chapter VIII.[13] The Council went on to support enhancement of the capacity of African states to contribute to peacekeeping operations and asked the UN Secretary-General to submit a report with concrete recommendations on the sources of conflict in Africa and ways to prevent and address these conflicts. Accordingly in 1998 the Secretary-General issued a *Report on the causes of conflict and the promotion of durable peace and sustainable development in Africa*.[14] This made proposals on peacekeeping operations in Africa; however, its overall approach is very cautious. The Secretary-General discussed three possibilities for UN support of regional and subregional activity. First, the authorization of the use of force by member states. But he said that this raised the problem of the ability properly to monitor such action. Second, the co-deployment of UN and regional forces. This might be modelled on the UNOMIL collaboration with ECOMOG in Liberia, but it could not be concluded that it would always be possible to delegate to regional organizations. The impartiality of member states could be open to question. Third, the strengthening of African capacity for peacekeeping. On the last possibility, assistance in the form of training, joint peacekeeping exercises, and partnerships between African states and donor states all had a role.[15] But the UN needed to ensure a consistent approach.

As envisaged in the *Agenda for Peace*, the Security Council has for the first time undertaken joint actions with UN and regional peacekeeping forces cooperating in Liberia, Georgia, Tajikistan, and Sierra Leone. It has also for

---

[10] S/PRST/1994/60 and 82. When the UN Secretary-General proposed a Chapter VII force in January 1996 no member state was willing to take the lead and Burundi was hostile to the deployment of a UN force: 1996 UNYB 73–89.   [11] SC Res 1072, 1996 UNYB 673.
[12] 1993 *Annual Register* 425; 1993 UNYB 304.   [13] S/PRST/1997/46.
[14] 37 ILM (1998) 913; also Secretary-General's *Report on the Enhancement of African Peacekeeping Capacity*, A/54/63.
[15] The Secretary-General said that the recommendations of the previous Secretary-General in S/1995/1911 remained valid on these points.

the first time acted under Chapter VII of the UN Charter to authorize the use of force by a regional arrangement or agency in the former Yugoslavia, Haiti, and Sierra Leone.

'REGIONAL ARRANGEMENTS AND AGENCIES'

All these recent resolutions and actions by the Security Council reflect a flexible approach to the once problematic question as to what counts as a 'regional arrangement or agency' under Chapter VIII. In the early days of the UN there was some controversy over this issue, reflected in the absence of any definition of regional arrangement in the UN Charter.[16] The UN Secretary-General, in his 1995 report to the General Assembly on cooperation with regional organizations, put a positive gloss on the absence of a definition; he said that the Charter had anticipated the need for flexibility by not giving any precise definition of regional arrangement or organization, thus enabling diverse organizations to contribute to the maintenance of peace and security.[17]

There was also in the early days of the UN some disagreement as to whether there should be any cooperation between the UN and regional bodies. Formal cooperation between the UN and regional organizations began in 1948 with the OAS, established the same year. This organization is expressly proclaimed in Article 1 of the OAS Charter to be a regional organization.[18] The General Assembly, in Resolution 253, invited the Secretary-General of the OAS to assist as an observer at General Assembly sessions. When Argentina initiated this proposal the Eastern bloc states were hostile, arguing that there was no provision in the Charter for such an arrangement. It seemed that they feared that it would reinforce Western domination of the UN. But the resolution was passed and the OAS was accepted by the UN as a regional organization under Chapter VIII. This was followed by an invitation to the Arab League in 1950. There was further controversy over the Arab League; this does not expressly claim to be a regional organization under Chapter VIII in its constituent treaty, but it had passed resolutions claiming this status.[19] Israel's challenge to the extension of an invitation to the Arab League and the subsequent debate led to some clarification of issues deliberately left unresolved in Chapter VIII, such as the question of what constitutes a regional agency or arrangement.[20] The subsequent acceptance of the Arab League as an observer amounted to an implicit rejection of Israel's arguments on this issue and

---

[16] Cot and Pellet (eds), *La Charte des Nations Unies* (1991) at 801, 810; Simma (ed.), *The Charter of the United Nations: A Commentary* (1994) at 691.   [17] 1995 UNYB 116.
[18] 119 UNTS 48; 33 ILM (1994) 981.   [19] Established in 1945, 70 UNTS 248.
[20] Cot and Pellet (eds), *La Charte des Nations Unies* (1991) at 795.

made it clear that the concept of region was flexible; that to qualify as a regional organization the Arab League did not have to be open to all the states in the region and that no express reference to Chapter VIII or even to the UN Charter in the constituent instrument of the regional organization was necessary. The OAU[21] and the Islamic Conference[22] were granted observer status as regional organizations in 1965 and 1975 respectively.

These invitations to regional organizations to be observers at the General Assembly were followed by General Assembly requests to report annually on what was being done to promote cooperation with these organizations. Even such an apparently innocuous request was the subject of some controversy in the cases of the Islamic Conference and the Arab League. On the former, some states expressed doubts because it served to promote one religion only; on the latter, Israel challenged the initial General Assembly requesting the Secretary-General to report, and twenty-three states abstained. From 1983 onwards Israel and the USA, with some support from the EC and Canada, resisted that part of the General Assembly's resolution on cooperation with the Arab League which requested the UN Secretary-General to intensify efforts towards the implementation of UN resolutions on Palestine and the Middle East.[23]

Since the end of the Cold War the CSCE and CIS have also been given observer status by the General Assembly. These organizations were not originally seen by their member states as Chapter VIII organizations.[24] The General Assembly resolution on observer status for the CSCE included express reference to Chapter VIII; that on the CIS did not.[25] The CSCE had declared at the Helsinki summit of July 1992 that it was a regional organization in the sense of Chapter VIII.[26] The CIS referred to itself in this way with regard to its action in Tajikistan in 1993; in 1996 it formally declared itself a Chapter VIII organization in its provision for peacekeeping.[27]

The Security Council has apparently taken a wide approach in its resolutions; it has expressly referred to the EC and CSCE in resolutions referring to Chapter VIII. The Security Council has also implicitly referred to NATO and the WEU as regional organizations in its resolutions on the former Yugoslavia and the Secretary-General included them in his meeting with regional organizations in 1994.[28]

---

[21] Established in 1963, 479 UNTS 70.   [22] Established in 1972, 914 UNTS 111.

[23] Gray, 'Regional Arrangements and the United Nations', in Fox (ed.), *The Changing Constitution of the United Nations* (1998), 91 at 94.

[24] The CSCE was established in 1975: 14 ILM (1975) 1292. The CIS was established in 1991: 31 ILM (1992) 138.

[25] On the CSCE, see 1993 UNYB 219, 1994 UNYB 610; on the CIS, see 1994 UNYB 255; 1994 (2) UN Chronicle 36.

[26] 31 ILM (1992) 1385; Bothe, Ronzitti, and Rosas (eds), *The OSCE in the Maintenance of Peace and Security* (1997).   [27] 1993 UNYB 516; 35 ILM (1996) 783.

[28] 1994 UNYB 88. The Secretary-General invited the CIS, the Commonwealth, CSCE, EU, NATO, Arab League, OAU, OAS, Islamic Conference, WEU, and ECOWAS.

However, it has become clear that the question whether an organization was expressly established under Chapter VIII, or was understood by its founder states to be a Chapter VIII organization, is of limited importance. The crucial factor is not the nature of the organization but the type of action that is undertaken and the attitude of the Security Council. Various peacekeeping operations have been undertaken by *ad hoc* groups of states and the legality of their actions has not been challenged on the ground that they were not regional organizations under Chapter VIII.[29] The most recent of these was the operation undertaken by MISAB, the Inter-African Mission to Monitor the Implementation of the Bangui Agreement, in the Central African Republic. It was established at the request of the Central African Republic and its legitimacy was assumed by the Security Council in its resolutions approving the conduct by member states of MISAB of operations in an impartial and neutral way to facilitate the return to peace and security; under Chapter VII it authorized the states participating in MISAB to ensure the security and freedom of movement of the force.[30]

THE CONSTITUTIONAL BASES FOR REGIONAL PEACEKEEPING

Similarly the question whether an organization has, under its own constitution, the power to take action involving the use of force has not in practice proved controversial in the majority of cases. It is striking that when most of the regional and subregional organizations were set up their constituent instruments did not make any express provision for peacekeeping activity or for enforcement action.[31] The OAU, Arab League, OECS, ECOWAS, SADC, CSCE, and CIS did not at their creation include in their constituent treaties the express power to take peacekeeping action. But recently, as awareness of the possibilities of regional action has increased,

---

[29] Wiseman,'The UN and International Peacekeeping: A Comparative Analysis', in UNITAR, *The UN and the Maintenance of International Peace and Security* (1987), 263 at 315; Brouillet, 'La Force Multinationale d'interposition à Beyrouth', 1982 AFDI 293.

[30] On MISAB, see *UN Chronicle* 1997 (4) 67, 1998 (1) 82, 1998 (2) 58; SC Res 1125, 1136. It was later replaced by a UN force, MINURCA, which was terminated in February 2000.

See also http://www.un.org/Depts/DPKO/Missions/car.htm.

[31] Only the *Rio Treaty* of the OAS, 21 UNTS 78, 43 AJIL Supplement (1949) 53, contains a provision that could possibly be interpreted to cover such action. Article 6 of the *Rio Treaty* provides:

If the inviolability or the integrity of the territory or the sovereignty or political independence of any American State should be affected by an aggression which is not an armed attack or by an extra-continental or intra-continental conflict, or by any other fact or situation that might endanger the peace of America, the Organ of Consultation shall meet immediately in order to agree on measures which must be taken in case of aggression to assist the victim of the aggression or, in any case, the measures which should be taken for the common defence and for the maintenance of the peace and security of the Continent.

some of these organizations have made new agreements expressly providing for peacekeeping powers. Thus the CSCE in 1992 at its Helsinki summit decided to provide itself with the capability to undertake peacekeeping operations. The member states declared their understanding that the CSCE is a regional arrangement in the sense of Chapter VIII. In the Declaration they laid down detailed rules on CSCE peacekeeping; such operations would be conducted within the framework of Chapter VIII.[32] The CSCE Declaration to a large extent codifies the UN rules on peacekeeping that have emerged through practice. It also clearly reflects the lessons learned from UN experience in Yugoslavia and Somalia.

The CSCE Declaration recognizes the wide variety of peacekeeping operations: 'a CSCE peacekeeping operation, according to its mandate, will involve civilian and/or military personnel, may range from small-scale to large-scale, and may assume a variety of forms including observer and monitor missions and larger deployment of forces. Peacekeeping activities could be used inter alia to supervise and help maintain cease-fires, to monitor troop withdrawals, to support the maintenance of law and order, to provide humanitarian and medical aid and to assist refugees.' The Declaration provides that the peacekeeping operations shall not entail enforcement action, and that they require the consent of the parties directly concerned. This formalizes the practice of the Security Council in recent years in seeking the consent not just of the government but of all parties involved in a conflict. This cautious approach is developed further in the requirement that certain conditions must be fulfilled before the decision to dispatch a mission is taken; an effective and durable cease-fire must be established, and the necessary memoranda of understanding must have been agreed with the parties concerned. As with UN peacekeeping, operations should be conducted impartially, and there must be a clear and precise mandate. Detailed rules are laid down on political control and the chain of command. Finally, the Declaration provides for cooperation with the EC, NATO, and the WEU; the CSCE will depend on them for troops and expertise. To date the CSCE has not conducted any peacekeeping operations apart from its dispatch of unarmed observers into Kosovo in 1998.

The CIS in 1996 agreed on the *Concept for Prevention and Settlement of Conflicts in the territory of states members of the Commonwealth of Independent States*.[33] They said that the CIS should, in its capacity as a regional organization, take the steps required to settle conflicts in the territory of member states in accordance with Chapter VIII of the UN Charter; this would include peacekeeping operations. They set out the essential conditions for the conduct of peacekeeping operations: like the CSCE Declaration, these follow the

---

[32] 31 ILM (1992) 1385 at 1399.   [33] 35 ILM (1996) 783.

general principles of UN peacekeeping and also build on recent UN experience.[34] Accordingly six of the member states adopted a Statute on Collective Peace-keeping force in the Commonwealth of Independent States.[35]

Other, subregional, organizations have also accepted or provided for the possibility of peacekeeping action.[36] ECOWAS was established in 1975 as a subregional organization of fifteen member states, concerned with economic matters.[37] Its constituent treaty made no provision for the establishment of peacekeeping forces, but two subsequent treaties expanded ECOWAS's concerns beyond the economic. These are the 1978 *Protocol on Non-Aggression* and the 1981 *Protocol on Mutual Assistance on Defence*.[38] The latter includes provision for the establishment of allied forces of the community to be used if there is a conflict between two member states or 'in the case where an internal armed conflict in a member state of the Community is actively maintained and sustained from outside likely to endanger the security and peace in the entire community'. These provisions may possibly be interpreted to allow peacekeeping forces. ECOWAS undertook such operations in Liberia, Sierra Leone, and Guinea-Bissau.[39]

[34] The signature of a cease-fire agreement by the conflicting parties and a clear expression by the parties of political will to settle the conflict by political means;
The consent of the conflicting parties to the conduct of PKO by CPF performing their appointed tasks, and the establishment of close cooperation between the parties and the CPF command for the conduct of such operations;
The acceptance by the parties to the conflict of their obligations to honour the international status, neutrality, privileges and immunities of CPF personnel in accordance with international law;
The open, neutral and impartial nature of peacekeeping operations;
The collective peacekeeping forces shall be formed on a coalition basis by the states which have agreed to take part in PKO . . .
The collective peacekeeping forces shall act under a single command, adhering strictly to the principles of impartiality, compliance with the laws of the host country, and respect for the traditions and customs of the local population. PKO may not be considered to be a substitute for settlement by means of talks;
In the conduct of PKO, the collective peacekeeping forces shall not take part in active combat. They shall make use, first and foremost, of peaceful means and instruments to promote appropriate conditions for the holding of talks and the reaching of mutually acceptable agreements on the settlement of conflicts. They shall refrain from the use of weapons except in cases of armed resistance to their discharge of the mandate to conduct PKO.
Enforcement measures in the settlement of conflicts (peace enforcement) shall be permitted only if such powers have been mandated by the UN Security Council in accordance with the Charter of the UN.

[35] 35 ILM (1996) 783.
[36] The SADC and IGAD were originally created to deal with development and drought; they have recently involved themselves with seeking diplomatic settlements to the conflicts in Sudan, Somalia, Lesotho, Angola, and the DRC (see, for example, Keesings (1998) 42115, 42426, 42538, 42539; (1999) 42929, 43050, 43093).   [37] 35 ILM (1996) 660.
[38] Weller (ed.), *Regional Peacekeeping and International Enforcement: The Liberian Crisis* (1994) at 18 and 19 respectively.
[39] The ECOMOG operation in Guinea-Bissau was established under the *Abuja Agreement* between the government and the junta that had opposed it: 38 ILM (1999) 28; ECOWAS communiqué, S/1998/638. This provided for the withdrawal from Guinea-Bissau of all foreign

But the fundamental question whether an organization has the power under its own constitution to engage in peacekeeping activities has been treated as unimportant in practice. When regional organizations have engaged in the use of force the legality of such action has been assessed by the rest of the world not in terms of the organization's own constitution but rather in terms of the UN Charter and general international law. Only in the case of Grenada was there any significant debate in the Security Council on this issue of the organization's own constitution.[40] Following a coup in 1983 in which a government sympathetic to Cuba and to the USSR seized power, the USA led a forcible intervention to 'restore government and order, and to facilitate the departure of those United States citizens and other foreign nationals who wish to be evacuated'. In a letter to the Security Council the USA claimed that its action was taken pursuant to an invitation by the OECS. It later elaborated on this in the Security Council debate on the intervention; the US position was that the OECS had sought its assistance to undertake collective regional action because of the vacuum of authority in Grenada. The consent to regional action had come from the Governor-General.[41] The representative of Grenada itself raised the point as to whether the action by the USA and OECS member states was legitimate under the OECS constitution; it argued persuasively that the OECS Treaty made no provision for peacekeeping action and that the US action went beyond what was allowed in the Treaty. The USA relied on Article 8 of the OECS Treaty as one of the justifications for its actions, but actually this clearly provides for collective self-defence against external aggression, not for intervention by a non-member state in the internal affairs of Grenada.[42] Many other states disagreed with the US

troops and the simultaneous deployment of ECOMOG interposition forces. The ECOMOG forces were to keep the warring parties apart, to guarantee security along the border with Senegal, and to guarantee free access to humanitarian organizations. That is, the regional force was to help a government without the military resources itself to maintain order and stability. The Security Council welcomed the deployment of ECOMOG to implement this peacekeeping mandate in SC Res 1233. However, a May 1999 coup ended the truce (Keesings 1999, 42924) and led to the withdrawal of ECOMOG: *Report of the Secretary-General Pursuant to Security Council Resolution 1233 (1999) relative to the Situation in Guinea-Bissau* (S/1999/741).

[40] 1983 UNYB 211; UN SCOR Meetings 2487–2491. On Grenada, see Gilmore, *The Grenada Intervention* (1984).

[41] The USA set out its position in S/16076; SCOR 2487th meeting para 52, 187; 2491st meeting para 51.

[42] Article 8 provides for the composition and functions of the Defence and Security Committee. Paragraph 4 provides that:

The Defence and Security Committee shall have responsibility for coordinating the efforts of Member States for collective self-defence and the preservation of peace and security against external aggression and for the development of close ties among the Member States of the Organization in matters of external defence and security, including measures to combat the activities of mercenaries, operating with or without the support of internal or national elements, in the exercise of the inherent right of individual or collective self-defence recognised by Article 51 of the Charter of the United Nations.

interpretation of Article 8.[43] However, the Security Council resolution calling for the withdrawal of foreign troops from Grenada was vetoed by the USA. It is striking that the actual member states of the OECS did not themselves adopt the same argument on Article 8 peacekeeping as the USA; they preferred to invoke the equally doubtful argument of 'pre-emptive defensive strike' under the OECS provisions for collective self-defence. However, most of the debate did not focus exclusively on the OECS Treaty; rather, states concerned themselves with the legality of the operation under the UN Charter.

Again in the Security Council debates on the OAS measures against Cuba in 1962 and the Dominican Republic in 1965 there was some discussion about whether the OAS Charter outlawed forcible intervention of the types undertaken.[44] However, there was no real discussion of the scope and application of Article 6 of the Rio Treaty or of the constitutionality of the action in terms of Article 6. The debate focused on whether the forcible interventions were compatible with the UN Charter and general international law. The Arab League intervention in Lebanon from 1976–83 was not discussed in the Security Council[45] and the OAU action in Chad in 1981 led to a split as to whether it was Chapter VIII regional peacekeeping or simply a domestic matter for Chad.[46] Thus neither episode was discussed by the Security Council in terms of its legality under the Arab League or OAU Charters. Therefore, by default, it seems to have been accepted by states during the Cold War that regional organizations have implied powers to establish peacekeeping forces, and also that they need not follow the formal procedures for decision-making laid down in the respective treaties, even if the peacekeeping action is taken in the name of the organization. Apparently the basis for this was that states can do together, even in the name of the organization, what they could do separately. That is, because individual states may undertake peacekeeping activities, groups of states acting through a regional organization may do the same; whether or not an entity qualified as a regional arrangement or agency under Article 52 did not affect its power to undertake peacekeep-

[43] Grenada, SCOR 2487th meeting at para 88. See also Mexico, Nicaragua, Cuba, Democratic Yemen, 2487th meeting. Also Poland and Ethiopia, 2489th meeting; Afghanistan, 2491st meeting.
[44] For a full discussion of these episodes, see Akehurst, 'Enforcement Action by Regional Agencies, with special reference to the Organization of American States', 42 BYIL (1967) 175.
[45] See Pogany, 'The Arab League and Regional Peacekeeping', 34 Netherlands ILR (1987) 54; Issele, 'The Arab Deterrent Force in Lebanon 1976–83', in Cassese (ed.), *The Current Legal Regulation of the Use of Force* (1986) at 179.
[46] UN Doc S/PV 2358. On Chad, see Naldi, 'Peacekeeping Attempts by the OAU', 34 ICLQ (1985) 593; Cot, 'The Role of the Inter-African Peacekeeping Force in Chad', in Cassese (ed.), *The Current Legal Regulation of the Use of Force* (1986), 167.

ing activities.[47] It seems to follow that only a member state of an organization may challenge the constitutionality of its peacekeeping action on grounds of non-compliance with the organization's constituent treaty. Otherwise, provided that the organization limits itself to peacekeeping and does not embark on enforcement action needing Security Council authorization, this would not be a ground for legal challenge by a non-member state.

This lack of concern over the constitutional basis for regional action may be seen also in the response to recent regional action. With regard to ECOWAS action in Liberia, other states did not go into questions of the ECOWAS constitution or the procedures followed.[48] This conflict and that in Sierra Leone will be discussed in detail in order to demonstrate clearly the application of Chapter VIII and the legal issues that have arisen in post-Cold War regional action. In December 1989 there was an uprising against President Doe, who had been in power since 1980. The uprising was led by Charles Taylor, a former member of the Doe government, who came from the Côte d'Ivoire with a small force (the NPFL). The rebels grew in number and were successful, though the opposition movement split in February 1990 when Prince Johnson broke away. By summer 1990 the rebels controlled about 90 per cent of Liberia and were advancing on the capital, Monrovia.

The government had sought UN intervention in June 1990, but the Security Council did not become involved until January 1991. Nor did the USA intervene, despite its major role in Liberia since its creation as a state in 1847. The USA had maintained and even increased its links with Liberia after Doe seized power in 1980. But when civil war broke out in December 1989 the USA ruled out direct intervention. In the absence of UN or US intervention ECOWAS stepped in. It established a Mediation Committee and in August 1990 the Committee called for a cease-fire and established ECOMOG with troops from Nigeria, Ghana, Gambia, Guinea, and Sierra Leone. About 3,000 troops went to Liberia and secured Monrovia against the NPFL. Various attempts were made to reach a peaceful settlement and at one of these conferences it was agreed to establish an interim government under President Sawyer. He was established in Monrovia in December 1990 and a cease-fire held from then until August

---

[47] Akehurst, 'Enforcement Action by Regional Agencies, with special reference to the Organization of American States', 42 BYIL (1967) 175.

[48] The following account of events in Liberia is taken from Gray, 'Regional Arrangements and the United Nations', in Fox (ed.), *The Changing Constitution of the United Nations* (1998), 91; see also Nolte, 'Restoring Peace by Regional Action: International Legal Aspects of the Liberian Conflict', 53 Zeitschrift für ausländisches öffentliches Recht und Völkerrecht (1993) 603; Weller (ed.), *Regional Peacekeeping and International Enforcement: The Liberian Crisis* (1994); Mindua, 'Intervention armée de la CEEAO au Liberia', 7 African Journal of International and Comparative Law (1995) 257.

1992. During this time attempts to produce a peaceful settlement continued and in October 1991 the *Yamoussoukro IV Agreement* was accepted by the Doe forces, the NPFL, and Prince Johnson. This provided for a cease-fire, the disarmament of the warring parties, and the encampment of all forces under the supervision of ECOMOG.

But in 1992 fighting broke out again; the NPFL forces attacked Monrovia and ECOMOG not only drove them off, it went onto the offensive and took territory formerly occupied by the NPFL in an action that appeared to go beyond peacekeeping. In July 1993 a peace agreement was concluded at Cotonou, Benin, but this was not observed and it was followed by a whole sequence of supplementary peace agreements. It was not until August 1996 that a final peace agreement was made; a year later elections were held and Charles Taylor was elected President by a large majority.

The crucial question of the legal basis for the ECOMOG operation was not much discussed by those involved or by the UN. Little attention was paid to the legality of the action under ECOMOG's own mandate and under its constitution. ECOMOG's mandate from the ECOWAS Mediation Committee was that 'ECOMOG shall assist the Committee in supervising the implementation, and ensuring strict compliance, of the cease-fire by all the parties to the conflict.' In its report to the Security Council on the establishment of ECOMOG Nigeria said that 'ECOMOG is going to Liberia first and foremost to stop the senseless killing of innocent civilian nationals and foreigners and to help the Liberian people to restore their democratic institutions. The ECOWAS intervention is in no way designed to save one part or to punish another.'[49]

Did ECOWAS have the power under its own constitution to establish peacekeeping forces? The 1981 *Protocol on Mutual Defence* offered a possible legal basis for the establishment of ECOWAS forces, given the apparent existence of outside involvement by Burkina Faso and Libya in supporting Charles Taylor and the NPFL. This was referred to in passing by the ECOWAS Mediation Committee when it first took action in August 1990, but was not subsequently mentioned by ECOWAS.[50] But, as with earlier regional operations, there was little international concern or express discussion about the legality of the ECOMOG operation in terms of ECOMOG's constitution. In ECOWAS's communications to the Security Council after the establishment of ECOMOG there was no mention of the legal basis for the establishment and deployment of ECOMOG.[51] Nor was this referred to in the Security Council statements[52] or resolutions[53] on

---

[49] S/21485.
[50] Weller (ed.), *Regional Peacekeeping and International Enforcement: The Liberian Crisis* (1994) at 67.　　　　　　　　　　　　　　　　　　　　　　　　　[51] S/21485, S/22025.
[52] S/22133, S/23886.　　　　[53] SC Res 788, 813, 856, 866.

Liberia, or in the first Security Council debate on the situation in Liberia in January 1991.[54] During this debate Liberia itself said nothing about the constitutional basis for ECOWAS peacekeeping. Nigeria said only that 'ECOWAS should be commended for promoting the principles of the UN Charter by stepping in to prevent the situation in Liberia from degenerating into a situation likely to constitute a real threat to international peace and security.'

In the second Security Council debate on Liberia in November 1992 there was again little interest in the legal basis of the ECOWAS action in terms of its own constitution and treaties.[55] The Côte d'Ivoire was alone in its express reference to the 1981 *Protocol on Mutual Assistance and Defence*. Sierra Leone referred to ECOWAS acting under the UN Charter and the Treaty of ECOWAS in sending a peacekeeping force. The USA said simply that the dispatch of peacekeeping forces had been a decision by ECOWAS governments on their own initiative. In his later report to the Security Council on events in Liberia the Secretary-General stated without elaboration that ECOWAS was acting under both the 1981 Protocol and the 1978 *Protocol on Non-Aggression* in establishing ECOMOG.[56]

Given the non-invocation of the latter Protocol as well as the fact that it provides for response to external attacks, it seems unlikely that the Secretary-General was correct in referring to the *Protocol on Non-Aggression* as a basis for ECOMOG. As for the 1981 Protocol, it is clear that the normal decision-making processes of ECOWAS were not followed. The decision to set up ECOMOG was not made unanimously by all ECOWAS member states. As in earlier peacekeeping operations, an extremely relaxed attitude, or indifference, on the part of those concerned is very noticeable with regard to this issue of the constitutional propriety of the creation of peacekeeping forces.

Even more striking was the lack of inquiry into constitutionality of the action in Sierra Leone in 1997. In May 1997 there was a coup overthrowing the government that had been democratically elected as part of the peace process ending the six-year civil conflict in Sierra Leone. There were already ECOMOG forces (Nigerian and Guinean troops) in Sierra Leone at the time of the coup, apparently there at the request of the government because of the overspill of the conflict in Liberia into Sierra Leone.[57] Nigerian forces were also present under a bilateral agreement with the government of Sierra Leone. After the coup Nigeria and Guinea sent more troops and, claiming to act under the aegis of ECOWAS, became involved in the conflict. The normal ECOWAS decision-making procedures do not

---

[54] SC 2974th meeting.   [55] SC 3138th meeting.
[56] Weller (ed.), *Regional Peacekeeping and International Enforcement: The Liberian Crisis* (1994) at 283; S/25402 para 15.   [57] Keesings (1991) 38136; (1992) 38900; (1995) 40491.

seem to have been followed at this stage; Nigeria and Guinea simply assumed the right to use force to resist the coup and to try to restore the legitimate government at the request of the deposed President. It was not until June 1997 that ECOWAS met and issued a formal statement. This said that ECOWAS's objectives were to reinstate the legitimate government, restore peace and security, and resolve the refugee problem. They called for non-recognition of the junta that had seized power and said that they would reinstate the democratically elected government by dialogue, sanctions, and the use of force. ECOWAS did not specify the legal basis for its operations.[58] But other states did not speak out against the Nigerian and Guinean military action on the ground that it was not really constitutional ECOWAS action. The use of force by Nigeria, ruled by a military junta that had seized power from a democratically elected government, to restore democracy in Sierra Leone met with a very muted response. There was not even much discussion of the legitimacy of the action in the light of UN and general international law rules on peacekeeping.[59]

A similar lack of concern was displayed over the constitutionality of CIS action in Tajikistan and Georgia. In the former, five of the CIS member states established coalition forces in Tajikistan in August 1993; they expressly stated that they viewed this as a regional arrangement, concluded in accordance with the principles and purposes of Chapter VIII of the UN Charter.[60] There was apparently no discussion of constitutionality of this operation in the UN. Similarly there were no inquiries into constitutional propriety with regard to the CIS operation established in 1994 in Abkhazia, Georgia.[61] Russian troops had remained in Georgia after the break-up of the USSR; they stayed there with the reluctant consent of the President of Georgia when it became clear that Georgian forces alone were not able to prevent the forcible secession of the Abkhaz people and their expulsion of the Georgian population from Abkhazia. These Russian forces were nominally transformed into CIS peacekeeping forces after a May 1994 cease-fire agreement between the Georgian and Abkhaz authorities; this provided that CIS forces would ensure respect for the cease-fire and for a weapons exclusion zone. Even though it is not clear that any formal decision-making process had taken place in the CIS the UN Security Council accepted the Russian troops as a CIS force and there was no discussion of constitutional propriety.[62] There was a similar lack of concern about the expiration of the mandate of the CIS peacekeeping force on 30 June 1998; the UN Secretary-General, after reporting a continuing good working relationship with the CIS forces, simply said that the

---

[58] S/1997/499.   [59] See below at 227.   [60] S/26610.
[61] 33 ILM (1994) 577; see also Greco, 'Third Party Peacekeeping and the Interaction between Russia in the OSCE in the CIS area', in Bothe, Ronzitti, and Rosas (eds), *The OSCE in the Maintenance of Peace and Security* (1997), 267.   [62] See below at 224.

expiry of the mandate had not affected its presence and that it continued to operate.[63]

THE LEGALITY OF REGIONAL ACTION IN TERMS OF THE UN CHARTER AND GENERAL INTERNATIONAL LAW

In practice, debate on the legality of regional action has centred on the compatibility of the use of force with the UN Charter and with general international law. During the Cold War the Security Council debates centred on fundamental issues such as whether the regional action was legitimate peacekeeping or whether it was enforcement action that needed Security Council authorization under Article 53, and the issue of what was meant by enforcement action under Article 53 of the UN Charter. Does the requirement in Article 53 of Security Council authorization for enforcement action apply to the imposition of economic measures by the regional organization? Does failure to condemn amount to authorization? These questions were crucial in the cases of Cuba and the Dominican Republic. In the former, the OAS responded to the 1959 socialist revolution which brought President Castro to power by suspending Cuba from the organization and imposing economic sanctions because Cuba's 'aims and principles were incompatible with the aims and principles of the inter-American system'; it subsequently authorized member states to take all measures including the use of armed force to ensure that Cuba did not receive from the USSR missiles that endangered the peace and safety of the continent. In the Dominican Republic the USA again responded to a socialist revolution by intervention; it initially sent in US forces, but later sought to transform its forces into an OAS force. The USA took a narrow view of enforcement action under Article 53 and claimed that the OAS was undertaking peacekeeping activities. It also took a wide view of authorization and relied on Security Council acquiescence as authorization under Article 53. These issues concerning the scope of peacekeeping and the need for Security Council authorization could not be authoritatively resolved by the Security Council during the Cold War.[64]

Other issues that emerged in practice during the Cold War with regard to the legitimacy of regional action related to the complex question of impartiality. Concern that one state would be able to manipulate a

---

[63] S/1999/60.

[64] See Pellet (ed.), *Les forces régionales du maintien de la paix* (1982); Akehurst, 'Enforcement Action by Regional Agencies, with special reference to the Organization of American States', 42 BYIL (1967) 175. The question of priority of jurisdiction as between the OAS and the UN was divisive during the Cold War, but has not been a problem in recent years; see Simma *The Charter of the United Nations: A Commentary* (1994) at 708, 710.

regional organization and use it to further its own ends arose in several cases during the Cold War. The role of the USA in the OAS action over Cuba and the Dominican Republic, of the USA (a non-member) in the OECS action in Grenada, and of Syria in the Arab League intervention in Lebanon all gave rise to serious criticism. Factors such as the composition, control, and financing of peacekeeping forces are all significant in this context.

Thus in Chad the OAU was in difficulties over the financing of the peacekeeping forces.[65] It appealed to the UN for financial help, the first such request from a regional organization. In April 1982 the Security Council responded by Resolution 504, calling on the Secretary-General to establish a fund to which UN member states could contribute in order to provide financial assistance to the OAU force.[66] In the event, the fund was not set up because the OAU intervention in Chad ended in June 1982. Only a limited number of states contributed troops to the OAU operation: Nigeria, Senegal, and Zaire. It is interesting that Senegal's troops were supported financially by France and those of Nigeria and Zaire received contributions from the USA. Such financial support inevitably raises questions about the independence of the regional decision-making and leads to doubts as to whether regional peacekeeping will really contribute to a greater democratization in international affairs as hoped by the UN Secretary-General in his *Agenda for Peace*.

Other issues concerning impartiality, now seen as a necessary characteristic of peacekeeping activity, concern the duty not to take sides in a particular dispute. The starting point of any examination of this issue is the mandate given to the force by the regional organization. In some cases there has been ambiguity. With regard to Chad, there was some uncertainty over the exact mandate. The relevant OAU resolution said that the task of the peacekeeping force was to 'ensure the defence and security of the country while awaiting the integration of government forces'. But the Chairman of the OAU said that the force's role was to enable the people of Chad to decide on a national government through free and fair elections supervised by the OAU with the help of the African peacekeeping force, and the OAU standing committee on Chad said that the force was to help the government maintain peace and security, and to help form a united national army. There were also agreements between the government of Chad and the OAU on the presence of the OAU forces providing

[65] On the OAU action in Chad, see Alibert, 'L'Affaire du Tchad', 90 RGDIP (1986) 368; Naldi, 'Peacekeeping Attempts by the OAU', 34 ICLQ (1985) 593; Cot, 'The Role of the Inter-African Peacekeeping Force in Chad', in Cassese (ed.), *The Current Legal Regulation of the Use of Force* (1986), 167; Wiseman, 'The UN and International Peacekeeping: A Comparative Analysis', in UNITAR, *The UN and the Maintenance of International Peace and Security* (1987), 263 at 309.   [66] 1982 UNYB 318.

that the forces should contain and moderate hostilities, safeguard the security of the states, and assist the government in the formation of a united national army. There was thus some ambiguity as to whether the role of the force was simply to act as a buffer between opposing forces or whether it was to help the government that issued the invitation to defeat the opposition.

The OAU forces had been invited in by President Goukouni in 1981, but when the civil war started to go against him they remained strictly impartial. President Goukouni became hostile to the forces because they would not support him and they withdrew. The OAU forces had chosen not to impose a military solution. There are radically opposing views of the success of this operation among the writers who discussed it: for Cot it was a success in that it permitted the orderly transfer of power and it reduced foreign intervention, but for Naldi it was an 'abject failure' in that it did not stop the civil war.[67] The UN implicitly legitimized the OAU intervention in Security Council Resolution 504, calling on members to support the fund to assist the operation, but there was no express reference in this resolution to Chapter VIII. The USSR argued that it was purely an internal matter for Chad. But the *Repertoire of the Practice of the Security Council* did include an account of the action under its section on Chapter VIII.[68]

In Lebanon similar questions arose over the scope of the mandate and the impartiality of the Arab forces. The initial limited Arab Security Force was mandated by the Arab League in 1976 to 'maintain security and stability' after the civil war; it was replaced by a much larger Arab Deterrent Force with a more ambitious mandate to ensure the observance of the cease-fire, separate the parties, implement the *Cairo Agreement*, and collect heavy weapons. The force was a very large one, and was overwhelmingly Syrian. When the Syrian forces exceeded their peacekeeping mandate and went beyond self-defence, taking action against Christian forces, other states withdrew their contingents and suspended their financial contributions. The force was now even more clearly Syrian-dominated, and doubts about its legality were strengthened when it remained in Lebanon even after the ADF mandate expired in July 1982. In theory the forces were under the control of the President of Lebanon, but in reality it was Syria that was in charge.[69]

---

[67] Naldi, 'Peacekeeping Attempts by the OAU', 34 ICLQ (1985) 593; Cot, 'The Role of the Inter-African Peacekeeping Force in Chad', in Cassese (ed.), *The Current Legal Regulation of the Use of Force* (1986), 167.

[68] *Repertoire of the Practice of the Security Council 1981–84*, 348.

[69] On the Arab League action in Lebanon, see Pogany, 'The Arab League and Regional Peacekeeping', 34 Netherlands ILR (1987) 54; Issele, 'The Arab Deterrent Force in Lebanon 1976–83', in Cassese (ed.), *The Current Legal Regulation of the Use of Force* (1986) at 179.

Liberia

With regard to the ECOWAS operation in Liberia, the question of impartiality arose again. Also, as in the cases of Chad and Lebanon, it is striking that not much attention was paid in the Security Council to the question of the legality of the operation under the UN Charter. The ECOWAS communications to the Security Council made no express reference to Chapter VIII of the UN Charter, but Nigeria spoke of ECOMOG as holding the fort for the UN in accordance with Chapter VIII.[70] States in the Security Council debates assumed that ECOWAS had legally established peacekeeping forces. The USA and China spoke simply of the peacekeeping forces set up by ECOWAS and appeared to assume their legality.[71] The first Security Council resolution on Liberia, Resolution 788 (passed in November 1992) imposing an arms embargo, was cautious in its language; it recalled Chapter VIII and commended ECOWAS for its attempts to secure a peaceful settlement, but did not mention ECOMOG by name.

In contrast, those resolutions passed after the *Cotonou Peace Agreement* in 1993 do refer to ECOMOG expressly and clearly assume its legality as a peacekeeping force. Resolution 866 establishing the UN observer force refers to ECOMOG as 'a peacekeeping mission already set up by another organization'. Later resolutions not only repeatedly commend the positive role of ECOWAS in its continuing efforts to restore peace, security, and stability in Liberia, but also call for states to contribute troop forces to ECOMOG, and then commend those that did this. They demand that all factions in Liberia strictly respect the status of ECOMOG personnel and urge member states to provide support for the peace process in Liberia through a UN Trust Fund for Liberia, in order to enable ECOMOG to fulfil its mandate.[72] These resolutions clearly indicate acceptance of the legality of ECOMOG's deployment under the *Cotonou Agreement* and later peace agreements.[73]

One central issue in establishing the legality of peacekeeping action is the need for the consent of the host state for the establishment and deployment of peacekeeping forces. In contrast to the stress on this need for consent in General Assembly Resolution 49/57, *The Declaration on the Enhancement of Cooperation between the UN and Regional Arrangements or Agencies in the Maintenance of International Peace and Security*,[74] on regional action, this was passed over in almost complete silence by states and in the

---

[70] S/PV 3138; The Head of State of Nigeria also made a speech outside the UN referring to Chapter VIII; see Weller, *Regional Peacekeeping and International Enforcement: The Liberian Crisis* (1994) at 105.   [71] S/PV 3138.

[72] SC Res 866, 950, 1014, 1020, 1041.

[73] Similarly with regard to Guinea-Bissau, the Security Council, after the *Abuja Peace Agreement*, was prepared in SC Res 1233 to mention ECOMOG by name and to assume the legality of its deployment.   [74] 1994 UNYB 124.

Security Council's statements and resolutions with regard to the initial deployment of ECOMOG in Liberia. It was not mentioned in the first ECOWAS communication to the Security Council in August 1990.[75] In their second communication in December 1990 ECOWAS said that an agreement between itself and Liberia was necessary on the status and operations of ECOMOG.[76] The ECOWAS authority mandated such an agreement to be made with the interim government under President Sawyer set up under the auspices of ECOWAS in December 1990.[77] Generally the UN treated the Sawyer government as the body with power to represent Liberia; the issue of the credentials of the Liberian representative to the UN was not raised. And the Secretary-General's reports spoke of the UN and the OAU as recognizing the Sawyer government until it was replaced by the Transitional Government under the *Cotonou Agreement*.[78]

At the time that ECOMOG was established and entered Liberia, there were newspaper reports that President Doe and Prince Johnson consented to its presence. But Charles Taylor, whose troops controlled 90 per cent of Liberia, did not consent and opposed the deployment. And in the Security Council debates on Liberia in January 1991 and November 1992 Liberia itself implied that consent was not necessary, at any rate for UN intervention. Liberia regretted that the UN had not involved itself earlier and called for a review and reinterpretation of the Charter, particularly of the provisions on non-intervention. It said that a strict application of this principle had hampered the effectiveness of the Security Council and its principal objective of maintaining international peace and security. In the second debate it said that opinion was divided between those supporting humanitarian intervention and those favouring classical conceptions of sovereignty, however anachronistic. It said that ECOWAS had taken a bold and courageous decision to deploy ECOMOG.

So there was considerable uncertainty on the consent issue as far as the initial deployment of ECOMOG was concerned. The readiness of the international community to acquiesce in the ECOMOG peacekeeping even in the absence of clear consent from the government and even though the government was no longer effective finds precedents in the flexible approach to the consent requirement in the cases of peacekeeping forces in Chad, Lebanon, and Somalia.[79] Subsequently it seems that the Security Council regarded the 1993 *Cotonou Peace Agreement* and its successors

---

[75] S/21485, Weller, *Regional Peacekeeping and International Enforcement: The Liberian Crisis* (1994) at 75.   [76] S/22025; Weller, ibid. at 121.
[77] S/25402; Weller, ibid. at 280.   [78] S/25402 para 17; Weller, ibid. at 280.
[79] Nolte, 'Restoring Peace by Regional Action: International Legal Aspects of the Liberian Conflict', 53 Zeitschrift für ausländisches öffentliches Recht und Völkerrecht (1993) 603; Wippman, 'Treaty-Based Intervention: Who Can Say No?', 62 University of Chicago Law Review (1995) 607, and 'Military Intervention, Regional Organization and Host-State Consent,' 7 Duke Journal of Comparative and International Law (1996) 71.

as providing legitimacy for the continued deployment of ECOMOG. Resolution 866 and later resolutions refer to ECOMOG expressly and note that the Peace Agreements assign to ECOMOG the primary responsibility of supervising the military provisions of the agreement.

Legal and practical problems have also continued since the end of the Cold War over the financing, control, and impartiality of regional forces. Thus in Liberia the question arose whether ECOMOG was really an impartial force. Was it a neutral force solely concerned to implement a cease-fire as Nigeria maintained, or was it a Nigerian-dominated force designed to stop Charles Taylor becoming President? Because Charles Taylor opposed its intervention, ECOMOG became involved in action against the NPFL and undertook action that seemed to go beyond peace-keeping and throw doubt on its impartiality. First, in October 1990 ECOMOG ousted the NPFL from Monrovia and established a security zone around the city. Much more far-reaching was its action in October 1992. After the NPFL attacked Monrovia, ECOMOG went on the offensive, using Nigerian planes to bomb NPFL positions outside Monrovia and driving them back to allow the Sawyer government to gain control of more territory.[80] The UN Secretary-General, in his March 1993 report, said that the NPFL attack had obliged ECOMOG to adopt a peace enforcement model to defend and protect the capital.[81]

The ECOMOG force was initially made up of troops from Nigeria, Ghana, Gambia, Guinea, and Sierra Leone, with the largest contingent coming from Nigeria. The original Ghanaian commander was removed and replaced by a Nigerian. At first the francophone members of ECOWAS were suspicious, seeing ECOMOG as designed to further Nigerian policy and to stop Charles Taylor from becoming President. Burkina Faso and the Côte d'Ivoire at first supported Charles Taylor. But there were newspaper reports that both were put under pressure by the USA to support ECOMOG and by November 1992 they had ended their opposition. Also Senegal was induced to contribute 3,000 troops to ECOMOG when the USA supplied funds for this purpose.[82] ECOWAS had difficulties in securing adequate funding for ECOMOG and its ability to carry out its responsibilities was hampered by the limited financing available.[83] The UN Secretary-General set up a trust fund to help support ECOMOG;[84] this again highlights the practical problem of turning to regional organizations in the absence of adequate resources.

Charles Taylor, not surprisingly, was hostile to ECOMOG and said that its intervention was an attempt by Nigeria to save the Doe government.

---

[80] Weller, *Regional Peacekeeping and International Enforcement: The Liberian Crisis* (1994) at 99, 100.   [81] S/25402 para 17; Weller, ibid. at 280.
[82] Weller, ibid. at 174.   [83] 1994 UNYB 379.   [84] S/26422; Weller, ibid. at 374.

He accused Nigeria of using Liberia to prove that it was an African super-power, criticized the composition of ECOMOG, and called for the UN to replace it. When a cease-fire was agreed at Cotonou in July 1993 the parties agreed to expand the participation of states in ECOMOG and to give the UN a role in establishing peace. As the Secretary-General commented in his March 1993 report, these measures were necessary because of the NPFL mistrust of ECOMOG and insistence on UN participation.

The problems that emerged in the Cold War over the meaning of 'enforcement action' and of 'authorization' under Article 53 did not give rise to controversy in the case of Liberia. When ECOWAS imposed economic sanctions on those factions that did not accept the *Yamoussoukro IV Peace Agreement* in October 1992, it asked the Security Council to make these sanctions mandatory for the entire international community. That is, it did not request Security Council authorization but simply assistance. The implication is that ECOWAS did not regard economic sanctions as enforcement action under Article 53, an issue raised earlier with regard to the OAS action against Cuba. The view that economic sanctions by a regional organization do not need Security Council authorization was controversial when the OAS took measures against Cuba,[85] but has been implicitly confirmed by the many sanctions imposed subsequently without recourse to the UN. This view is confirmed by the action with regard to Haiti. The OAS imposed sanctions in 1991. The UN General Assembly supported this, but the Security Council did not act until June 1993 when it passed Resolution 841 unanimously imposing an oil and arms embargo on Haiti. Thus without discussion it was assumed that OAS economic sanctions did not require Security Council authorization.

With regard to Liberia, the Security Council did not go so far as to make the ECOWAS sanctions mandatory for all states, although it did impose an arms embargo. It unanimously passed Resolution 788; this recalled Chapter VIII, commended ECOWAS for its efforts to restore peace in Liberia, reaffirmed the *Yamoussoukro IV Peace Agreement*, and condemned the continuing armed attacks against the peacekeeping forces of ECOWAS by one of the parties to the conflict. It requested all states to respect the measures established by ECOWAS to bring about a peaceful solution to the conflict in Liberia.

ECOWAS did not seek UN Security Council authorization for ECOMOG. It seems, therefore, that ECOWAS did not regard ECOMOG action as enforcement action for which Article 53 authorization was necessary. Nor did any state in the Security Council claim that ECOMOG needed its

---

[85] Akehurst, 'Enforcement Action by Regional Agencies, with special reference to the Organization of American States', 42 BYIL (1967) 175; Simma, *The Charter of the United Nations: A Commentary* (1994), 732.

authorization. But ECOWAS did inform the UN of its actions, even if its initial report came some months after the deployment of ECOMOG. Approval was given by the Secretary-General and by the Security Council in statements and resolutions commending ECOWAS for its actions. The Security Council did not demonstrate concern that ECOMOG had gone beyond legitimate peacekeeping even after its 1992 offensive. Later resolutions such as Resolution 911 recognized that the *Cotonou Peace Agreement* assigned ECOMOG to assist in the implementation of the Agreement. Later peace agreements gave ECOMOG and the Transitional Government 'peace enforcement powers' and the Security Council welcomed the action of ECOMOG in helping to defeat a coup attempt in September 1994.[86]

In Resolution 866 (1993), following the *Cotonou Peace Agreement*, the Security Council established UNOMIL, a UN peacekeeping force to complement ECOMOG. The resolution actually spelled out that this was the first time the UN had undertaken a peacekeeping mission in cooperation with a force set up by another organization. A clear understanding about the roles of the two forces was crucial.[87] Under the Peace Agreement[88] ECOMOG, which was initially to be 4,000 strong, had the primary responsibility for supervising the implementation of the military provisions of the Agreement. It was to be stationed at entry points, ports, and airports to ensure compliance with the Resolution 788 arms embargo; and also to be deployed throughout the country to supervise the disarmament and demobilization of the combatants. African states from outside the region were to contribute forces.[89] Like the establishment of a UN force, this provision for other states to contribute was designed to overcome the mistrust of those who saw ECOMOG as not truly impartial. Tanzania, Uganda, and Zimbabwe agreed to provide troops. The Agreement provided that ECOMOG was to be a neutral peacekeeping force. It included a heading 'peace enforcement powers', but in fact this made no express provision for the use of force except in self-defence. ECOMOG was to ensure the safety of UNOMIL observers.

Under Resolution 866, UNOMIL, a force of 300 military observers, was to monitor compliance with the cease-fire and the Peace Agreement and, '*without participation in enforcement operations*, to coordinate with ECOMOG in the discharge of ECOMOG's separate responsibilities both formally and informally'. This express exclusion of a peace enforcement role for

[86] 1994 UNYB 380.

[87] The Secretary-General made a report defining the respective roles of UNOMIL and ECOMOG: S/26422, Weller, *Regional Peacekeeping and International Enforcement: The Liberian Crisis* (1994) at 374; an agreement was subsequently concluded: S/26868, Weller, ibid. at 440.

[88] *The Cotonou Agreement*, S/26272; Weller, ibid. at 343.

[89] S/26868, Weller, ibid. at 440; S/1994/168, Weller, ibid. at 455. A Trust Fund was established to help pay for the ECOMOG forces. The USA, the UK, and Denmark contributed.

UNOMIL seems to refer to the Peace Agreement and to imply that ECOMOG could undertake peace enforcement. But it does not amount to an express authorization of enforcement action by ECOMOG under Article 53 of the UN Charter and so the implication seems to be that peace enforcement is not enforcement action under Article 53. The Security Council seems to assume that some legal basis exists for peace enforcement operations by ECOMOG, that peace enforcement is not incompatible with peacekeeping.[90] The *Cotonou Peace Agreement* described ECOMOG as a peacekeeping force.

UNOMIL was to monitor the various implementation procedures in order to verify their impartial application. The UN involvement contributed significantly to the eventual implementation of the Peace Agreement and served to underline the international community's commitment to conflict resolution in Liberia. In all its subsequent resolutions on Liberia the Security Council stated that UNOMIL's ability to carry out its mandate depended on the capacity of ECOMOG to discharge its responsibilities.

But the peace process ran into repeated difficulties; there were delays in the establishment of an effective Transitional Government and hostilities prevented ECOMOG and UNOMIL from carrying out their respective mandates. UNOMIL was reduced in size at the end of 1994 and the peace process was at a standstill.[91] Its mandate was subsequently adjusted to reflect the breakdown of the *Cotonou Peace Agreement* and the succession of subsequent peace agreements, but in essentials UNOMIL's functions remained the same.[92] Later resolutions stressed the need for close contacts and enhanced coordination between ECOMOG and UNOMIL. They also called for ECOMOG to intensify the necessary action to provide security for UNOMIL.[93] It was not until August 1996, after another outburst of fighting, that the final *Abuja II Peace Agreement* was concluded and ECOMOG and UNOMIL were able to discharge their responsibilities. After elections were held and President Taylor came to power UNOMIL was terminated in September 1997. ECOMOG remained to help the Liberian government not only to provide security throughout Liberia, but also to restructure the Liberian army and police.[94]

The ECOWAS intervention in Liberia may be seen as a success in that it helped to secure a cease-fire and a political settlement. Alternatively, it may be seen as a Nigerian-inspired operation that merely prolonged the

---

[90] This type of uncertainty may be traced to the UN Secretary-General's categorization of peacekeeping in his *Agenda for Peace*. He has later, in his Lessons Learned Report on *Cooperation between the United Nations and Regional Organizations/Arrangements in a Peacekeeping Environment* (1999) para 36, stressed the need for a uniform terminology, common to the UN and to regional organizations.   [91] S/1995/158; 1994 UNYB 371, 1995 UNYB 350.
[92] SC Res 1020.   [93] SC Res 1014, 1020, 1041, 1059, 1071, 1083.
[94] Final Report of the Secretary-General on UNOMIL, S/1997/712.

conflict and postponed the coming to power of Charles Taylor. It highlights the problems over consent and impartiality; there was considerable
uncertainty about the Liberian consent to the ECOMOG intervention and
also controversy over ECOMOG's role in the civil war. A regional organization may run into the danger of seeming to take sides and of being
dominated by one powerful member state. A condition of the Peace
Agreement was the inclusion of states from outside ECOWAS in ECO-
MOG; UN involvement also proved necessary to secure the commitment
of all the parties to the peace process. There were also financial problems,
which throw doubt on the ability of regional or subregional organizations
to carry out extensive peacekeeping operations. The UN had to establish
a special fund and bilateral aid was also provided.[95] Nevertheless, there
was much talk of the ECOWAS operation being an important precedent
for future regional action and for UN/regional cooperation.[96]

The former USSR

This precedent of cooperation between a regional and a UN force was followed in the cooperation between the CIS and the UN in the former
USSR, in Tajikistan and Georgia. In both operations a small UN force of
military observers was supplemented by a larger regional force which
was to maintain security. This division of labour reflects that adopted in
Liberia. It seems that the cooperation in Tajikistan was regarded as
relatively unproblematic, whereas at the inception of the operation in
Georgia there was some concern about the impartiality of the CIS forces.

   After the outbreak of civil war in Tajikistan in May 1992 Russia wrote to
the Secretary-General in April 1993 proposing the deployment of a military
contingent of forces from Kirgizstan, Kazakhstan, Russia, Tajikistan, and
Uzbekistan.[97] The five states made a formal Declaration after a summit
meeting in August 1993; they said that the CIS would undertake regional
peacekeeping under Chapter VIII. They agreed that the conflict was essentially an internal one, but that there was cross-border infiltration from
Afghanistan.[98] There were already CIS border forces in Tajikistan deployed
to act in collective self-defence of that state. The Security Council welcomed
these efforts by the regional states.[99] The five states then made the *Moscow
Accord* in September 1993 to establish a coalition force in Tajikistan; again
they spoke of this as a regional arrangement concluded in accordance with
the principles and purposes of Chapter VIII of the UN Charter.[100] Tajikistan
was a party to the agreement and hence clearly consented to the deployment of this force and welcomed it as an important step in de-escalation

[95] Above note 26.   [96] S/PV 3138; S/24815.   [97] S/25720.   [98] S/26290.
[99] S/26341; 1993 UNYB 514.   [100] S/26357; S/26610.

of the conflict. But nevertheless it asked the Security Council to consider giving the CIS forces the status of UN peacekeeping forces. The Security Council did not accede to this request, although it was repeated many times during the conflict and may indicate not only the relief from the financial burden to the CIS, but also the higher status and perhaps also the clearer impartiality of UN forces.[101] Throughout 1993 and for most of 1994 there was fighting within Tajikistan and across the border. In September 1994 the parties concluded the *Tehran Agreement*; this provided for a temporary cease-fire and for the cessation of hostile acts across the border.[102]

After the *Tehran Agreement* the UN established a new UNMOT, to replace earlier temporary missions; this was to be a small team of observers with the mandate under Resolution 968 to monitor the cease-fire, investigate reports of cease-fire violations, and to provide its good offices. It was to liaise closely with CIS peacekeeping forces and with the border forces. In this resolution the Security Council made no reference to Chapter VIII. As regards the role of the CIS forces, it showed less enthusiasm than it had with regard to ECOWAS in Liberia and later in Sierra Leone; the Security Council merely acknowledged positively the readiness of the collective peacekeeping forces of the CIS in Tajikistan to work together with UN observers to assist in maintaining the cease-fire and underlined the importance of close liaison between UNMOT and the CIS collective peacekeeping forces and the border forces.

In later resolutions it also expressed satisfaction over the close liaison between UNMOT and the CIS forces; it underlined the need to pursue this and develop it further. Later it expressed its satisfaction at the regular contacts between UNMOT and the CIS forces and the border forces.[103] But it was not until after the conclusion of the *General Agreement on the Establishment of Peace* in 1997 that the Security Council expressed any gratitude to the CIS forces, and then it was only for their readiness to assist in providing security for UN personnel at the request of UNMOT.[104] By 1998 they had become more appreciative; in Resolution 1167 they welcomed the cooperative liaison between UNMOT and the CIS forces and encouraged them to continue discussion of options for improving security cooperation. Resolution 1206 welcomed the continued contribution by the CIS peacekeeping in assisting parties in the implementation of the General Agreement, and in a statement the Security Council welcomed the readiness of the CIS forces to arrange for the guarding of UN premises in Dushanbe.[105]

---

[101] 1994 UNYB 591.   [102] Ibid.   [103] SC Res 1030, 1061, 1089.   [104] SC Res 1128, 1138.
[105] S/PRST/1998/4. The mandate of UNMOT was expanded after the 1997 Peace Agreement and it was given a security unit to protect its personnel. But progress in establishing peace was slow and the situation remained precarious. The first multi-party elections were held in March 2000: UN Press Release SC/6827. UNMOT was terminated in May 2000.

The UN was at first even more cautious in expressly regulating the relations between the UN force and the regional force in Abkhazia, Georgia. In this conflict the UN observer mission pre-dated the official establishment of the CIS forces (although Russian forces that later made up the CIS forces had remained in Georgia after the break-up of the USSR). Abkhaz claims for secession grew while Georgia was riven by civil discord; in August 1992 armed conflict broke out. Georgia accused Russian forces of siding with the Abkhazians.[106] In July 1993 the UN Security Council began to plan the deployment of military observers; Resolution 849 planned to deploy observers once a cease-fire was implemented. It welcomed the participation of Russia as a facilitator in the UN Secretary-General's attempts to launch a peace process. In August 1993 the Security Council in Resolution 858 established UNOMIG to verify compliance with the July 1993 cease-fire and to investigate reports of violations. However, the cease-fire broke down and the Abkhaz offensive led to their occupation of almost the whole of Abkhazia and the displacement of the Georgian population. Accordingly UNOMIG could not carry out its original mandate; the Security Council produced a revised interim mandate for UNOMIG in Resolution 881: it was to maintain contacts with both sides and also with the Russian military contingents. In December 1993 Resolution 892 welcomed the readiness of Russia to help ensure the security of UNOMIG.

In May 1994 a more lasting cease-fire was agreed. This gave formal authority not to the Russian troops but to the 'CIS peacekeeping force'. This marks the transformation of the Russian forces into CIS forces, with the mandate to ensure respect for the cease-fire and the weapons exclusion zone.[107] Russia wrote to the Secretary-General, reporting that the CIS had decided under Chapter VIII to send a collective peacekeeping force to Abkhazia. The advance contingent of Russian troops already in Abkhazia would be deployed immediately.[108] The Security Council was willing to take this at face value and did not inquire into constitutional propriety; in Resolution 934 it noted with satisfaction the beginning of CIS assistance in zones of conflict, in response to the request of the parties on the basis of the May Agreement in continued coordination with UNOMIG. However, the Security Council made no reference to Chapter VIII. Further coordinating arrangements with UNOMIG were to be agreed and the Secretary-General was to report on these arrangements. Resolution 937 welcomed the May Agreement; it recognized that the deployment of the CIS peacekeeping force was predicated upon the request and consent of the parties to the conflict. It noted with satisfaction the readiness of Russia

---

[106] S/26031, 1993 UNYB 506.   [107] S/1994/583.
[108] 1994 UNYB 582, S/1994/476, S/1994/732.

to continue to inform the members of the Security Council on the activities of the CIS peacekeeping force. It expanded UNOMIG and gave it the mandate of monitoring and verifying the implementation by the parties of the May cease-fire; to verify respect for the security zones and to monitor the withdrawal of troops and patrol and investigate violations of the Agreement.

UNOMIG was also 'to observe the operation of the CIS peacekeeping force'; this apparently reflects a perception that it was necessary to secure the impartiality of the CIS operations because of suspicion about the role of Russia. This provision for observation of the operation of the CIS force goes beyond any provision on the relation between UNOMIL and ECOWAS or UNMOT and the CIS forces. But many subsequent resolutions reported satisfaction at the cooperation and coordination between the two forces.[109] Resolution 1150 welcomed the contribution that the CIS forces had made to stabilizing the situation in the zone of conflict and noted that the cooperation between UNOMIG and the CIS was good and had continued to develop. Resolution 1187 was similar. Resolution 1225 went even further and noted that the working relationship between UNOMIG and the CIS peacekeeping force had been good at all levels.[110]

SIERRA LEONE

Some of the questions about constitutionality and impartiality that arose with regard to the ECOWAS action in Liberia arose again with regard to Sierra Leone. Here also a UN force was established to work with the regional force after the restoration of the democratically elected government. In contrast to Liberia, there was clear consent to the presence of the Nigerian and Guinean troops in Sierra Leone from the democratically elected President, both before the coup in May 1997 and after he was overthrown. But there are doubts as to whether the action taken in the name of ECOWAS did in fact constitute regional peacekeeping. ECOWAS, in June 1997, called for the restoration of the democratically elected government. It said that there were three means of achieving this: dialogue, sanctions, and, if necessary, the use of force. But the actual use of force seemed to go beyond impartial peacekeeping action; ECOWAS used force to remove the junta and restore democratic government. In contrast to the Security

---

[109] From SC Res 971, 993.

[110] The political deadlock in Abkhazia has proved impossible to resolve, but the Secretary-General reported that without the presence of UNOMIG and the CIS forces there would be conflict (1995 UNYB 614, 1996 UNYB 349). The situation deteriorated in 1998: UN Press Release SC/6523.

Council's express authority to use force in Haiti to restore democratic government, it did not expressly authorize a comparable use of force by ECOWAS. There is therefore controversy as to the legal significance of this ECOWAS action.

The first Security Council reaction to the coup was prompt but limited. It issued a statement on 27 May 1997 expressing concern. Especially given that the UN had assisted the attempts at reconciliation in Sierra Leone, the Security Council deplored the attempt to overthrow the democratically elected government and called for the immediate restoration of constitutional order.[111] The first ECOWAS communiqué was issued when ECOWAS met in June 1997, some time after the involvement of the Nigerian and Guinean forces in the fighting in Sierra Leone.[112] This said that the ECOWAS objectives were to reinstate the legitimate government, restore peace and security, and resolve the serious refugee problem. It called for non-recognition of the junta and said that it would reinstate the previous government by force if necessary. It set up a Committee to monitor developments. Nigeria then requested a meeting of the Security Council; it said that the countries of the subregion had once again risen to the challenge of serving the cause of peace and security in the neighbouring country of Sierra Leone. It referred to the ECOWAS communiqué of June 1997; it acknowledged that some delegations had expressed concern about the use of force, but argued that negotiation and sanctions could not be achieved without the use of some military force. The meeting of the Security Council in July 1997 was held in closed session.[113] The product was a statement, expressing concern at the atrocities committed by the supporters of the junta against civilians, foreigners, and members of the ECOWAS monitoring group.[114] It welcomed the mediation efforts initiated by ECOWAS and said that it would monitor the progress of efforts aimed at the peaceful resolution of the crisis; it was ready to consider appropriate measures if constitutional order was not restored. It is clear that the Security Council's language endorsing ECOWAS attempts at peaceful settlement was very cautious and stopped far short of an authorization of the use of force.

This pattern was repeated in the subsequent Security Council statements and resolutions. It was not until Resolution 1132, imposing sanctions on Sierra Leone in October 1997, that the Security Council gave any express legitimation to the use of force by ECOWAS. From the time of the coup ECOMOG forces had imposed a *de facto* embargo on Sierra Leone through interception of ships and aircraft. This was formalized in the June 1997 meeting of ECOWAS. In October 1997 ECOWAS sought Security

---

[111] S/PRST/1997/29.   [112] S/1997/499.   [113] S/1997/531; S/PV 3797.
[114] S/PRST/1997/36.

Council support for its efforts. Nigeria reported that the junta was intransigent and the situation was a threat to international peace and security. The subregion was anxious to avoid a costly and long engagement like that in Liberia and sought UN support and endorsement for the ECOWAS sanctions and for enforcement of those sanctions.[115] The Security Council passed Resolution 1132 unanimously under Chapter VII; this expressed strong support for the efforts of the ECOWAS Committee to resolve the crisis and imposed sanctions against the members of the junta designed to restrict their freedom of movement. It also imposed an oil and arms embargo on Sierra Leone. An express exception was made allowing the import of oil by the previous government and ECOWAS forces, but (apparently through an oversight) at first no comparable exception was made for the supply of arms to the previous government or ECOWAS.[116] Resolution 1132 also invoked Chapter VIII, as well as Chapter VII, specifically authorizing ECOWAS to ensure the strict implementation of this resolution by halting inward shipping. Member states could provide technical and logistical support to ECOWAS to carry out these responsibilities. This follows the precedents of the authorization to member states acting nationally or through regional organizations to use force to secure compliance with arms embargoes on Yugoslavia and Haiti. But, unlike these earlier resolutions, it referred to the relevant regional organization by name. The authorization was not to UN member states acting nationally or through regional agencies or arrangements but only to ECOWAS itself, not to individual members of ECOWAS. The matter was not discussed in the Security Council debate leading up to the resolution, but it seems that the intention was to ensure that ECOWAS acted collectively.

The language of Resolution 1132 was cautious and did not amount to an authorization for enforcement action apart from that needed to implement the sanctions. However, the reference to ECOWAS could be taken as an endorsement of Nigeria's claim to be acting through the regional organization rather than unilaterally. The debate leading up to the resolution also shows some caution.[117] Several states spoke of their support for ECOWAS attempts to bring about the return of the government *through negotiations*. Russia in particular spoke of the need to strengthen coordination between the Security Council and ECOWAS; it said that its main premise was that the Charter required that enforcement action could not

---

[115] S/PV 3822.

[116] The sanctions regime was later modified to allow the supply of arms to ECOMOG and the legitimate government in SC Res 1156 and 1171; later SC Res 1299 extended this exception to UNAMSIL. On the breaking of the blanket arms embargo by the UK, see the UK government publication, *Report of the Sierra Leone Arms Investigation* (1998).   [117] S/PV 3822.

be undertaken by regional organizations without the authority of the Security Council.

After the imposition of sanctions the parties agreed on the *Conakry Peace Agreement* in October 1997, on the basis of a peace plan produced by the ECOWAS Committee. This provided for ECOMOG to monitor and verify the cessation of hostilities, disarmament, and demobilization.[118] This peace plan was welcomed by the Security Council, but there was no immediate cease-fire.[119] ECOMOG continued to be involved in the conflict; it used force extensively, but in its reports to the Security Council under Resolution 1132 it was careful to claim to be acting in self-defence or in enforcing the arms and oil embargo.[120] Nigeria also reported to the Security Council, saying that ECOMOG forces had been the target of attacks by the junta. They claimed that the final engagement which led to the overthrow of the junta was the direct result of unprovoked attacks on ECOMOG.[121] On 12 February 1998 ECOMOG forces ousted the junta. The democratically elected government was returned and the peace agreement was implemented.[122]

The Security Council, in Resolution 1162, commended ECOMOG on its important role in the ongoing restoration of peace and security. For the first time in a resolution it expressly referred to the ECOMOG forces. As in the case of Liberia, this express reference to ECOMOG and the apparent acceptance of the legality of its operations followed the conclusion of a peace treaty between the parties. The Secretary-General, in his reports on the situation in Sierra Leone, avoided any pronouncement on the legality of the ECOMOG action; his report on the action leading to the restoration of the President in March 1998 does not challenge the legality of the final ECOMOG action even if it did not expressly accept at face value the ECOWAS claims to be acting in self-defence. He said that 'responding to an attack by the junta forces, ECOMOG launched a military attack on the junta which culminated approximately one week later in the collapse of the junta and its expulsion by force from Freetown after heavy fighting'. ECOMOG subsequently took control of almost every major town. The Secretary-General commended the contribution by ECOMOG officers and men to the removal of the military junta.[123]

The ECOMOG forces were then supplemented by UNOMSIL, a small UN force of 70 military observers established in June 1998 by Resolution 1181 to monitor the military and security situation, and the disarmament and demobilization process, including the role of ECOMOG in the provi-

---

[118] S/1997/824.   [119] S/PRST/1997/52.

[120] S/1997/895, S/1998/14, S/1998/107, S/1998/170; see also address by President Kabbah of Sierra Leone, S/1999/186, saying that ECOMOG forces were acting in self-defence.

[121] S/1998/123; S/1998/170.   [122] S/1998/215; SC Res 1156.

[123] Fourth Report of the Secretary-General on the Situation in Sierra Leone, S/1998/249.

sion of security and in the collection and destruction of arms. This express injunction to monitor the regional peacekeeping force mirrors the precedent of the mandate of UNOMIG in Georgia and may reflect a suspicion of Nigeria comparable to that of Russia; at least it reflects the primacy of the United Nations and the need to secure the propriety of ECOMOG's actions. The combination of a small UN force and a larger, pre-existing regional force follows the precedents of Liberia, Tajikistan, and Georgia.

The rebels returned to the attack and occupied the capital, Freetown, in January 1999. ECOMOG played a major role in driving them back from the capital and in launching a counter-attack.[124] Again the traditional requirement of impartial peacekeeping was difficult to maintain in the situation where one side in a civil conflict refused to accept a cease-fire. ECOMOG's role was to defend the legitimate government that it had helped to restore; it seems rather far-fetched to claim that this action could constitute self-defence of ECOMOG.[125] But no concern was expressed about the ECOMOG action. The UN Secretary-General said that ECOMOG was to be congratulated on its success in repelling the rebels from Freetown and restoring a measure of order to the city. Donor governments, the Netherlands, Canada, the UK and the USA, were also thanked for their logistical support.[126] The Security Council, in Resolution 1231, also commended the efforts of ECOMOG towards the restoration of peace, security, and stability, and called on all member states to provide ECOMOG with financial and logistical support. Thus there was clear support for ECOWAS and apparent acceptance of the legality of its actions, but without any discussion of their legal basis.

In July 1999 the warring parties concluded the *Lomé Peace Agreement*.[127] This stipulated the adoption of a new mandate for ECOMOG; it was to cover four areas: peacekeeping; security of the State of Sierra Leone; protection of UNOMSIL; and protection of disarmament, demobilization and reintegration personnel. Also a timetable was to be drawn up for the phased withdrawal of ECOMOG; it was to be replaced by a neutral peacekeeping force comprising UNOMSIL and ECOMOG.[128] In August 1999 ECOWAS accordingly adopted a revised mandate for ECOMOG and

---

[124] Fifth Report of the Secretary-General on UNOMSIL, S/1999/237.

[125] Also, it may be that some states were willing to accept the legality of this operation because of the fact that there had been foreign support for the rebels from Liberia (S/PRST/1991/1). On the accusation by Sierra Leone against Liberia, see S/1999/73. This argument was used by the UK to justify its substantial aid to the democratically elected government and to ECOMOG (Private notice question answered by the Foreign Secretary, House of Commons, 19 January 1999). Liberia denied intervention and attributed the actions to mercenaries (S/1999/17, S/1999/193).

[126] Fifth Report of the Secretary-General on UNOMSIL, S/1999/237.

[127] S/1999/1073.

[128] Seventh Report of the Secretary-General on UNOMSIL, S/1999/836.

Nigeria indicated that it intended to withdraw its forces by December 1999.[129]

The Security Council approved this revised ECOMOG mandate in Resolution 1270, but it did not refer to Chapter VII or Chapter VIII. The implication is that it did not regard ECOMOG as an enforcement force needing authorization under Article 53 and that it saw it as deriving its legal basis from the *Lomé Peace Agreement*. In contrast, the Security Council did invoke Chapter VII with regard to UNAMSIL. This new 6,000-strong UN force was to replace UNOMSIL. It was to cooperate with the government and the other parties to the Peace Agreement in the implementation of the agreement. Its main purpose was to assist the government in the disarmament and demobilization and the creation of conditions of confidence and stability. The force was not mandated to ensure the security of Freetown and the international airport or to provide protection for the government. These tasks and 'operations against rogue elements' would remain the responsibility of ECOMOG.[130] Under Chapter VII UNAMSIL was authorized to take the necessary action to ensure the security and freedom of movement of its personnel and, within its capabilities and areas of deployment, to afford protection to civilians under imminent threat of physical violence.

The division of functions between the two forces was agreed. The initial mandate of UNAMSIL under Resolution 1270 rested on the assumption that ECOMOG would continue. But Nigeria decided in December 1999 to withdraw its forces.[131] Accordingly the Security Council, in Resolution 1289 in February 2000, expanded the numbers of UNAMSIL to 11,000 and redrew its mandate to allow it to take over the functions of ECOMOG. It was given increased powers under Chapter VII, but the Secretary-General stressed that these tasks would not fundamentally change the nature of the mandate, which was based on the requirement in the *Lomé Agreement* for a neutral peacekeeping force.[132] ECOMOG forces were subsequently incorporated (rehatted) into UNAMSIL.[133]

Thus in Sierra Leone a regional force operated with Security Council initial acquiescence and later express approval to restore a democratically elected government and to maintain it in power when the national army was not able to do so on its own. It was clear, through its repeated commendations of ECOMOG's role in the restoration and maintenance of

---

[129] Eighth Report of the Secretary-General on UNOMSIL, S/1999/1003.

[130] SC 4054th meeting; see also Press Release SC/6742.

[131] First Report of the Secretary-General on UNAMSIL, S/1999/1223.

[132] Second Report of the Secretary-General on UNAMSIL, S/2000/13; Press Release SC/6800.

[133] Third Report of the Secretary-General on UNAMSIL, S/2000/186; UN Press Release SC/6821.

peace and security, that the Security Council approved the regional action, but did not make clear the legal basis for this. In the absence of express provision or illuminating debate the most plausible solution seems to be that this was created as a regional peacekeeping force, operating with the consent of the democratically elected President. It was authorized to use force to implement the Security Council embargo, but apart from this the Security Council made no further reference to Chapter VII or VIII with regard to ECOWAS. ECOWAS itself based its use of force on this resolution and on self-defence. Subsequently it could base its legal authority on the more far-reaching provisions of the peace agreements.

Some have claimed that this episode shows acceptance of a regional right to use force to restore democracy, comparable to the Security Council authorization in the case of Haiti, and perhaps even supporting a unilateral right to use force to further democracy, but this seems open to doubt. In the absence of express or even implied Security Council authorization under Chapter VII to allow the restoration of democracy, and in the absence of any discussion of this question in Security Council debates, this is another example of reinterpretation of state practice, looking at what states did and not at what they said. The 'restoration of democracy' was an aim of ECOWAS, but not the express legal basis for their action. ECOWAS did not itself claim a legal right of pro-democratic intervention; its use of force was based on the implementation of Resolution 1132, self-defence, and the various peace agreements.

SECURITY COUNCIL AUTHORIZATION OF USE OF FORCE BY REGIONAL ORGANIZATIONS

The flexible approach of the Security Council to the question of what counts as a regional arrangement or agency under Chapter VIII was apparent in its practice in the former Yugoslavia. The Security Council apparently viewed the EC, CSCE, and possibly also the WEU and NATO as regional bodies in that it referred to Chapter VIII to commend their activities or to authorize force by them.[134] In Yugoslavia the Security Council for the first time used its powers to authorize enforcement action

---

[134] As regards the EC and the CSCE, typically resolutions said: 'Recalling also the provisions of Chapter VIII of the Charter of the United Nations, commending the efforts undertaken by the European Community and its Member States, with the support of the States participating in the CSCE, to restore peace and dialogue in Yugoslavia.' The implication was that the EC and the CSCE are regional organizations. Similarly some of the resolutions authorizing member states to use force refer to Chapter VIII; although there was no express reference to NATO, it was understood by the member states that it would be NATO, that implemented the resolution.

by a regional organization. The Security Council's early response to the situation in Croatia and later in Bosnia was to impose an arms embargo on the whole of the former Yugoslavia. It subsequently, in May 1992, imposed a complete trade embargo on Serbia and Montenegro; in November 1992 it reinforced these sanctions in Resolution 787: 'Acting under Chapter VII and Chapter VIII, the Security Council calls upon States acting nationally or through regional agencies or arrangements, to use such measures commensurate with the specific circumstances as may be necessary under the authority of the Security Council to halt all inward and outward maritime shipping in order to inspect and verify their cargoes and destinations and to ensure strict implementation of the provisions of resolutions 713 and 757.' Under this authorization NATO and the WEU intercepted ships in the Adriatic and on the Danube.

The Security Council also authorized the use of force to secure the implementation of an embargo under Article 41 of the UN Charter in Haiti and Sierra Leone. In response to the 1993 coup in Haiti the Security Council imposed an oil and arms embargo; in Resolution 875 'Acting under Chapters VII and VIII of the Charter of the United Nations, Calls upon Member States, acting nationally or through regional agencies or arrangements, cooperating with the legitimate Government of Haiti, to use such measures commensurate with the specific circumstances as may be necessary under the authority of the Security Council to ensure strict implementation of the provisions of resolutions 841 (1993) and 873 (1993) . . . and in particular to halt inward maritime shipping as necessary to inspect and verify their cargoes and destinations.' In Resolution 917 it extended this to outward shipping. These resolutions on Yugoslavia and Haiti do not refer to any regional organization by name in the operative paragraphs quoted above. They could nevertheless be seen as the first use by the Security Council of Article 53 of the UN Charter in that they authorize member states of regional agencies or arrangements to take enforcement action. But no express reference is made to Article 53 and it is typical of the Security Council not to concern itself with the exact article under which it is acting if this makes no difference to its powers. The Security Council action with regard to Sierra Leone seems even more obviously to fall within Article 53 in that it 'authorizes' rather than 'calls on' states to take action and it expressly refers to the regional organization, ECOWAS, by name. But even this resolution makes no express reference to Article 53. As was mentioned above, the Security Council in Resolution 1132, 'Acting also under Chapter VIII of the Charter of the United Nations, authorizes ECOWAS, cooperating with the democratically elected Government of Sierra Leone, to ensure strict implementation' of the oil and arms embargo.

The Security Council has also gone further than authorizing force to implement a trade embargo. With regard to the former Yugoslavia in Resolution 770, acting under Chapter VII, it called upon states acting nationally or through regional agencies or arrangements to take all measures necessary to facilitate the delivery by relevant UN humanitarian organizations and others of humanitarian assistance. In Resolution 816 it authorized member states 'acting nationally or through regional organisations' to take measures to ensure compliance with the ban on flights in Bosnia's air-space. In this resolution the Security Council said that it was acting under Chapter VII, but it also recalled Chapter VIII. The authorization to member states to use force made it clear that they were under the authority of the Security Council and subject to close coordination with the Secretary-General and UNPROFOR. Also member states were required to coordinate their activities, including their rules of engagement, with the Secretary-General and UNPROFOR and to inform the Secretary-General of any measure taken. Resolution 836 on the use of force to protect the safe areas established by the Security Council is slightly different in that it did not make any express reference to Chapter VIII.[135] It not only expanded UNPROFOR's mandate by authorizing it to use force in reply to attacks on the six designated safe areas, but also authorized member states acting nationally or through regional organizations or arrangements to take 'all necessary measures' through the use of air power to support UNPROFOR under the authority of the Security Council. Again the Security Council called for close coordination between member states, the Secretary-General, and UNPROFOR. Under these resolutions NATO deployed planes to monitor the no-fly zones and safe areas. Early in 1994 NATO took its first action. For NATO, these resolutions and subsequent military actions are a new departure; they represent its first out-of-area action and its first use of force.[136]

It seems that the question whether the Security Council has authorized states to use force under Article 53 of Chapter VIII or under Chapter VII is not of any great legal significance, though it may be of symbolic importance for the role of regional organizations. The use of Article 53 may constitute an acknowledgement of the importance of their contribution. When the resolutions refer to member states of a regional agency or arrangement rather than to the organization itself, this may reflect a lack of concern with any question of constitutionality; in contrast, the reference with regard to Sierra Leone to ECOWAS rather than its member

---

[135] Later SC Res 908, 1037, 1120 on Croatia also refer only to Chapter VII, not to Chapter VIII in authorizing force by member states acting nationally or through regional agencies to protect UNPROFOR and its successors in Croatia.
[136] UN Publications, *The Blue Helmets: A Review of United Nations Peacekeeping* (1993) at 531.

states may be taken as showing greater concern that the member states should act collectively. But this may be reading too much into the difference of terminology.

CONCLUSION

The optimism of the Secretary-General in the *Agenda for Peace* has proved to overestimate the role to be played by regional organizations and to underestimate the difficulties. The later report of the Secretary-General in June 1993 looking further into the implementation of the recommendations of his *Agenda for Peace* is much more cautious with regard to the role of regional organizations. There he said that his call in the *Agenda for Peace* for stronger reliance on regional organizations came before regional organizations and arrangements had fully adjusted to the end of bipolarity. It was now clear that there were new tensions and that 'in this time of change not all regional arrangements may prove willing or able to take on the challenges confronting them'. Nevertheless, he reported significant progress in strengthening mechanisms for cooperation and in effective joint ventures in the field. In the later *Supplement to the Agenda for Peace* the Secretary-General again shows a cautious optimism. He said that regional organizations have much to contribute. They can cooperate with the UN through consultation, diplomatic support, operational support such as NATO's provision of air support to protect UNPROFOR in the former Yugoslavia, co-deployment such as that in Liberia and Georgia, and joint operations such as that in Haiti. But he regarded the co-deployment operations as experimental; he said that if they succeeded they might herald a new division of labour between the UN and regional organizations, under which the regional organization carries the main burden but a small UN operation supports it and verifies that it is functioning in a manner consistent with positions adopted by the Security Council. The political, operational, and financial aspects of the arrangement gave rise to delicate questions.

The Secretary-General supported a flexible, informal approach; 'given their varied capacity, the differences in their structures, mandates and decision-making processes and the variety of forms that cooperation with the UN is already taking, it would not be appropriate to try to establish a universal model for their relationship with the UN'. Nevertheless, it is possible to identify certain principles on which the cooperation should be based. These stress the need to respect the primacy of the UN, to clearly define the division of labour, and to secure consistency in dealing with common problems such as standards for peace-keeping operations.

The wide variety of recent developments with regard to regional action —the cooperation between the UN and regional organizations in seeking peaceful settlement of disputes, as reflected in the large number of Security Council resolutions referring to regional action; the joint peace-keeping actions in Liberia, Sierra Leone, Georgia, and Tajikistan; the use of regional organizations for enforcement action, possibly under Article 53; the expanded conception of what constitutes a regional arrangement or agency—suggests that regional arrangements will play a larger role in international peacekeeping and enforcement in the future. Although it is now clear that regional organizations may contribute to a deeper sense of participation, consensus, and democratization, as the UN Secretary-General had envisaged in his *Agenda for Peace*, there is a need for caution.

The problems in securing agreement within the EC and NATO over action in the former Yugoslavia make it very clear that it will not neces-sarily be any easier for a regional organization to come to an agreement than it is for the UN. The Liberian and Sierra Leone episodes show the problems of one powerful state dominating, or being thought to domi-nate, an organization, and many states members of regional organizations will continue to prefer UN to regional intervention. As with the authori-zation to UN member states to use force, so the authorization to the mem-ber states of a regional organization raises issues of UN supervision and control. It is also clear that some problems handled initially at the regional level cannot be resolved at that level, but will require the greater author-ity and resources of the UN. Regional organizations were the first to become involved in Liberia, Sierra Leone, Tajikistan, and Georgia, but later were supplemented by the UN, partly to guarantee their impartial-ity and to remove fears of sphere of influence peacekeeping.[137]

---

[137] Report of the Secretary-General on the Work of the Organization, A/54/1 at para 112.

Index